Iconic Communication

Edited by
Masoud Yazdani
Philip Barker

intellect™
Bristol, UK
Portland OR, USA

First Published in Paperback in UK in 2000 by
Intellect Books, PO Box 862, Bristol BS99 1DE, UK

First Published in USA in 2000 by
Intellect Books, ISBS, 5804 N.E. Hassalo St, Portland, Oregon 97213-3644, USA

Consulting Editor:	Masoud Yazdani
Cover Design:	Yahia Badawi
Editorial Production:	Claire Leslie
	Robin Beecroft
Copy Editor:	Wendi Momen

A catalogue record for this book is available from the British Library

ISBN 1-84150-016-X

Printed and bound in Great Britain by Cromwell Press, Wiltshire

Contents

Preface

Part 1: Foundations

1. Human Communication Processes   1
    Philip Barker

2. On the Possibility and Impossibility of a Universal
    Iconic Communication System   17
    Andrew J King

3. The Limits of Iconic Communication   29
    John Roscoe

Part 2: Background

4. Some Pictorial Symbol Systems for Public Places   42
    Ian McLaren

5. Double Vision   51
    Michelle Gausman and Clive Chizlett

6. Communication through Icons   63
    Masoud Yazdani

Part 3: Proposals

7. Do You See What I'm Saying?   68
    Stuart Mealing

8. IconText: An Exploration of the Limitations of Iconic Languages   79
    Colin Beardon

9. Visualisation of Textual Structures   92
    Graziella Tonfoni

Part 4: Development of Prototypes

10. The Augmentation of Textual Communication with User-created Icons   111
    Leon Cruickshank and Lon Barfield

11. VIL: A Visual Inter Lingua   126
    Lee Becker and Paul Leemans

Part 5: Research Outcomes

12. Icons in the Mind   143
    Philip Barker and Paul van Schaik

13. Designing and Evaluating Icons   161
    Philip Barker and Paul van Schaik

14. Evaluating Appropriate Interface Metaphors   178
    Paul Honeywill

Preface

Communication is one of the most important activities in which people become involved. It may involve gestures, touching, talking and listening, writing and, of course, drawing. The advent of various types of technological support (such as telephones, cameras, computers and so on) has changed the basic ways in which we perform these activities. These developments have also made possible new approaches to communication. For example, using a computer system it is possible to send messages anywhere in the world virtually instantaneously. As well as being of a textual nature, these messages could also embed visual images of various sorts and sound effects. Modern forms of human communication through the medium of computers are rapidly taking on a 'multimedia' nature.

Bearing in mind the above developments we need to be aware that some information is communicated better by one medium, than another, as each medium has both constraining and enabling features, while other information is communicated better by a combination of media. This situation demands that we ask a number questions. For example:

- Do pictures really enhance the communicative power of text?
- Is it possible to design purely visual languages?
- What would be the basic building blocks of a visual language?
- If a multimedia approach is used, what combination is best?
- How should we select and apportion content to different media?
- How do we coordinate media to ensure that given communicative goals are achieved by any resulting artifact?
- How do we combine words with pictures to communicate across cultural barriers?

As our society is becoming a more visual culture day by day we need to address the above issues. This book offers a critical framework within which 'iconic communication' systems could be developed to bridge linguistic and cultural gaps and to provide effective computer-based systems for conveying information on a global scale.

Iconic communication offers possible solutions to some of the questions that were posed above. For many people, 'icons' are a familiar form of communication both in computer and in non-computer contexts. Despite their familiarity and popularity as communicative aids, there are a number of fundamental issues that we need to think about. For example:

- How do we design a really good icon or icon set?
- How can icons be combined in ways that create more meaningful messages?
- What happens when a user is exposed to an icon (or set) within a graphical user interface?

Contributors to this book, with insights from the Information and Communication Technologies, deal with these issues. Their audience is primarily graphic designers and human-computer interface developers.

Foundations

1. Human Communication Processes

Philip Barker

Introduction

The primary purpose of this initial 'foundation' chapter is to 'set the scene' for the material that is to be presented by the other authors in the subsequent chapters of this book. This initial scene-setting activity is undertaken in the four sections that follow this introduction. These make up the main body of this chapter. Each of these sections provides a different, but important, perspective on 'iconic communication'. Additional foundation material is also presented in the other two chapters which, together with this one, make up the first part of this book, which follows immediately after these opening remarks. The second section of this chapter is used to describe a number of simple but powerful 'foundation' models. Together these provide much of the context and framework for the subsequent discussions of iconic communication that are presented in this book. These models have been derived by applying (to human activity systems) some of the graphical techniques that are often used to teach general systems theory and its applications. In using these representational techniques, particular emphasis has been given to the various communication processes in which people become involved.

In order to understand why people communicate with each other, another simple model is needed. Quite naturally, any attempt to explain human communication processes cannot be based on an understanding of technology alone. Consideration must be given to the human participants that are involved. For this reason, the third section of this chapter attempts to explain human communication in terms of two important psychological perspectives. First, the motivational factors that underlie communication processes and, second, the cognitive processes that we believe form the underlying basis for conversational activity. The main topic discussed in this section is the role of mental models – and how they can be used as a basis for explaining human communication processes.

In the opening part of their book, Sassoon and Gaur (1997) suggest that 'the present connects the past with the future – knowing about the past provides a basis from which we can plan'. Because of the importance of earlier work on iconic communication techniques, the fourth section of this chapter reflects briefly on past activities that are relevant to the development of icons and iconic languages. Particular emphasis is given to the growing importance of icons within the graphical user interfaces that are now used in many software packages. Some consideration is also given to the underlying metaphors that are often embedded within these interfaces.

For most people, the future will be far more important than the past. Therefore, following on from the short 'historical perspective', the fifth part of this introductory chapter is given to speculation. Here, an attempt is made to predict some of the potential application areas for (and developments in) iconic communication that we might see in the immediate, short-term future – the next 10 to 20 years. These speculations are based both on our own research activities (see, for example, the descriptions that are given at our World Wide Web site – the address for which is http://www.isrg.co.uk) and on the developments that are taking place in other relevant areas of communication and information technologies.

Finally, in the conclusion to this chapter, an attempt is made to summarise and bring together the important concepts that have been discussed – with a view to providing an appropriate foundation and framework for the other contributions to this book.

Foundation Models

In order to understand the significance and importance of iconic communication within modern-day settings, two important models need to be introduced. The first of these attempts to describe (in a graphical way) the various relationships that exist between people and the technologies that they use to perform the various tasks that they need to undertake in order to realise the goals that they wish to achieve. This model is illustrated schematically in Figure 1.

The model presented in figure 1 places 'people' at the central focus of all the implicit and explicit relationships that exist between the different components of the diagram. Closely 'bonded' to the people component of Figure 1 are the 'interfaces' that people use when they interact with each other and with technology.

Human activity is one of the most fundamental aspects of many important natural and quasi-natural systems. As was stated above, purposeful human activity normally involves the execution of tasks. These can be executed in either an aided or an un-aided way (Banerji, 1995; Beacham, 1998). Aided execution of a task involves the use of some form of technology to facilitate the fulfilment of that task. As is suggested in figure 1, one of our basic premises is that all human interaction must be mediated by suitably designed 'interfaces'. These may be based on the use of hardware and/or software resources, they may involve people and they may be of a procedural or a linguistic nature. These interfaces facilitate any control and communication activities that are necessary for the successful execution of a task – in both aided and unaided contexts. These types of communication and control activity are probably most obvious in situations where some form of technology (such as a computer) is used to facilitate task execution.

The second model that we need to introduce is one which reflects the importance of technology as a framework for providing support for human communication processes. This model is illustrated in a diagrammatic way in Figure 2.

In this diagram there are four different types of communication represented. The directed arc on the left-hand side of the diagram represents human–human

Human Activity

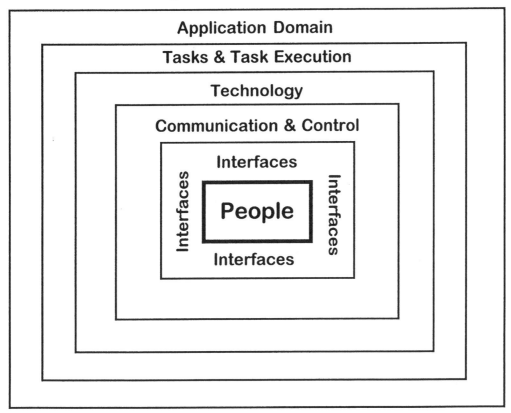

Figure 1: Human activity expressed in terms of tasks and technology

communication (HHC). This could involve either 'self-communication' (within the context of an individual) or 'group communication' when it involves two or more communicating partners. The two outermost arcs joining the 'people' and 'technology' nodes of the graph represent various forms of technology-mediated communication (TMC) as might take place through the use of telephones, facsimile machines, electronic mail or video-conferencing equipment. The inner arcs that join together the two nodes represent human–machine (HMC) and machine–human communication (MHC). Examples of these types of communication are: switching on a radio and pressing the buttons on a numeric keypad to select a particular broadcast frequency (HMC) and the various sound effects that a mobile phone makes in order to alert its user to an incoming call or a 'battery low' condition (MHC).

Of course, for communication to take place some form of linguistic framework is necessary. This could be based on simple tactile interaction or the use of spoken utterances. Alternatively, it could be based upon some sort of visual activity such as

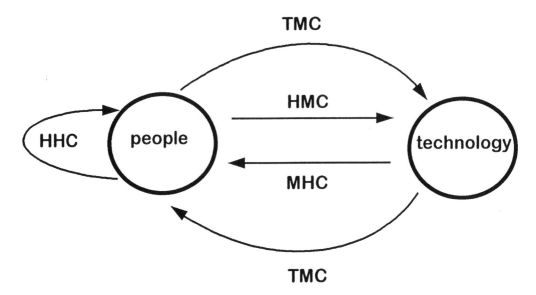

Figure 2: Types of human communication process

gestures, head or eye movement. The communication that takes place could also be multimodal – that is, involving the simultaneous or sequential use of two or more communication channels. In all cases, there is usually some form of underlying syntax and semantic rules that control how communicative events are made, controlled and interpreted.

A communication event can be thought of as the passage of a message from one person to another. Naturally, if the communication process that is involved is to be meaningful to its participants, it must embed three basic principles. First, messages must be coded within a suitable linguistic framework with which each participant is familiar. Second, the exchange of messages must be organised and structured according to an agreed protocol. Third, the exchange of information should take place in a purposeful way and be directed at the achievement of some common goal.

The importance of control flow in a dialogue process is illustrated graphically in Figure 3. This shows how two people (A and B) participate in a communication process.

While A is speaking, B listens to what is being said by A. At an appropriate point in the conversation (usually indicated by an embedded signal from A – or an interruption by B), B takes on the role of speaker while A takes a turn at listening. This 'swapping' of roles takes place throughout the dialogue process until the conversation ends.

Of course, as the number of people involved in a conversation increases, so the importance of the control model increases – if the onset of chaos is to be avoided. Depending upon the context in which a conversation takes place, the number of people involved and the modalities that are used, a wide range of control protocols are available in order to ensure the successful exchange of messages between dialogue participants.

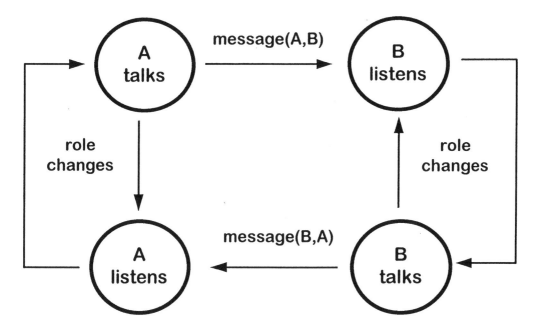

Figure 3: Simple control model for a dialogue process

The Role Of Mental Models

People communicate with each other in a variety of ways for a multitude of reasons and purposes. They employ numerous linguistic conventions and use many different dialogue protocols. Much of this communication activity is driven by a number of basic, underlying motivational forces which are closely related to the goal-seeking activity that underlies human behaviour. A good example of the effects of this motivational drive are the conversational processes that arise as a result of our desire (or need) to find out more about 'things' that are of interest to us. This type of 'question-based' communication is motivated by our inherent inquisitiveness about the many objects and entities that exist in the environments of which we form a part. The questions that we ask each other in a conversation may be quite explicit or they may be disguised in various ways in order to hide our underlying curiosity.

Of course, there are several other powerful motivational factors that are often responsible for many of our communication activities. Included amongst these are: the need to express emotion or pain; the desire to participate in an argument or a debate; and the need to give instructions to someone. Other examples of motivationally driven communication include: the processes of 'showing' and 'telling' a person something; and exercising control over the various situations in which we become involved.

As was suggested in the previous section, communication involves the generation and/or receipt of messages and/or signals by a group of people who are involved in a conversation with each other. The exchange of messages usually takes place using one or more suitably configured, shared communication channels.

As people engage in conversation with each other (be this in a face-to-face mode or using some form of technology), it is important to consider the effects that received messages have on the cognitive activity of their recipients. A message can be regarded as a stimulus that causes some form of 'mental' processing to take place. The outcome of this processing activity will normally result in some form of action being taken – usually, a response of some kind will be made. That is, the recipient of a message will generate a new message that will be sent back to the relevant dialogue partner(s). In most cases, there will be some form of relationship between the messages that a person receives and the messages which that person responds with – although this need not necessarily be so. The response that a person makes to a particular message will invariably depend upon the knowledge that the respondent has relating to the topic of discourse.

Bearing in mind what has been said above, a useful way of explaining the 'stimulus-response' activity involved in a dialogue or conversational process can be derived by invoking the concept of mental models (Rogers, Rutherford and Bibby, 1992; Seel, 1995; Barker, van Schaik and Hudson, 1998). Essentially, mental models are cognitive structures that encode much of the knowledge that we acquire as a result of the various experiences to which we are exposed.

It is our thesis that all the learning activities in which we engage ourselves lead to the creation, augmentation and/or refinement of mental models (Barker, van Schaik and Hudson, 1998). Once we have acquired these models we use them to solve problems. These mental models also influence the ways in which we behave within the different situations in which we find ourselves. The importance of mental models with respect to dialogue and conversation processes is depicted in Figure 4.

Within Figure 4, there are three basic roles that mental models perform. First, they control conventional dialogue processes (both with self and others). Second, they facilitate the use of technology-mediated communication (telephone, computer, fax and so on). Third, they stimulate and guide teaching/learning processes (both individual and group-based) towards the successful acquisition of skill and knowledge within the bounds set by natural and/or augmented capabilities.

In order for two (or more) people to talk about a topic in a purposeful way, they must have relevant mental models that relate to the topic of conversation. The 'richness' of the mental models that a person has about a particular topic determines the level of discussion in which he/she can become involved. Examples of some of these different levels of discussion can be seen in the types of conversation that take place between: two experts in a given domain, an expert in that domain and a novice, and two novices to the area. We believe that the transition from novice to expert in a given domain is accompanied both by the acquisition of greater skill levels and by the development of richer and richer mental models that are relevant to that domain. As this transition takes place, so the depth of conversation that can be achieved using these models increases correspondingly.

The Evolution Of Iconic Communication

In the previous parts of this chapter, much of what was said referred to conventional human communication as might take place through the exchange of spoken utterances.

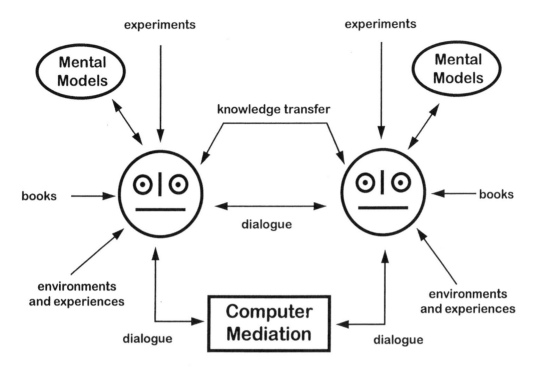

experiments   experiments

Mental Models   Mental Models

knowledge transfer

books   books

dialogue

environments and experiences   environments and experiences

Computer Mediation

dialogue   dialogue

Figure 4: Mental models as a driving force for communication

Of course, another important possibility is that the communication processes depicted in Figure 2 could involve various forms of 'written' expression. These might be based on the use of words, phrases, diagrams and/or sketches. Naturally, it is this type of framework wherein icons are normally used. Although they are important, this book does not consider the use of auditory icons (or earcons).

Bearing in mind the comments that have been made above, as far as this book is concerned, we regard an icon as being a graphical representation of some object or process. The object that is represented could have a concrete existence (such as a traffic signal or an aeroplane) or it could be abstract in nature – such as a thought, a concept or an idea. The use of icons (in conjunction with text or sound augmentation) for communicative purposes is therefore the basic domain with which this book is concerned. Some authors use the term 'iconography' to refer to the study and use of icons. For convenience, in the remainder of this book the terms 'iconic communication' and 'iconography' are used synonymously.

Extensive research into the origin, historical development and evolution of icons as a vehicle for communication has been undertaken both by Sassoon and Gaur (1997) and by Honeywill (1999). As well as their historical perspectives, each of their books also contains a discussion of some of the more contemporary uses of icons – both within conventional computer applications (Sassoon and Gaur) and in systems that are intended for use on the World Wide Web (Honeywill). Another useful treatise on current applications of icons in computer systems can be found in *The Icon Book* by William Horton (1994).

In their book, Rosemary Sassoon and Albertine Gaur discuss at some length the early origins of iconography. They refer to some of the primitive uses of icons (for formulating and recording thoughts and ideas) that date back to as long ago as 35,000 BC. These authors then trace both the functional evolution of icons and their application within areas such as calligraphy, religion and art.

In his book, Paul Honeywill also makes numerous references to the historical evolution of icons. However, his primary interest seems to be their use within early Mayan communities. His main purposes in introducing the Mayan hieroglyphs within his book is to show the 'ancestry' of icons and to illustrate, from a designer's perspective, how these early icons (along with other aspects of Mayan culture) can be used as an influence on modern design activities. He describes, for example, how Mayan hieroglyphs can be used to influence the development of character fonts and logos for use on printed stationery.

Because of their communicative power, icons are now used in a wide variety of situations in order to inform people about particular conditions or to give instructions. Although much of this book is about computer icons, iconic communication does not deal exclusively with this type of icon. As we shall see in several chapters of this book, there are very many different 'non-computer' situations in which icons can be employed for communication with good effect. Typical examples of their use appear in many public information spaces, in trains, aeroplanes and cars and, increasingly, in printed books. Figures 5 and 6 illustrate two applications of icons taken from this latter domain.

The first of these examples (Cyberkath, 1997, p. 192) shows the use of icons on a printed page to indicate the nature and extent of the facilities that are available in different cybercafes. Working from left to right across the page, these icons represent the number of computer workstations available at a particular cafe, a black and white printer, a colour printer, scanning facilities, video-conferencing facilities (CU-SeeMe™), the availability of AOL (America Online) software and various 'special offers' that are available to the owner of the book (such as discounted connect time).

The second example of the use of icons in conventional books is taken from an introductory text on Microsoft's OUTLOOK – an electronic personal information manager (Price, 1998). In this book, the icons (shown in Figure 6) are used to draw readers' attention to particular conceptual aspects of the material that is being presented in the textual narrative. The three icons depicted in Figure 6 represent a handy tip, something to remember and things to be cautious about.

So far, within this chapter, much of the previous discussion relating to communication processes has been orientated towards the HHC activities that were depicted in Figure 2. If we now focus on human communication with machines and other devices (such as computers) it will be interesting to see how iconic communication (in the context of computer-based systems) has emerged and continues to evolve (Schlack, 1997). This evolution is depicted in a diagrammatic fashion in Figure 7.

This figure depicts a number of important trends that have taken place with respect to human-computer interaction. In the 'early days', users of computers communicated

USA, BIRMINGHAM (MICHIGAN)

CyberCafe@birmingham

750 South Old Woodward Ave Ph: +1 248 433 3135 Fax: +1 248 433 3620
mail@bigweb.com; http://www.bigweb.com

Location and Access
Birmingham is in the Detroit area. The cyber-
cafe is located near the 555 Bldg in down-
town Birmingham across from Borders.
Bus: 450, 460; ask for George St.
Nearest cross streets are Maple and 14 Mile.

Hours
Mon-Thu   7:30am-10pm
Fri-Sat   7:30am-midnight
Sun   10am-8pm

Prices
$7.50 per half hour
$15 per hour
AmEx, Disc, MC, Novus, V
Student, child, and senior discount available

Nearby Places to Visit
Detroit Zoo, Cranbrook Institute of Science
and Planetarium, the Holocaust Museum at
the Jewish Community Center

Figure 5: The use of icons in printed books

with them by means of simple 'binary state' switches, buttons and numeric (octal or hexadecimal) keypads. As interface technology improved, this mode of interaction was superseded by the use of QWERTY keyboards which enabled the construction of command line interfaces. These could embed a variety of different linguistic structures. As the complexity of these grew, they became more difficult to learn and remember.

Fortunately, it was found that much of the complexity of command line interfaces could be removed through the introduction of appropriately designed 'dialogue boxes'. Such graphical representations could be used to depict the structure and content of a command line interface in a pictorial way. Dialogue boxes thus enabled users to simply key-in relevant parameters into the data entry 'slots' that were contained in the graphical representations of the underlying commands. Provided people understood what they were doing, meaningful dialogue with a computer could now take place without the need to remember complex command line structures.

Over the last few years, the growing sophistication of dialogue boxes has given rise to the birth of graphical user interfaces (GUIs). These have substantially reduced the amount of typing that needs to be performed when using a computer. Instead, users just point to objects (such as icons and pictures) on the screen and select required options from lists; most often (but not always), a mouse is used to perform these pointing and selection tasks. Increasingly, the use of icons within GUIs is reducing the need to use text in lists and menu options. In addition, customisable toolbars (that embed iconic representations of commands – in the form of clickable 'buttons') are now becoming an important component within graphical user interfaces.

The increased use of icons (and iconic communication) in software packages can be seen in the trends that have taken place in the nature of the end-user interfaces to word-processing packages such as Microsoft's Word for Windows (Microsoft, 1991;

Figure 6: Further examples of the use of icons in printed books (Published previously in MS OUTLOOK *in Easy Steps. Published here with the kind permission of Computer Shop.)*

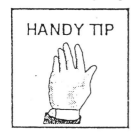

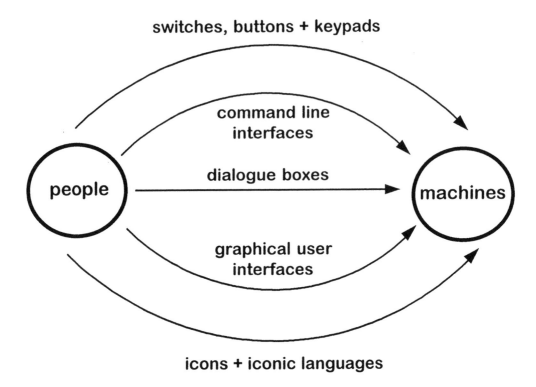

Figure 7: The evolution of iconic communication

Borland, 1997). As an illustration of some of the developments that have taken place, an example will be given from the domain of macros (Microsoft, 1994). A macro is essentially a stored program that can operate on the various objects contained in an electronic document. Once it has been created, a macro is given a name and is then stored in a library. Subsequently, a macro can be invoked when it is needed by issuing a 'run command' that contains the name of the macro to be executed. Early versions of Word for Windows also allowed a keyboard 'short-cut'(such as Ctrl/A or Ctrl/Alt/Z) to be used to invoke a particular macro. In addition to this mode of interaction, more recent versions of Word (such as Word 97) also allow a macro to be assigned to a 'button' (or icon) that can be placed on a toolbar. Facilities exist within Word 97 (for example) to enable users to create and edit icons and then place them on custom generated toolbars. In many ways, these developments reflect the power of the end-user interface to enable end-users to create their own low-level iconic languages that can be used for particular types of word-processing applications.

Because of the growing importance of icons within graphical user interfaces, it is necessary to give considerable thought to how they are designed and the factors that govern their effectiveness. In this context, William Horton's book provides a very relevant contemporary treatment of icons and contains a great deal of useful background material (Horton, 1994). It deals with such issues as why we should use icons, how they work and how to design them. He also discuses the development of simple iconic languages, the use of colour within icons and creating icons for specific purposes. A very important aspect of Horton's treatment of icons is the emphasis that he places on the need for evaluation and testing of individual icons and icon sets.

One of the many other attractive features of Horton's book is the computer diskette that accompanies it. This contains a collection of 500 icons that can be copied, edited and used within relevant applications. Incidentally, there are large numbers of icon collections now starting to become available from various sources on the World Wide Web (for example, http://cuiwww.unige.ch/eao/www/gif/gif.html). Of course, Paul Honeywill's book is also a useful starting point for locating sources of Web-based icon collections (Honeywill, 1999).

Before concluding this section, one other important topic needs to be mentioned: metaphors – and their importance within graphical user interfaces. Within the domain of human-computer interaction (particularly, end-user interface design) metaphors have been extensively studied (Carroll, Mack and Kellogg, 1988; Richards et al, 1994; Falkner, 1998). Metaphors play an important role in interfaces (both with respect to their design and their subsequent use) because they can act as 'cognitive transfer agents'. That is, they enable people to use knowledge (for example, which is represented in mental models) that they have about one particular domain (with which they are familiar) in another domain with which they are less familiar. The important role of metaphors is well-illustrated by the famous 'desktop' metaphor that has been used in many early graphical user interfaces. Essentially, this metaphor allows people to use the knowledge that they have about everyday desktop objects in an office environment (such as a telephone, fax machine, filing cabinet, notepad and so on) to predict the behaviour and properties of objects that appear on their computer screens.

Much of the 'ease of use' of a computer system often depends upon the power of the metaphors that are embedded within its end-user interfaces. Naturally, within the context of graphical user interfaces, there is an obvious and important 'reciprocal' relationship between metaphors and icons. This relationship is one of suggestion and reinforcement. The metaphor should help end-users to deduce the meaning of the icons that are used in an interface and the icons themselves should be designed in such a way that they reinforce the messages that are inherently embedded in the interface metaphor. As we will discuss later in this book, the metaphors contained in an application's end-user interface are used in order to project a 'system image' to the end-users of that application. This system image plays an important part in building the mental models that are subsequently used to facilitate problem-solving and task execution within the target domain with which the application deals (Norman, 1988).

What Next?

The rudimentary historical perspective on the evolution of icons and iconic communication that was presented in the previous section has naturally skipped over much important work that is relevant to the development of modern-day practice in iconography. However, much of this 'missing' material will be reported on later by other contributors to this book. Bearing this in mind, this section now considers some future possibilities for iconography.

Quite naturally, taking into account what was said in the earlier sections of this chapter, any attempt to predict future developments with respect to iconic communication should be based on an understanding of the types of human activity in which this technique is likely to be used. Therefore, once again taking 'people' as the central focus of importance, it is fairly easy to identify some of the important areas of technological development which are likely to involve some form of iconic communication. These areas and the relationships between them are illustrated graphically in the concept map that is presented in Figure 8.

Readers who are not familiar with concept maps or 'mind mapping' techniques are referred to for further details to the treatments presented by McAleese (1999) and the various contributors to a special issue of the Journal of Interactive Learning Research (Kommers, 1997).

Essentially, in Figure 8 six main areas have been identified wherein developments in icons and iconic languages are likely to be of importance. The nodes representing these important areas of development are labelled 1 through 6. Naturally, bearing in mind what has been said earlier in this chapter, communication processes will figure highly in the list of important future developments. Other important areas where icons will

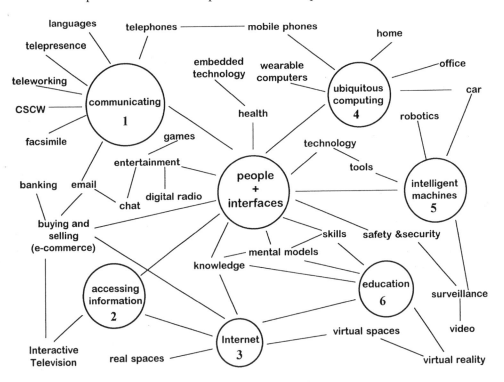

Figure 8: Potential areas of application for icons and iconic languages

have an important impact are accessing information, Internet software, ubiquitous and mobile computing equipment, interfaces to intelligent machines and devices and in education – as a consequence of their importance within the context of mental models (Barker et al, 1998).

In keeping with the major theme of this book, if the communication node in Figure 8 is now selected as the underlying 'theme for the future', there are two broad situations that need to be considered. These involve the use of iconography to support human–human communication and its use to facilitate human–machine dialogues. Because of the graphical nature of icons, their use in communication processes (of necessity) involves some form of underlying representational 'technology' – be this parchment, paper, a control button or a computer screen. Obviously, it is this latter technology that is of primary concern to us here. Bearing this in mind, some of the possible situations for potential developments relating to iconographic communication are illustrated in a 'generic' way in Figure 9.

The situation shown in the upper part of this figure represents the role of iconic communication in the context of an individual communicating with his/her computer workstation (or some other device such as an interactive TV set or a hi-fi system) in order to control some local or remote process. An example of the type of iconic languages that could be used in this sort of situation has been given previously in this chapter (see the description of macros – within the context of the Microsoft Word 97 end-user interface).

The second important situation (shown in the lower part of Figure 9) depicts a much more demanding and sophisticated example of the potential roles for iconic communication. In this example, two basic types of iconic language could be in use – either private (to a particular person at a specific workstation) or public (for common, shared use). These languages are used to facilitate group communication via a shared local or global network system. The example depicted in the lower part of Figure 9 is important because it can be thought of as forming the basis of an important form of teleworking – namely, computer-supported collaborative working (CSCW). The basic communication channels needed to support a CSCW scenario are illustrated schematically in Figure 10.

This diagram shows a number of people collaborating with each other and communicating about a problem that they are working on. Naturally, as has been suggested previously, each participant in the dialogue process has to have an appropriate set of mental models in order to communicate in a meaningful way. These models will relate to: (a) the problem being solved and (b) the way in which the CSCW system works and the functions that it provides.

The underlying network facility inherent in Figure 10 has to perform two important functions. First it has to provide a shared workspace in which to host the problem being solved; this can be either a real or a virtual space. Second, the network has to support a variety of different communicative functions. The physical links that inter-connect the various workstations therefore have to provide support for mechanisms which will allow each user to see (or 'visualise') the problem space, enable them to 'talk' about it (one to another) and, when necessary, influence it in various ways.

13

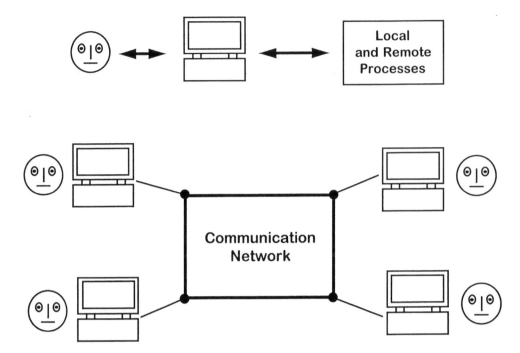

Figure 9: Potential application areas for iconography

Obviously, each of these requirements will need appropriately designed linguistic frameworks. Naturally, there is much scope here for using a variety of multi-dimensional icons and languages that are based upon them. Of course, the effective realisation of the type of situation that is depicted in figure 10 will require very sophisticated and powerful multimodal, graphical user interfaces that offer full support for network-centric computing activities. Some of these systems are already starting to appear in the form of 'network user interfaces' (Halfhill, 1997).

Conclusion

Human communication processes play many necessary and fundamental roles in virtually all areas of human endeavour. Increasingly, much of this communication is becoming mediated by machines – especially those that embed a computer system. To a large extent these machines support communicative exchange via sonic utterances (for example, a telephone or a two-way radio) and textual messages (such as typewritten documents, electronic mail and many computer-based conferencing systems). It is anticipated that in the future much greater support for visual communication techniques will become available. Within this context, iconic communication is likely to play an important role.

As will be seen from some of the material that is presented later in this book, the evolution of iconic communication is likely to take place in two distinct ways. First,

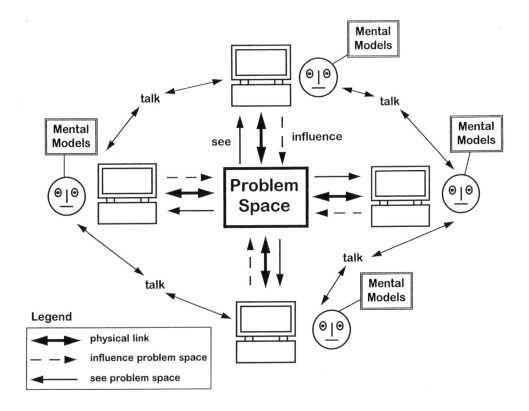

Figure 10: Human activity expressed in terms of tasks and technology

through the incorporation of icons within other more general communicative frameworks (for example, their use within graphical user interfaces for different products such as word-processors, spreadsheets, web browsers, graphics packages and animation tools). Second, through the study of the communicative power of icons themselves and iconic/pictorial languages based upon their use – as is illustrated by the work of Otto Neurath (1978), Henry Dreyfuss (1972, 1984), Adrian Frutiger (1989), Otl Aicher (1999), Barker and Manji (1997, 1989), Mealing and Yazdani (1990), Yazdani and Mealing (1995) and Colin Beardon (1995). Each of these different approaches and many of the implications of this work are discussed in detail in subsequent chapters of this book.

References

Aicher, O. (1999). Details of Otl Aicher's work are given at the following World Wide Web address: *http://www.hfg-archiveulm.de/*.

Banerji, A.K. (1995) *Designing Electronic Performance Support Systems*, PhD Thesis, Interactive Systems Research Group, Human-Computer Interaction Laboratory, University of Teesside, UK.

Barker, P.G. and Manji, K.A. (1987). 'Pictorial Communication with Computers', *International Journal of Man-*

Machine Studies, 27, 315-36.

Barker, P.G. and Manji, K.A. (1989). 'Pictorial Dialogue Methods', *International Journal of Man-Machine Studies*, 31, 323-47.

Barker, P.G., van Schaik, P. and Hudson, S.R.G. (1998). 'Mental Models and Lifelong Learning', *Innovations in Education and Training International*, 35(4), 310-18.

Beacham, N.A. (1998). *Distributed Performance Support Systems*, PhD Thesis, Interactive Systems Research Group, Human-Computer Interaction Laboratory, University of Teesside, UK.

Beardon, C. (1995). Discourse Structures in Iconic Communication, *Artificial Intelligence Review*, 9(2/3), 189-203. Also available at the following World Wide Web address: *http://www.esad.plym.ac.uk/personal/C-Beardon/papers/9508.html*.

Borland, R. (1997). *Running Word 97*, Microsoft Press, Redmond, WA, USA.

Carroll, J.M. Mack, R.L. and Kellogg, W.A. (1988). 'Interface Metaphors and User Interface Design', 67-85 (Chapter 3) in *Handbook of Human-Computer Interaction*, (M. Helander ed.), Elsevier Science Publishers, BV (North-Holland), Amsterdam, The Netherlands.

Cyberkath (1997). Cybercafes – *A Worldwide Guide for Travellers, The Wandering Traveller*, San Francisco, CA. (E-mail: cyberkath@traveltales.com)

Dreyfuss, H. (1972). *Symbol Sourcebook*, McGraw-Hill, New York, USA.

Dreyfuss, H. (1984). *Symbol Sourcebook: An Authoritative Guide to International Graphic Symbols*, Van Nostrand Reinhold, New York, USA.

Faulkner, C. (1998). *The Essence of Human–Computer Interaction*, Prentice Hall, London.

Frutiger, A. (1989). *Signs and Symbols: Their Design and Meaning*, Van Nostrand Reinhold, New York, USA.

Halfhill, T.R. (1997). 'Good-Bye GUI, Hello NUI', *BYTE*, 22(7), 60-72.

Honeywill, P. (1999). *Visual Language for the World Wide Web*, Intellect Books, Exeter, UK

Horton, W. (1994). *The Icon Book – Visual Symbols for Computer Systems and Documentation*, John Wiley & Sons, Inc, New York, NY, USA.

Kommers, P. (1997). Concept Mapping, *Journal of Interactive Learning Research*, vol. 8, issues 3 & 4, 281-502.

McAleese, R. (1999). Concept Mapping: *a Critical Review, Innovations in Education and Training International*, 36(4), 351-60.

Mealing, S. and Yazdani, M. (1990). 'A Computer-based Iconic Language', *Intelligent Tutoring Media*, 1(3), 133-36.

Microsoft (1991). *Microsoft Word for Windows* (Version 2.0) User's Guide, Microsoft Corporation, Redmond, WA, USA.

Microsoft (1994). *Microsoft Word for Windows Developer's Kit* (2nd edn.), Microsoft Corporation, Redmond, WA, USA.

Neurath, O. (1978). *International Picture Language*, University of Reading, Reading, UK.

Norman, D. (1988). *The Psychology of Everyday Things*, Basic Books, USA.

Price, M. (1998). *Microsoft OUTLOOK in Easy Steps*, Computer Step, Southam, Warwickshire, UK.

Richards, S., Barker, P.G., Banerji, A., Lamont, C. and Manji, K. (1994). 'The Use of Metaphors in Iconic Interface Design', *Intelligent Tutoring Media*, 5(2), 73-80.

Rogers, Y., Rutherford, A. and Bibby, P.A. (1992). *Models in the Mind: Theory, Perspective and Application*, Academic Press, London.

Sassoon, R. and Gaur, A. (1997). *Signs, Symbols and Icons – Pre-history to the Computer Age*, Intellect Books, Exeter, UK.

Schlack, M. (1997). 'Why Interfaces Matter', *BYTE*, 22(7), 12.

Seel, N.M. (1995). 'Mental Models, Knowledge Transfer and Teaching Strategies', *Journal of Structural Learning*, 12(3), 197-213.

Yazdani, M. and Mealing, S. (1995). 'Communicating Through Pictures', *Artificial Intelligence Review*, 9(2/3), 205-13.

2. On the Possibility and Impossibility of a Universal Iconic Communication System

Andrew J King

Impossibilities

The tendency of verbal languages to branch and split over time – in the process dividing humanity into mutually incomprehensible camps – has always been felt to be a curse, a frustrating limitation on the enormous instrumental power of language. The aetiological myth of the Tower of Babel found in the Old Testament explains it as a divine punishment for the technological hubris of mankind.

The apparent potential of images to cross cultural and linguistic boundaries, to be recognisable in a way that spoken and written words are not, makes them a tempting tool to seize on in the struggle to overcome the alienation of language.

The idea which suggests the feasibility of such a project (an anti-Babel device, in effect) is the experience of recognising, in a pictorial image, a familiar object. This in turn gives rise to the feeling that an iconic language could have a universal intelligibility, that it could form the basis of a Universal Symbolic System – one which requires little or no learning but is self-explanatory. Clive Chizlett's paper in this volume notes the fascination of some European thinkers with the potential 'universality' of ideographic symbols, apparently so different in concept from their own.

Systems of communication based on icons have, after all, been successfully employed almost since the dawn of human civilisation. Chinese, Egyptian, Mayan and other forms of writing have all used pictorial imagery to encode meaning. No one, however, is likely to claim that these writing systems are universally intelligible. Iconic signs are in fact bound by certain limitations common to all language systems. Perhaps the easiest way to argue this is to begin with an extreme case:

The Problem of Xenocommunication

Since 1971 attempts at iconic communication with alien beings have been making their way out of our solar system and into deep space, fixed to the side of the Pioneer and Voyager space probes. Examination of these plaques reveals some curious features. They assume (albeit unconsciously) a fairly high degree of familiarity with late 20th-century Western hemisphere human conventions of representation for example: the representation of three-dimensional objects (the human figures) by means of line-drawing; the convention of the directional arrow, incomprehensible to anyone who has no experience of the weapon from which its metaphor is drawn, yet so familiar to some of us as to be regarded as an intrinsically and naturally 'meaningful' image. The plaque also combines several different codes or conventions of representation, some superimposed on each other.

The plaque is an attempt at the intriguing problem of what might be called 'xenocommunication' and it reveals in the various strategies it deploys the key problem of xenocommunication. The establishment of communication between two intelligences requires, in the first instance, common experience. The resources of science are used in the Pioneer plaque to try to identify objects of common experience: the hydrogen atom, the most common element in the universe, and the pattern of pulsations of pulsars observable both from Earth and other solar systems. Even with a shared repertoire of objects to communicate about however, the establishment of an agreed code of representation is still required and here the xenocommunicator faces a really serious problem: the Pioneer and Voyager plaques will only encounter their readers (if they ever do), hundreds if not thousands of years from now, across distances

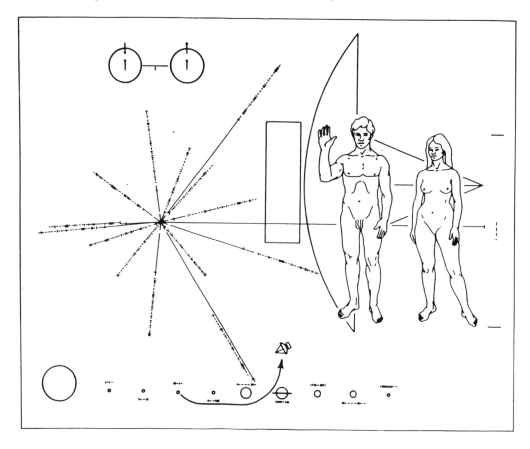

Figure 1: Pioneer Plaque. The plaques attached to the Pioneer space probes use multiple conventions of representation that depend on a particularly human cultural context.

which preclude exchange in reasonable time. It is a one-way message. It can only work as a communication, therefore, if its readers happen to have developed codes of representation sufficiently similar to our own to be able to detect or hypothesise correspondences – assuming in the first place that representation is an activity they engage in at all.

As a solution to the problem of fitting a lot of information into a small space using the limited medium of engraved metal, it does its designer some credit. One cannot help feeling, however, that it makes more sense as a public relations exercise to fellow earthlings than as a putative Rosetta Stone for extra-terrestrials. After all, was it not astronomer Fred Hoyle who pointed out that if we do ever encounter alien life forms, they are likely to be not only stranger than we imagine but stranger than we can imagine? The Pioneer plaque, on the other hand, assumes that aliens will in fact be very like us.

The Problem of Meaning

The problem of xenocommunication highlights, through an extreme case, the problem of meaning. Here on Earth, in the period spanning the end of the 19th-century and the beginning of the 20th, a number of thinkers in different times and places and from widely differing perspectives began to examine how language works and to attempt to formulate a theory of meaning. Until then the nature of meaning had been a problem almost as mysterious and intractable as the problem of the nature of consciousness is to us. If the problem was considered at all, meaning was generally held to be inherent in things, or in the things that represented them, or else already present in the mind, waiting only for the right stimulus to evoke it. It was also felt that representational signs had some kind of natural correspondence with the real world.

It was Ferdinand de Saussure[1] in the late 19th-century who pointed out the inherent arbitrariness of the linguistic sign, its total lack of any kind of 'indexical' connection or logical correspondence with the real world. Saussure, and the many theorists of language and culture who followed in his footsteps, concluded that meaning is not inherent in things but is constructed through a social contract. Saussure describes the linguistic sign as a kind of binary pair: a mental concept or idea, and the code element that represents it. Each helps to define and delineate the other from the formless chaos of infinite possibility, and the link between the two, and their differentiation from what surrounds them, is maintained by a kind of social contract or agreement. This agreement can differ widely from culture to culture – evident from the fact that different languages do not merely have different words but frequently also divide the world of subjective experience into different categories, hence the difficulties encountered by translators.

Saussure felt that the linguistic sign was a special case and that there existed also a category of 'indexical' signs, of which iconic images would be an example. These, he felt, did have some sort of logical correspondence with the things represented. Subsequent thinkers were not so sure. Even the photograph, that paradigm of truthful indexical representation of the real world, was shown by theoretical reflection and anthropological fieldwork to require a cultural consensus as to its codes of representation before it could be 'read'.[2]

Saussure is, of course, not the only thinker to have addressed the problem of meaning. An alternative tradition emphasising the importance of grammatical structures and of intention to communicate exists in the thought of Wittgenstein and associated figures, referred to in Colin Beardon's contribution to this volume. But it is largely owing to Saussure that the arbitrary and culturally constructed nature of almost any form of representation is a fundamental tenet of belief for Postmodern cultural theorists.

The Tower of Babel and the 'Toilet Door Problem'

An example of this problem can be seen in the widely used (in the Western hemisphere) toilet door symbols for men and women. These are so ubiquitous and their meaning so generally agreed, despite individual variations of style, that we forget on what an artificial convention of representation they are based. The 'man' is shown with forked, separate legs, indicating trousers, the woman with a skirt. This despite the fact that a small number of Western men wear kilts, and a large number of women wear trousers. The convention works well enough, however, in a culture in which the dress or skirt is still a clear signifier of femininity. The use of the male/female figures themselves is also conventional: the presence of sexually differentiated doorways is inferred by the user as a euphemistic reference to the evacuatory functions. As Paul Honeywill notes elsewhere in this volume, quite other symbols have from time to time been proposed.

Iconic communication systems apparently cross language barriers because they are based on a cultural consensus that is broader than that on which verbal languages are constructed. Broader, but at the same time vaguer, less rigorously enforced, less consistent and more diffuse. The Western hemisphere's toilet door symbols cross language barriers but only within a larger cultural grouping to which a certain number of languages belong: that in which a skirt-type garment has been, within living memory, a reliable signifier of 'femaleness'. Even if we were to switch to an anatomical symbol, while the meaning might be clearer to a wider cultural grouping, there would still be plenty of real and theoretical exceptions, as studies of cultural gender theory indicate.

The Problem of 'Indexical Drift'

Such a move would be an attempt to reinforce the 'indexicality' of the symbols, yet history indicates that even apparently indexical symbols have a tendency to become rapidly more arbitrary over time. The ideographic writing system of ancient Egypt was indecipherable to Europeans for hundreds of years, despite the ability to recognise clearly depicted objects still present in the Egyptian environment. The simplification of ideographs by scribes to facilitate writing tends to turn them back into arbitrary symbols, but even if that is not the case, it is necessary to add 'metasignificances' to object-symbols. It is necessary to express the properties of objects, processes, abstract concepts. The relationship between the chosen object-symbol and its abstract correlate is inevitably arbitrary, in the linguistic sense.

In the Chinese ideographic system, the image of a sword is simplified to a brush-stroke but it is also used as the correlate of the abstract concept 'nobleman'. Chinese ideographic writing does indeed display some of the claimed advantages of iconic communication. Because it operates at the level of the concept rather than of the word, it is possible for speakers of different verbal languages to share the same script. Spoken Mandarin and Cantonese are mutually unintelligible, but speakers have no difficulty communicating with one another across the barrier in ideographic script. However, it is evident that the same cannot be said for English speakers. The ideographic script exists in the context of a wider cultural consensus than the spoken languages, but it is still far from being a universal consensus.

Problems of Cultural Drift: 'What Things Are'

Iconic images also suffer from cultural drift. An amusing extrapolation of this is used in William Gibson's 'cyberpunk' novel *Idoru*. In it, the main protagonist, a teenage girl, lives a great part of her life in the virtual reality environment of her own computer. In a virtual room is a virtual coffee table, having on it various objects which are icons for application programmes or system software. Because she lives so far removed from the world of 'real things' she is beginning to lose touch with the real-world objects that the virtual icons use as metaphors for software artifacts and functions. In a kind of 'object illiteracy' that echoes the decline of traditional forms of verbal language, she is forced to consult an 'icon dictionary' entitled 'What Things Are'.

Secrecy, Elitism and Exclusion: Object Languages

One of Rudyard Kipling's *Plain Tales from the Hills*, short stories about the interaction between the British and Indians in the Raj, hinges on the use of a traditional 'language of objects'. A young British man learns this traditional symbolism and uses it to carry on a romantic correspondence with a young Indian woman in the traditional state of strict seclusion known as purdah. The 'letters' are inevitably discovered. In entering a closed circle of users of this particular set of symbols in this way, the young man has unwittingly transgressed another set of conventions and the object of his attentions is held by her relatives to be dishonoured and suffers a dreadful punishment.

The code of objects – nuts, flowers, etc., is intentionally exclusive. The according of a particular significance to them by a constrained social group is a deliberate act of exclusion – manipulating the social contract by restricting its members is what gives the language intelligibility within the group and unintelligibility outside the group, enabling it to act as a 'secret' code. Far from being an automatically universal language, any system of symbols, if (like most Western codes, such as tourist amenity symbols) it depends on knowledge of experiences accessible only to relatively few, then it will be seen by the rest of the world as a secret, exclusive code.

Inherent Ambiguity: The Tradition of 'Imprese'

The ambiguity and lack of inherent meaning in visual symbols has also been exploited in the past, not just to create secret codes but secret arcana. The elaborate heraldic visual metaphors called 'imprese' by the Italian Renaissance philosopher–princes for whom they were a favourite game were an elitist 'secret language' that also became a key to secret knowledge. The symbols themselves are ambiguous – without the Latin mottoes that accompany them, they are unintelligible. Even then, understanding often depends on a knowledge of the political circumstances under which they were created.[3]

The Neo-Platonist tradition of thought from which imprese came also included magic, and divination. Ambiguity is a key component of divination systems and the use of imprese as deliberately vague and oracular statements, at first for use in metaphysical meditations and later for cruder divination and fortune-telling systems, is a feature of this curious sub-genre of the graphic art.

Ambiguity is also essential to the creative use of any communication code. The literary critic William Empson wrote a famous analysis of its use in literature under the title *Seven Types of Ambiguity*.[4] Ambiguity forces the brain to supply meanings of its own or to search between possible alternative meanings – thus creating rich resonances of thought. Divination systems are a cruder use of the same principle. Here the ambiguity is used as a 'crystalliser' or catalyst of a hesitant thought process: 'what might the future hold, what do I want it to hold?' The point for our investigations is that ambiguity is not merely a flaw, but an inherent and necessary feature in all systems of symbolism -an ambiguity that comes from the shifting and provisional nature of the social contract that supports meaning.

Figure 2: The Renaissance tradition of imprese depended on insider knowledge for their interpretation, often being used as a badge to identify those who shared that knowledge.

The Problem of Neologisms and New Languages – Critical Mass and Inertia in Collective Cultural Artifacts

Even if, in the face of these difficulties, one sets out to create a universal iconic language, there remains the fascinating problem of critical mass. One of the curious features of language noted by the founders of linguistic science is that while languages constantly change over time, it is normally beyond the power of any given individual to introduce arbitrary change. Language falls into a peculiar class of social artifacts which are created collectively and unconsciously and therefore are not normally open to self-conscious, individual intervention and change – to design, in fact. This problem

Figures 3/4: In an elaborate architectural joke, the images carved on the metopes of The Circus, Bath, by 18th century British architect John Wood are thought to be derived in part from Wither's Emblemes, a fortune-telling book based on imprese. (Mowl and Earnshaw, John Wood, Architect of Obsession, 1989.) Far from being immediately intelligible, the ambiguity of such symbols is essential to the game.

affects the possibility of creating new languages from scratch. The limited success of such deliberately created universal languages as Esperanto is a commonplace example.

That is not to say that the language cannot be changed in small ways: especially by the influence of a small, tightly integrated 'outsider' sub-group. The sub-groups of surfing and of computer programmers have contributed an amazing number of new words and phrases to the speech of people who live hundreds of miles from the sea or have never written code in their lives. Ethnic groups can and do have a similar influence. A relatively small and tightly integrated sub-group can renegotiate the social contract of language, within certain limits, with individual innovations quickly taken up and rapidly spread throughout the group. In the age of mass communications, if the sub-group attains a certain prestige (or notoriety) its innovations will be imitated and incorporated into the contract of the larger group.

It is also not to say that whole new languages cannot be established in special circumstances. The British and American variants of sign language for the deaf constitute a flourishing linguistic culture, with a unique literature and 'voice' of its own. The special case of sign language is based upon the existence of a de-facto sub-

Figure 5: The apparent literalness of alchemical symbols provided a puzzling decoy to distract attention from the metaphysical ideas, while providing a set of fruitfully ambiguous mental images for adepts to base their meditations upon.

group with a vested interest in communicating via the visual rather than the auditory channel. Once the historical isolation of deaf people in society was overcome by the provision of facilities for social interaction, the ground was prepared – a social group ready to form a contract – the language itself the means by which the contract is formed. Or rather language is itself a contract. It can be a contract between two, as in the secret languages developed by twins brought up in isolation by non-speaking parents, or between many, as in a national tongue, but it remains in its fundamental essence a social contract. The actual code is merely the vehicle or medium through which the contract, and thus the group itself, is forged. Without it, it is merely a set of sounds, shapes, movements or objects. Indeed, the experimental designs for a set of 'modifier' icons to supplement written computer communication put forward by Cruikshank in his contribution to this book assumed from the start the active involvement of a defined user group.

The importance of the social contract perhaps suggests another reason why iconic languages have rarely achieved much success: they are not normally used, with the same ubiquity, intensity and sheer frequency as verbal language. The drawing of pictures is always less fluent than the writing of stylised ideograms, phonetic symbols or the use of hand movements or speech. This lack of fluency limits the opportunity for the everyday use and familiarity needed to enable the creation, negotiation and passing on of a contract of meanings. Only with the establishment of a worldwide community of computer users has some kind of rudimentary and still inconsistent language of screen icons developed. Barker and van Schaik have noted that their attempts to study the efficacy of icons as a means of communicating software skills (described in this volume) were often hampered by the reluctance of their subjects to devise, draw and use icons outside of the computer context in which they were learnt.

Threats
Before we leave the consideration of the impossibilities, two threats to the project of building a universal iconic language deserve mention, one from the verbal side and one, paradoxically, from the visual.

The 'Visualisation' of Culture through TV and Telematics
Professor Barbara Maria Stafford of the University of Chicago studies the global shift towards what she calls 'visual modalities', as evident in the internet and other digital media.[5] Her work asks what the implications are for the arts, education and a range of other disciplines of a culture which increasingly emphasises visual intelligence and visual modes of communication. In the context of such an approach, the project of an iconic language is seen to be a subset of a wider field of visual communication, a field which has ways of thinking and talking that might ultimately make such a specific approach to the problems of visual communication seem unduly limiting.

The Threat of 'Universal English'
Is the whole project likely to be overtaken by universal English? English, despite the counterclaims of other languages, is the most common second language on the planet. It has been for many years the language of business, of international aviation and, through the internet, of telematic communications. Could the dominance of 'world English' render the development of visual iconic languages unnecessary?

Possibilities
It is now time to switch from pessimism to optimism and to consider what factors might give the project of a universal iconic language some currency.

If we accept, with the semioticians, that meaning depends on a social contract, then it follows that universal meaning requires a universal contract. What are the possibilities in a global culture? Are the spread of Coca-Cola, Mickey Mouse, Big Macs, Hilton Hotels and global marketing actually the key to the success of this project? Has international advertising already begun to establish just such a global code of icons?[6]

Multimedia as a Language – objects and spaces – filmic language
The perspective provided by Stafford, referred to above, also of course provides an avenue of possibility, albeit for a form of visual communication more loosely based on existing modes of 'visual discourse' than on a specific code of symbols, however elaborated. The long established 'language' of film-making is one example, the less well-developed extensions of it into interactive multimedia and immersive computer games potentially provide users simultaneously with a shared experience and a language with which to articulate it. Insofar as the conventions of the 'movie' or the computer game are internationally understood, they suggest possible modalities for international communication.

25

Possibilities of Chomskyan 'Deep Grammar' and a 'Language Instinct'; Language as Evolved Behaviour

The possibilities discussed so far remain nested within the cultural matrix we have identified as an essential prerequisite for language. There are some areas of thought about language, however, which posit an element of linguistic function which is in some way 'pre-cultural', operating at an instinctive or even neurological level, as a result of evolutionary development of 'language behaviour'. The idea, in short, is that there exists 'hard-wired' into the human brain, a pre-existing functional matrix for language on top of which particular culturally constructed language forms are erected by social behaviour. This concept of 'natural language' is a highly controversial one but it holds out the possibility that there is a stratum of grammatical structures[7] which are common to all human beings, regardless of race or culture, and which might therefore form a basis for some sort of universal communication system.

Jungian Archetypes

The psychologist Carl Jung proposed the idea of 'archetypal' images and themes – common to the human race as a whole because they express experiences common to the human condition regardless of culture. Many widespread ancient symbols are thus claimed by Jungians to have roots in the subconscious. Such a theory, while again controversial, provides an obvious starting point for investigating the possible existence of a small lexicon of truly universal symbols. If the theory is correct, such symbols would, however, be likely to deal with very fundamental ontological/existential themes rather than the trivia of practical day-to-day communication.[8]

'Epistemology of the Body'

A final enabling possibility to consider lies in recent developments in the field of epistemology. Mark Johnson[9] has put forward the notion that the physical human body and its functions provide a set of basic concepts common to all human beings which he terms 'kinaesthetic image schemas' and which he suggests are the basic 'building blocks' of human knowledge. If this were true, such concepts would exist a priori to cultural constructs but would nevertheless be common to all humans, again, forming a possible base for the erection of a limited but universal symbolic system.

Conclusions

Universal Symbolism and the Modernist Utopia

Mealing and Yazdani[10] have cited the Isotype system as an early example of success in the construction of an iconic language. Isotype was born in the 1930s out of a felt need to create visual representations of population data. The use of a fixed code of icons was to a great extent a product of the printing technology of the time. It was restricted largely to the visual representation of quantitative relationships.

The Isotype system was in many ways a quintessentially Modernist project, an attempt to impose logic, order and rationality, to disseminate universally valid knowledge by universally valid means. Indeed, the creation of universal languages or systems of one sort or another has been a characteristically Modernist project – one which implies a much more stable world of thought than that in which we now exist.

Culture, Context and Interpretation – Linguistics and Postmodern Critical Theory

The development of linguistics as a discipline has been the foundation-stone (if such a metaphor is not inappropriate) for much of postmodern theory. Its revelation of the socially constructed, and therefore contingent, ephemeral and arbitrary nature of ideas and values that were previously (and often still are) held to be 'natural', 'universal' and rational, has opened up radically new perspectives on cultural activities of all kinds, both in sciences and arts. It has provoked in some quarters a pessimistic relativism, a feeling that if we cannot have timeless and universal truths and values, then we are doomed to have none. In other quarters it has provoked a virulent reaction against such pessimism, characterised by attempts to deny the insights of linguistic cultural theory and to re-establish permanent values.

An approach which is perhaps more justified by the nature of the insights involved sees the change in perspective as a devolution of responsibility: no longer are cultural artifacts, theories, values seen to be universal, validated by reference to absolutes outside of human culture and thus imprisoning: tools of domination, exploitation or exclusion. Instead, theories and values are recognised as cultural processes, in a state of constant flow and mutation, valid for particular groups, circumstances and times but in a process of constant re-negotiation.

To view the project of an iconic language in such a context is to recognise that the challenge in establishing communication is not one of simply designing a code and transmitting information but a human, social and political problem of establishing and maintaining cultural consensus, of convening a 'group', an act which in itself involves negotiating a 'system of differences', a shared way of dividing up and structuring the world of experience and thus giving it meaning – a shared worldview.

The problem of motive power was not to devise a perpetual motion machine but to devise one that would efficiently transform an input of energy into an output of motion. For the promoters of a universal system of communication, the problem is not to create a supposedly indexical and therefore universally intelligible set of symbols, having a clear relationship to the real world – that is as much a chimera as perpetual motion. The problem is rather to facilitate the negotiation and ownership, by the widest possible group, of a 'structure of differences' of which the symbols are ultimately only an arbitrary expression.

Aliens and Alienation

Meaning is not inherent, nor are the codes by which meaning is transmitted inherently rational. Meaning is a social contract – yet such conclusions never seem to fully explain its power. When we encounter it in a meaningful word or symbol, or sense its lack, we focus on the symbol itself as having or not having meaning. In this a peculiar type of alienation is at work. When experiencing language, we forget we have (collectively and unconsciously) created it. We forget also that it has been created 'immanently'. That is to say, language does not come about like a designed object, conceived, originated and implemented; rather it is continuously, incrementally and without any profound discontinuity marking 'beginning' existent. We forget that it is not a 'system' 'out there' but a social grouping to which we do or do not belong. Universal meaning implies a universal social contract and is therefore a social, cultural and political issue.

The director of the SETI Institute[11] which scans the skies for radio signals that might indicate intelligent life has expressed the thought that the discovery of extraterrestrial intelligence will unite divided human cultures. Perhaps Pioneer holds the key after all: human cultural unification in response to contact with the 'other'.

Notes

1. Saussure, Ferdinand de. (1960) *Course in General Linguistics*, trans. Wade Baskin, London.
2. For an accessible example, see the discussions of oriental reactions to western perspective in Gombrich, *Art and Illusion*, chap. 8.
3. For example, see Praz, Mario. (1981) 'The Gonzaga Devices' in: *Splendours of the Gonzaga*, Chambers and Martineau (eds.), Victoria and Albert Museum.
4. Empson, William. (1930) *Seven Types of Ambiguity*, London.
5. Stafford, Barbara Maria. *Good Looking: Essays on the Virtue of Images*, University of Chicago.
6. Yazdani, M. and Mealing, S. (1995) *Communicating Through Pictures*, Exeter University, Department of Computer Science, (an example based on hotel booking – a westernised and westernising concept that is likely to be part of any emerging 'global culture'.)
7. Chomsky, Noam. (1972) *Language and Mind*, 2nd edn. New York.
8. For a recent discussion of these ideas, see Stevens, Anthony. (1988) Ariadne's Clue: *A Guide to the Symbols of Humankind*, London.
9. Johnson, Mark. (1987) *The Body in the Mind: The Bodily Basis of Meaning, Imagination and Reason*.
10. Mealing, S and Yazdani, M. (1990) 'A Computer-based Iconic Language', in *Intelligent Tutoring Media*, vol.1 no 3, pp.133-36.
11. SETI (Search for Extra Terrestrial Intelligence) Institute, Mountain View. California. For an account of more recent attempts at xenocommunication and the problem of representation see *Lets Learn Lincos* in *New Scientist* magazine, 18 September 1999, pp. 36-9

Illustration acknowledgements

Figure 1.   NASA
Figure 2.   V&A Picture Library
Figure 3/4.   Millstream Books
Figure 5.   Thames & Hudson

3.   The Limits Of Iconic Communication

John Roscoe

The contributors to this volume are all to some degree the inventors of what are intended to be iconic languages (or at least fragments of such languages). Now the business of inventing languages has a long history in which parts have been played by some of the very greatest thinkers, men such as Descartes, Newton and Leibniz, but it has also been the province of innumerable cranks and fanatics. These have included at the very least one man who was barking mad. His name was Urquhart; he was a colonel in the Royalist cavalry and rode into the Battle of Worcester with the manuscript of a treatise on an iconic language in his saddle-bags. Weighed down by these 1,200 foolscap pages, he was, of course, very quickly captured by Cromwell and the pages of his manuscript met what was, to judge by Urquhart's surviving writings, a quite appropriate end: they were used by the soldiers of the New Model Army for what a contemporary chronicler delicately describes as 'an essential military purpose'.

No time need be wasted on the details of Urquhart's essay in iconic communication; as far as can be judged, he quite failed to grasp what he was about: the man had no clear notion of what communication is and none at all of what an icon might be. His modern successors ought to be sure of having clear answers to these same questions before attempting to communicate using icons. We may otherwise be trying to do something that cannot be done and our projects may deserve no less ignominious a fate than that suffered by Urquhart's.

Communication

The reader may think he has grasped the meaning of the chronicler referred to; that is to say, he may think he knows what the chronicler had in mind. The present author is communicating with the reader now to the extent the reader thinks he knows what the author had in mind. As he put pen to paper, he was thinking about Urquhart, and if this thinking was like anything other than itself, then it was like having a certain picture come before the mind.[1] The reader too was made to think about Urquhart; a similar picture was put into his mind. Communication, it seems, is most usefully seen as the transferring of a picture from one mind into another – although there are important ways in which these pictures are very unlike pictures that might be drawn on a piece of paper. Human beings are not telepathic creatures, and because they are not, some physical intermediary must be used to effect such transfers. If this suggestion be accepted, then iconic communication becomes something quite precise. It is this: the use of icons in transferring pictures from one mind to another. This pronouncement may have an air of obviousness but this is something that must be said clearly if the limitations on iconic communication are to be understood. These limitations will still not be grasped until it has been said just as clearly exactly what an icon is.

Icons

For this to be clearly said, attention must first be drawn to the character of the world that human beings share. (Because for them it is the world, they do not often notice what it is like.) It is a world full of things. Urquhart was one of these things, this book is another and so too are the reader's room and its chairs and tables. The important thing to notice is that whilst each of the things mentioned is an individual thing, each also belongs to a specific type of thing. Urquhart was a human being; the author and his reader too are human beings: they are all of the same type as Urquhart, the type which bears the name 'Human Beings'. The chairs in the reader's room are not human beings but each of them is of the same type as all the others, the type whose name is 'Chairs'. One can remind oneself of all this by saying that the world shared by human beings is a world typified, by which is intended that everything in it is of some type or other. The philosophically inclined stop in wonder at this point; one wants to ask why there should be types and not just things. But then one becomes grateful that the world is typified and that it is typified in the same way for each of us, for it is apparent as soon as one starts to consider the matter that had it not been so, we humans should not have been able to communicate with one another at all.

Marks

Amongst the types of things that humans find in this world are not just people and chairs but also marks. Marks do occur naturally – moss and lichens mark stones, for example – but of far greater importance to us are the marks we make ourselves: marks smeared by our primitive ancestors on the walls of their caves in the blood of mammoths, marks made by our historical selves on papyrus, parchment and paper, and marks caused by our modern selves to appear on computer screens. Something else calculated to arouse the philosopher's wonder is this: that not only are marks typified but marks and things are typified in precisely the same way. Here, for example, is a mark which is easily made in a book:

it is a mark of the same type as any other picture of a human being. 'Pictures of Human Beings' is the name of a type of mark, just as 'Human Being' is the name of a type of thing. The marvellous fact is that a type of mark corresponds to each type of visible thing. Other individual marks of the same type as '⚲' might have been exhibited here but this particular individual mark was chosen because whilst it is unambiguously of the type to which it belongs (it is unambiguously a picture of a human being), it is the simplest individual of that type which can be contrived. (The reader who is not satisfied that this is so is at liberty to substitute for '⚲' any mark which he feels better fits the description.) Being a very simple individual of the type called 'Pictures of Human Beings', it is certainly not a picture of any particular human being (it no more depicts Urquhart, for example, than it does the reader – but no less so either). It is a mark that hardly corresponds to a thing in the way that the painting of Urquhart in the National Portrait Gallery corresponds to him. This individual mark corresponds not to an individual but to a type: this mark is an icon.

Several other icons will be needed in the course of the present discussion. The reader may not always see without being told to which type of thing each corresponds but that is only because the business of making icons is really rather difficult: in principle, there is no need for anything to be said. The correspondence between icons and types of things is a natural one; it is one valid for all human beings.

Iconic Communication

A clear statement can now be offered of what iconic communication would be: it would be the use in transferring pictures from one human mind into another of tokens of types of marks which, for human beings, correspond naturally to types of things. What must next be clarified is how such transfers could be accomplished. The thought of Urquhart riding into battle can certainly be communicated by making a picture of Urquhart riding into battle but that is hardly what one has in mind with iconic communication. But communication would be established iconically if icons were used in making pictures. How could this be done? – Well, a picture is always a complex thing; a picture has parts. Each of the parts of a picture is itself a picture, as the reader will discover by inspecting the picture already inside his own mind.

The parts of a picture of Urquhart riding into battle (Figure 1), finding himself in dire straits and beating his horse to drive it on, for example, are pictures of such things as a man, a horse, a bulging saddle-bag, an enormous manuscript and so on. The picture of a man which is a part of this great picture has in its turn such parts as pictures of an arm, pictures of a leg and a picture of a head. The picture of a head in its turn has such parts as pictures of an eye. A picture could then be made by reproducing some of the parts of the original with icons. Figure 2 (in which use has been made of an iconic man and an iconic horse) might be a part of that picture: What is seen is a man on a horse. Such a reproduction of a mental picture by a spatial arrangement of icons on, let us say, a computer would be one way of communicating the thought iconically. But such a procedure would be of little use for communicating anything other than spatial relations: the icons would be spatially arranged much as the component parts of the original picture had been. But not only has the proper pictorial arrangement of things become somewhat distorted (here Urquhart is not sitting properly on his horse) but the individuality of things has been completely suppressed. The result is

Figure 1

Figure 2

Figure 3

a picture of a man on a horse; what was wanted was a picture of Urquhart on his horse. To make this a picture of a particular man, the iconic man will have to be labelled. If the only marks allowed for use are icons (as they should be if what is intended is iconic communication), then it will be necessary to show that the icon which labels the man is being used in a special way, namely as a label. This might be done by using a different fount of iconic signs or a different weight or colour or even by putting a ring around icons being used in this special way, to isolate them, as it were, from the picture composed from the other icons (see Figure 3).

Urquhart's horse was called 'Soldier' which is the name in our language of a type of visible thing, so the iconic horse in the reconstructed picture above has been labelled using an iconic soldier (the reader will notice the banner proudly held aloft).

However, the ease with which this is done rather confuses the real issue. 'Urquhart' is an antique name in the unfamiliar language of the Highland Scots; for the Sassenach, the word has no meaning and lacks an iconic equivalent. But it does not matter what iconic name we give Urquhart. The function of a name is to identify something in our mental pictures and then to re-identify it as the same individual when it appears in other pictures. We can use any icon as a name provided only we always use the same one. Urquhart might be given the name 'Bear', for instance, because an iconic bear is easily contrived (Figure 4).

Recipes for Making Pictures

There might well be certain special uses for such a system (it might be a fragment of an iconic language) but it could not be a universal system of communication (as natural languages are), for there is also the need to communicate non-spatial relations. To do this, the things related have to be pick-out and an indication given of which relation it is that connects them. This too is something easily done using icons. Thus in the case of the picture of a man on a horse, the iconic man would not be placed above an iconic horse (as was done just now); rather, an icon would be introduced which corresponded not to a type of thing (as do both '𐅀' and '𐅆') but to a type of relation between things, namely to the type of relation we call 'Being On'. Just as Urquhart and the reader and

Figure 4

author are all things of one and the same type, so are Urquhart's-being-on-a-horse and the-reader's-being-on-a-chair and the author's-being-at-his-writing-table all relations of one and the same type. Here is another picture of a human being:

Whereas the figure in '⚡' is simply being the thing he is, this new iconic man is behaving in a special way: he is standing on something. (It can be seen that he is by the way his feet are turned out.) In human communication, this icon might be used in such a way that it was not an alternative iconic man but an iconic something-on-something-else. An icon employed in this way is rather different from '⚡' or '⌐' used as they have been above: they brought to mind things of the same visual type, whereas what is done by '⚡' (used in the way now intended) is to bring to mind certain abstract things of the same conceptual type. In the picture of Urquhart, a man (whose iconic name is 'Bear') is on his horse (whose iconic name is 'Soldier'); that is the picture intended to be brought before the reader's mind with the following arrangement of icons:

It is necessary to show which type of thing is related to which other type of thing; to identify the individual things in question; to show what type of relationship obtains between them – and indeed, an arrow is needed to make this clear, for a picture of a man on a horse is not at all the same as one of a horse on a man.

Given such a system, the iconic communicator is no longer restricted to merely spatial relations. In the picture to be tranferred, Urquhart is also beating his horse; Urquhart and horse stand to one another in the 'Beating' relation as well as the 'Being-on' relation. This can be communicated iconically using an iconic thug (a human being behaving as a thug and thrashing something with his stick) in the manner shown in Figure 6.

What has been done here might be described as the iconic reduction of an ordinary picture of a man beating the horse which he is riding. This is still a two-dimensional

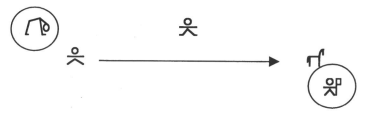

Figure 5

arrangement of icons but it is not so much a picture as a recipe for making a picture. The recipe constituted by this complex of marks is followed by making a mental picture of a man, arranging it in the attitude of a rider, putting it on a horse and having it beat the animal with a stick. At the same time, the picture is related to any others the reader may have seen in which either a man called Urquhart or a horse called Soldier make their appearances.

These simple means are enough for the iconic reduction of pictures in which things are related in the most complex ways (pictures in which the relations are 'polyadic', as a logician would say). Thus a picture of Urquhart handing over Soldier to somebody else (whose name we do not need to know) might be reduced as in Figure 7.

Here this icon, '◌̃', has been used not as an iconic hand releasing a ball but as an iconic something-relinquishing-something; and similarly this icon, '◌', not as an iconic hand grasping a ball, but as an iconic something-acquiring-something. (An important feature of this scheme lies in the immediate way in which it tells us to make a picture of the same horse being related in different ways to two different people.)

Titles

Any way of making use of the two-dimensions available for iconic communication would be some variation on this scheme. But there is quite another way in which to make a recipe for making a picture. The recipes in question now are of the sort we call titles. The phrase, 'A man on horseback' is the title used in spoken English when a speaker wants his audience to make for itself mental pictures of a man on horseback. An iconic title would make use not of English words but of the icons which correspond to parts of the mental picture.

The only familiar titles are those which can be made using natural languages. The important difference between a picture and a natural language title is this: whereas the picture is a two-dimensional entity, the title is essentially only one-dimensional. The title somehow reduces the picture from two dimensions to just one. A natural language title has to do this because a speech utterance is only one-dimensional: it consists of a linear sequence of sounds, 'man' – 'on' – 'horse', for example. But icons are essentially two-dimensional entities. If an iconic title were just a sequence of icons, then an opportunity to exploit the second dimension which the computer screen (unlike the medium of spoken language) possesses would seem to have been squandered. But has

Figure 6

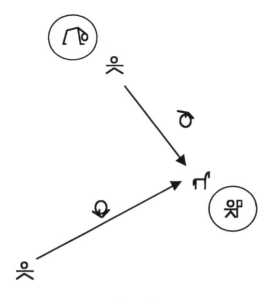

Figure 7

anything been squandered? – does the two-dimensionality of our iconic medium present us with new possibilities?

Consider how one-dimensional iconic titles might be made. The problem is clear: the two-dimensional spatial organization of the iconic reduction of the ordinary picture of a man on horseback with which we began has to be replaced by the sort of one-dimensional syntactical organization found in language. In the two-dimensional case, the iconic reduction is essentially a labelled and directed line (a labelled vector, as a mathematician would say). It is only necessary to write down its label together with the icons which are its end points in the order in which these three occur as one moves along the vector to do as language does and reduce the two-dimensional picture in Figure 8 to a single dimension, as in Figure 9.

This feels very natural to a speaker of English because in this sequence, icons occur in the same order as English words do in the title 'Man on Horse'. This is also the order in which words occur in a title written in Chinese, the other of the great human languages, but not for, example, in Japanese or many other languages. In this sense, this iconic title and the corresponding English or Chinese titles are all of one and the same type. If the reader be told, as he now is, that the titles which follow are also of that type, then he will construct for himself the mental pictures, as in Figure 10, it is

Figure 8

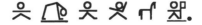

Figure 9

intended he should. The present author has now communicated with his reader iconically – purely iconically: there is nothing in these examples but icons. They are expressions of a rudimentary language, one which is clearly quite autonomous in respect of any natural language. The interesting thing about this autonomous language is its semantics, the source, that is, of the meaningfulness of its sentences: they have been derived directly from two-dimensional iconic reductions of ordinary pictures. (To appreciate the importance of this, the reader is invited to attempt an explanation of where the English word 'man' gets its meaning let alone the phrase 'a horse on a man'.) Here we have a first indication of the power and the real value of iconic communication. Of course, a lot remains to be done before titles can be made with the same precision as in a natural language – things need to be identified by their names but if we know which icons are being used as iconic things and which as iconic relations, then we can simply put the iconic name of a thing beside it in the sequence, like in Figure 11 (rather than being ringed, the icons being used as names have been underlined; this seems more appropriate in writing). Here it is Urquhart again who is on Soldier; and in Figure 12, Urquhart is not only mounted on Soldier but is also beating the animal. To deal with polyadic relations, it is necessary to allow simple titles to be combined as the title of a complex picture; that is the function of the systems of punctuation used in writing down complex sentences of natural language. In the case of the picture of the horse being handed over, there were two partial titles, which are

Figure 10

Figure 11

Figure 12

36

shown in Figure 13. This, for example, might now be done, using a colon to combine the reductions of individual vectors, as in Figure 14.

These are sentences from what is still a very rudimentary language; if we used it to communicate, we should quickly feel the lack of the natural language devices which enable us to identify and re-identify particular individual things which have no names, or whose names are unknown (as the words 'a' and 'the' do in English).

Saying 'that'

The reader who recognizes the figure inspired by Rodin's Penseur in Figure 15 might have supposed that the intention in making it was to supply the title for a picture of someone thinking about a picture; the intention was actually to give its title to a picture of someone having a thought. Mental pictures, like the example in Figure 16, are clearly more elaborate than ordinary pictures could be. For example, the people in mental pictures may be behaving in such special ways as saying something in particular; they may even be thinking secret thoughts. If the ordinary pictures we draw on paper are to show such things, then they must be elaborated by exploiting the second dimension of the picture surface. This is what the cartoon artist does with his speech – and thought – bubbles. The thought that Urquhart was thinking about beating his horse might be communicated by making a picture of Urquhart and adding a second picture contained within a bubble coming out of his head, this time the picture of Urquhart beating the horse.

The two-dimensional iconic reduction of such a picture, as in Figure 17, is interesting; the iconic picture ('□') which appears in the title must be identified as the particular picture it is – just as the iconic man has been identified as Urquhart: the picture too must be given its own iconic name, represented in Figure 18.

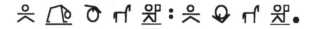

Figure 13

Figure 14

Figure 15

37

Figure 16

What could the name of this picture be? – Well, there is no need to invent names for pictures, for what is the title of a picture if not its name? Any recipe for making the picture bubbling out of Urquhart's head could be used to name the picture within a picture above. The whole picture could then be reduced iconically in the manner seen in Figure 19.

The thought which corresponds to it is a thought of one of the most abstract sorts that we humans have (it is concerned with what philosophers call a mental intention); nevertheless, its one-dimensional reduction is easily accomplished. We already have the device we need: we can write our title in the manner of Figure 20: underlining the icons which make up the title of the inner picture to mark them as a name.

Figure 17

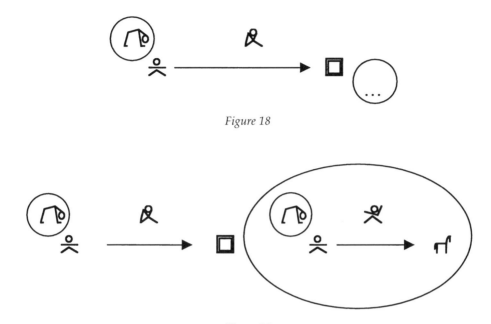

Figure 18

Figure 19

Modality

Observe that this device makes the iconic picture of a picture, '□', function like the English word 'that'. Enabling a system of communication to say 'that' is actually of fundamental importance: it enables one picture to be embedded inside another. For if a system of iconic communication is to be universal, then it must be able to express what is expressed in familiar natural languages by the tenses and other modalities of the verbs in a sentence. Once we can say 'that', the rest easily follows. For we can then say that Urquhart rode on horseback rather than that he is riding or will be riding, by showing how a picture of a man on horseback is related to some part of the abstract entity we call time. The iconic reduction of a timeless picture of Urquhart thinking about beating his horse has just been presented. A picture identified by the iconic reduction of a picture of the man beating his horse was related to Urquhart as an act of thinking. In a picture in which Urquhart's beating of his horse is in the past, the same picture is related not to Urquhart but to time past, and the relation is one not of beating but of being included in. What is the two-dimensional iconic reduction of that picture? – Well, it would be something like Figure 21. Here a mental picture (identified by its

Figure 20

39

name-giving title as one of Urquhart beating his horse) is related, in some way that cannot yet be written down, to some similarly embarassing entity. Whilst an icon might be made with which to replace the question mark, '?', labelling the vector, a closed fist, for example, (something which might have something else enclosed within it), '□', none could be made to replace the first question mark. Iconic men and iconic horses can be produced without much difficulty; so too can iconic people behaving in many different ways. But no iconic time past, or iconic time present, or iconic time future could be made. This is not, of course, a limitation only upon the two-dimensional system, for it recurs in the one dimensional reduction, seen in Figure 22.

Conclusion

Here then is the limit of purely iconic communication. If either of the two systems sketched above is to be exploited, the vocabulary of icons will have to be supplemented with marks which do not have natural meanings. The one dimensional title can still be translated word-for-word into English more or less intelligibly as 'Past-time has that man beating horse' but a mark which is purely arbitrary, a conventional sign, will be needed to take the place of 'time-past'. This means that a purely iconic system of communication could be at best the first stage towards a universal language. (There are, incidentally, good reasons for thinking that even natural languages must have begun their evolution as purely iconic systems.)

The titles which were embedded within other titles functioned syntactically just like such iconic names as 'Bear' or 'Soldier'. The difference is that whereas the names were simple signs, the titles were complex ones: each consisted of a series of signs. These complex signs are conventional, by which is meant that it is not enough just to be a sighted and otherwise normally endowed human being to understand them. They are, however, also systematic in the sense that anyone who knows what the component

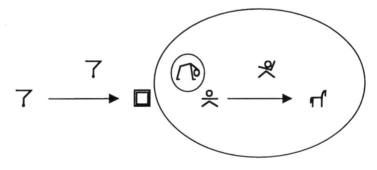

Figure 21

Figure 22

parts are intended to mean can work out the intention behind the sign as a whole. Most of the icons we see on our computer screens today are precisely arrangements as a single sign of iconic components. Most projects for iconic communication do in fact use conventional signs which are systematic combinations of iconic components, although not combined by the sort of linguistic syntax that has been explained above. (They are usually either unstructured ensembles of icons or else their components are pictorially arranged. They are usually intended to remind one of a meaning which must either be guessed at or discovered by some indirect means.)

It has been shown, first, that despite what might have been supposed, the second dimension of the medium of iconic communication does not offer opportunities for saying anything that could not be said in a one-dimensional language; and, secondly, that a purely iconic language could not constitute a universal vehicle of communication. This is not, of course, to say that an iconic system could not be a very useful fragment of a universal system. Indeed, it has also been indicated that its great strength lies in revealing immediately when it is the same thing and when different things that occur and recur in very complex relationships.

But an intriguing possibility does suggest itself in the case of a language which has an iconic core, without restricting itself to iconic signs. It is this: that whereas in the present paper a language has been sketched with a similar structure to that of many natural languages, one might be invented which in its initial iconic stage had a structure so novel by the standards of natural languages that were this core to be supplemented with the conventional signs necessary to make it as universal as a natural language, it would be possible for us to write down the titles of pictures which have no natural language titles. It might then be that this new language could provide us with titles which were recipes for making mental pictures which we otherwise could never have brought to mind. It would be the vehicle for thinking entirely novel thoughts. One can at least coherently conceive of this possibility; whether it is a real possibility is a profound question for the philosophy of mind which is not on today's agenda.

Incidentally, that 'essential military purpose' to which our chronicler referred was making cartridges for Cromwell's musketeers – but the reader, of course, understood that all along. Communication really is best understood as the transferring of picture's from one mind to another, but we should resist the temptation to suppose that we understand so very much more than just that about the whole business. The road to understanding may prove to go by way of languages we invent rather than by way of the languages we grow up speaking.

Reference

Roscoe, John (1999). Ideography, Stavanger University Press

Notes

1. But this is mere façon de parler: whilst thinking is like having a picture come before the mind, I do not want to be understood as committing myself to the reality of mental pictures, or, indeed, to that of any of the 'cognitive structures' discussed in this volume in Barker and von Schaik's Icons in the Mind. The issue is addressed in detail in my Ideography (and particularly in Parts I and VI).

Background

4. Some Pictorial Symbol Systems for Public Places

Ian McLaren

Otto Neurath and the 'Isotype Movement'

Neurath initially developed his method of visual presentation of statistical information as an educational medium using pictograms in Leipzig during World War One. Later he returned to Vienna where after their enthusiastic acceptance at a co-operative for one-parent housing, he was responsible for the inauguration of the Museum for Housing and Town Planning in 1923. This museum developed a wider function and adopted the title 'Social and Economic Museum in Vienna' ('Wirtschaftsmuseum in Wien'). Neurath later married his first employee at the museum and the names Otto and Marie Neurath were inseparable throughout the evolution of what became known as the Isotype Movement. This employed a schematised form of representation of pictorial symbols to illustrate social and economic data. Originally called the 'Vienna Method', following the Neuraths' move to Holland was later anglicised to 'international system of typographic picture education' – hence ISOTYPE. A central concern therefore of the Isotype system is the representation of quantities for public information (Figure 1). In the catalogue of the exhibition prepared at Reading University during 1975, Twyman refers to this as 'pictorial statistics' (Edwards and Twyman, 1975).

A basic principle of the Isotype system is that each symbol represents both a topic and a designated quantity. Neurath clearly conceived the system as a pictorial language, with its own syntax. One of his earliest publications was entitled 'Statistical Heiroglyphs' (Neurath, 1926). In 1936 he published 'International picture language: the first rules of Isotype' (Neurath, 1936). From 1928 onwards, with the help of Gerd Arntz – a German artist who produced woodcuts and linocuts, he systematically developed and compiled the collection of symbols (Figure 2). The reference document for this was known as the 'Symbol Dictionary'. The first was produced principally by Arntz using hand-cut linocuts. It was necessary to compile a second version as a result of their flight from Holland. This version employed metal line blocks, which presumably would have been photoengraved from line drawings.

United States, Wheat Trade

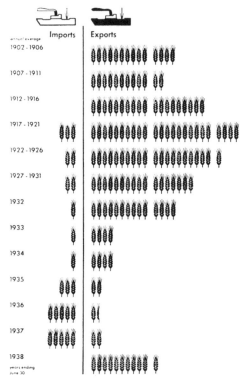

Each symbol represents 10 million bushels of wheat and flour
Flour expressed in corresponding quantity of grain

Figure 1. Neurath Isotype diagram A classic example of Isotype presentation. (From Neurath's 'Modern Man in the making', 1939; London: Secker and Warburg. New York: Alfred A Knopf)

A characteristic of the Isotype system is that it permits symbols to be 'compounded'. Obviously, the individual symbols are designed in such a way that they may be used in association with others, to produce more complex designs. But they were also conceived with a view to it being necessary both to qualify a symbol, by the addition of supplementary detail, or to combine two or more symbols (e.g. 'man' + 'mining' = mine worker).

When the Neuraths moved to London during 1940 the main thrust of their work shifted to the production of print media and, after 1945, to documentary and educational films (for Paul Rotha). They were also invited to train teams in Russia and Nigeria, where their work was relevant to audiences with lower literacy levels.

Twyman quotes Neurath as saying 'pictures make connection, words make division' (Edwards and Twyman, 1975). He also suggests that 'the Isotype movement deserves to be considered as one of the pioneers of modern graphic design. In my view it occupies much the same position in relation to pictorial composition this century as the pioneers of the New Typography do to verbal communication.'

I have a vivid personal recollection of the Neurath's work as a child during the forties and fifties, before I had any aspiration to be involved in graphic communication.

Otl Aicher

Aicher was the principal figure behind the establishment of the Hochschulefür Gestaltung in Ulm, Germany (High School of Design / 'HfG Ulm') during the late fifties. As a result of his responsibility for the visual identity of the Olympic Games in Munich (1972), he was invited to undertake other significant assignments simultaneously, one of which was for Frankfurt Airport (Flughafen Frankfurt). For both of these he developed and extended the system of symbols proposed originally for the Tokyo Olympics (Figure 3). I had the good fortune to know Aicher as a student at the HfG Ulm and in Munich where I was one of his deputies. With Gerhard Jocksh's assistance, Aicher developed the Tokyo symbol set on a more 'geometric' basis. He also

Figure 2. Gerd Arntz woodcut, 1926 From 'Graphic Communication through ISOTYPE', 1975, University of Reading

extended significantly the range of symbols to form a comprehensive and coherent set.

The geometry of Aicher's symbols was derived in part by initially using articulated manikins made of cutout cardboard with jointed limbs. The design of individual characters was systematised and geometricised and therefore assumes a somewhat more rigid appearance than that employed by the Neuraths and Arnzt. The individual designs conform largely to a background geometric grid.

The set developed for the Olympics amounted to approximately 180 symbols, of which 21 were for the Olympic sports at that time (more sports subsequently have been given Olympic status). During the Munich Olympics these were applied to over 2,600 signs required for the Olympic sites; the majority of these signs included the pictograms. The number of applications in printed matter must have exceeded this by at least a factor of ten and the symbols were also applied as comparatively decorative elements in buildings, to produce an appropriate 'ambience'.

Subsequently, ERCO Leuchten (ERCO Lighting) of Lüdenscheid, Germany, worked with Aicher to produce a set of nearly 900 symbols. These are available in different sizes and as adhesive and illuminated signs (Figure 4).

Aicher referred to his symbols as a 'Ziechensprache'. (Interestingly the German word 'Zeichen' can mean both 'symbol' and 'drawing', and 'character' – as in font, 'reference', etc. Hence this can translate as 'symbollanguage' or 'drawn language'). As a consequence of ERCO's effective international marketing, Aicher's 'drawn language' has been applied worldwide. It has also been adopted by and adapted unofficially (and clumsily) to an even greater number of sports-related buildings and organisations.

ISO / BSI

The International Organisation for Standardisation (ISO) and the International Electrotechnical Commission (IEC) had by 1995 standardised approximately 1,450 symbols for international use. These are compiled respectively in ISO 7,000 'Graphical symbols for use on equipment – Index and synopsis' and IEC 417 'Graphical

Figure 3. Otl Aicher Photographed during the Munich Olympics, 1972(Photo, Ulmer Museum / HfG Archive)

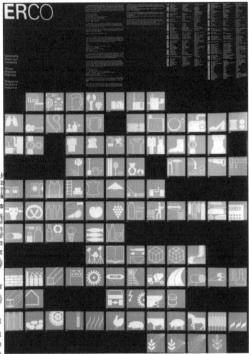

Figure 4. ERCO Lighting Poster (original A1), one of a set illustrating the 750 symbols available.

symbols for use on equipment – Index, survey and compilation of the single sheets'. BSI has compiled a synopsis of both of these, together with other related symbols 'PD 6578; 1995' shown by (ISO 7001). This provides the 1,450 symbols standardised by ISO and the IEC, together with comparable symbols published by both of these organisations, as well as further symbols standardised by BSI and CEN relating to safety and fire safety and public information.

In the majority of cases there may be more than ten 'related' symbols. Hence the figure of 1,450 symbols is deceptive. In fact, the number of symbols which have been standardised by BSI, ISO, IEC and CEN amounts to more than 8,000.

For example, the first item listed in PD 6578 (0001) depicts a simple arrow pointing to the right. It lists after this a further eight symbols which have a similar appearance, but are drawn differently.

0001 is designated as:

'Limited rectilinear motion'.

The following eight related symbols with the same visual appearance denote the following:

'Limited rectilinear motion' (BS 3641:1971)
'Limited rectilinear motion in one direction' (BS 5951: 1982)
'Limited rectilinear motion' (ISO/R 369: 1964)
'Movement in arrow direction: limited' (ISO 5232: 1988)
'Non-decimal tabulating on typewriters for languages written from left to right' (ISO 1090: 1981)
'Limited rectilinear motion' (IEC 878: 1988)
'Nature, limited; linear' (ISO 4196:1984)
'Non-decimal tabulating on typewriters for languages written from right to left' (ISO 1090: 1981).

Hence the same (or similar) visual image has been standardised by nine different committees working in isolation at different times to denote a variety of meanings, not all of which have any relation to each other.

The foreword to PD 6578 states '. . . it recognises the need not only to standardise symbols, which may be compared with words, but also to evolve a grammar or syntax'. There is evidently a long way to go in this respect.

Of the more than 8,000 symbols included in PD 6578 only a mere 56 have been tested for public recognition. Not only have the 'Public Information Symbols' been tested, but the tests have been conducted internationally. I am pleased to have been associated with this process. One of the reasons that the testing process has been protracted is that the testing methodology relied upon existing symbols, which had to be collected from participating countries. Regrettably, in many cases the design of these were extremely varied and in many cases the testing results would probably have been different had the test materials been prepared in a way which sought to present examples of comparable graphic quality. Moreover, in several cases there were very few examples available to test. It is regrettable that the psychologists who formulated the testing process did not allow for either the provision of improvements to test materials or, more critically, the design of symbols for which there was an absence of available material. Several of the designers associated with the process (myself included) were frustrated at being obliged to offer designs on a voluntary basis.

The 56 Public Information Symbols comprise:

1	Direction
2	Smoking allowed
3 & 4	Helicopter
5 & 6	Tram
7 & 8	Bus
9	Male
10	Female
11 & 12	Telephone
13 & 14	Petrol station
15	Drinking water
16	Stairs
17 & 18	Taxi
19	Waiting Room
20	Fire extinguisher
21	Toilet
22	Toilet for men
23	Toilet for women
24	Rubbish receptacle
25	Do not dispose of rubbish here
26	Currency exchange
27	Elevator, lift
28	Aircraft

29	Parking for a specified type of vehicle
30	Boat
31	Nature reserve
32	Way in
33	Way out
34	Left luggage
35	Sporting activities
36	Accommodation
37	Restaurant
38	Hospital
39	Cable car
40	Cable car, small capacity
41	Cable railway, ratchet railway
42	Chair lift
43	Close overhead safety bar
44	Open overhead safety bar
45	Close safety bar
46	Open safety bar
47	Line up two by two
48	Line up three by three
49	Raise ski tips
50	Ski lift
51	Bath
52	Shower
53	Tennis
54	Squash / racket ball
55	Lost property
56	Tickets

In reality there are a mere 49 Public Information Symbols, as seven of the 56 are duplicates intended for reproduction at small scale. The high proportion of symbols relating to winter sports is a reflection of the interests of those countries which provided the initiative and funds for the testing to be conducted.

One of the largest providers of test materials has been the British Tourist Authority (BTA), which over the years has established a library of nearly 450 symbols for tourism related purposes. These are available as both hardcopy and on disk (British Tourist Authority, 1973).

Sadly, although BSI, with the support of the BTA, initially took the lead in introducing international testing of symbols, in recent years it has decided that the process is too protracted. Subsequently the British have been instrumental in introducing an international policy of reducing testing to a point where in practice it is no longer conducted.

One of the positive features of the Public Information Symbols (ISO 7001) is that the standard is not the visual representation but the verbal description of what is to be depicted. Readers assume that the standard is the visual image reproduced in the standard document. In fact, different countries have the latitude to portray local uniforms and rolling stock to reflect local conventions. For example, I have had occasion to design symbols to depict national organisations such as the police and fire services in France. In both cases the headgear, a distinguishing feature, is markedly different from the British equivalents (Figure 6). Similarly, when designing symbols for public transport, in several critical cases the depiction of vehicles is heavily dependent upon local forms; for example French city buses tend to be single decker, with an unusual and visually conspicuous shape to the windscreen. Hence the double decker profile appropriate to London and the United Kingdom would not be appropriate for a French location. It is my contention that it is futile to seek a 'universal' symbol for such services, where local uniforms and vehicles provide an inherently strong means of identification.

Personal Experience

At a personal level, over the years I have worked on various assignments, mostly in France, where sets of symbols have been required. Much of the symbols work with which I have been associated has related to public sector organisations and the signing of public spaces. I have accumulated a set of 168 designs for such symbols.

In the domain of public transport I have worked on signing for both the Lyon Métro (Métro de Lyon), and the Parisian public transport authority (Réseau Autonome des Transports Publics – RATP). Because the latter includes underground, rapid transport rail services and buses, this set is the most comprehensive of those with which I have

been associated (Figure 7). A total of 68 were required. Several subsidiary sets were included, such as those which indicate different methods of payment, as well as some which are very demanding to depict visually, such as 'Alarm', 'Audio Signal' and 'Intercom'. It proved difficult to differentiate visually between the latter.

The next largest set I have worked on was for economic cartography for the Lorraine development agency. In this case the set numbered 51; and included some challenging aspects, such as having to depict the difference between 'Metal processing', 'Iron smelting', 'Steel processing', 'Foundry' and 'Brass

Figure 5. Standard reference sheet ISO 70001, 1980; and BS 6034, 1981.The standard is in fact the verbal description of 'Standard image content' in this example 'toilet for women'.

Armée	Pompiers	Police, gendarmerie	SNCF
Armed forces	Fire service	Police	Railway
Armee	Feuerwehr	Polizei	Eisenbahn

Figure 6. Braunstein et McLaren, 1979. Symbols for the French national public purchasing authority. Note the depiction of headgear as an identifier.

Foundry'. Cartographic symbols have to be reproduced in quite small sizes; in this case, only three millimetres high. This makes for a challenging assignment. In my experience, cartographic applications present a good test for the legibility and intelligibility of visual symbols. (If one can differentiate clearly between iron and steel processing at a height of three millimetres, the symbols will have to be pretty clear!) (Figure 8)

Conclusion

I have sought here to present three of what I believe are important examples of symbol design and to add a note on symbol design from my own experience working internationally. The sheer number of symbols in current circulation is surprisingly large. It is unfortunate that only a small proportion are well designed and that so few have been tested on international audiences.

Figure 7. 'RATP Pictogrammes' Symbol set for signing and publications for the Parisian public transport authority. Plan Créatif, 1993 (Designers Claude Braunstein and Ian McLaren).

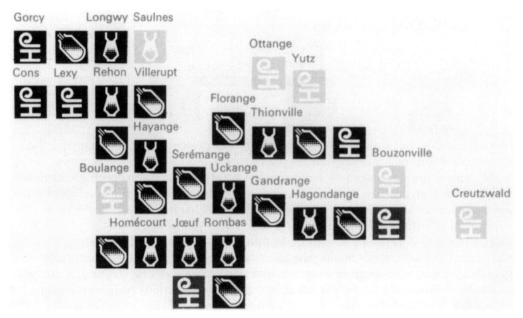

Figure 8. 'La Lorraine Aujourd'hui', 1976. One of a series of cartographic diagrams, page size A4. The individual symbols are designed to be legible at a height of 3mm.

Notes

1.   BSI, London 'Published Document PD 6578: 1995. Guide to British, European and international graphical symbols, for use on equipment, for safety and fire safety, and for public information, in relation to ISO 7,000 and IEC 417'.

2.   British Tourist Authority. (1973 and subsequent editions) 'Symbols for tourist guides, maps and countryside recreation'

3.   Edwards J and Twyman, M. (1975). Graphic communication through ISOTYPE. University of Reading, Reading.

4.   ISO 7001 'Public Information Symbols'. Also published by BSI, as a UK national standard.

5.   Neurath, O. (1936) 'International picture language: the first rules of Isotype' Basic English Publishing (Psyche miniatures, general series, no 83).

6.   Neurath, O. (1926) 'Statisitische Hieroglyphen', Gemeinde Zeitung.

7.   ERCO UK, 38 Dover Street, London W1X 3RB. www.erco.com (then 'products' & 'pictograms'), or www.piktogramm.com/erco

5. Double Vision

Michelle Gausman and Clive Chizlett

It is unorthodox, but situationally reasonable in this present case, that we review the credentials of our two investigators.

Michelle Gausman is aged 25. Following her BA (Hons) course in graphic information design at the University of Westminster, she went on to complete her research degree at the University of Middlesex in 1998. She has also benefited from a work-experience scheme: an information design studio and an in-house publishing office.

Her research dissertation inquires into difficulties experienced by first-time wayfinders in built environments. She identifies two broad categories of difficulty: *boundaries* arising from cognitive and sensory impairments among wayfinders; *barriers* which are imposed upon all wayfinders: thoughtless distractions and inconsistent, incomplete and illogical provision of guidance systems.

Some three years ago it was diagnosed that Michelle Gausman was born dyslexic. Her disorder tends to affect spatial and orientational awareness and to make the acquisition of automatic, unconscious skills difficult, prolonged and tiring. Consequently, she has needed to develop compensatory insights and strategies. Clive Chizlett, her colleague, reports her to be remarkably observant and questioning, persistent and ingenious when dealing with problems. Incidentally, her interests include playing as an orchestral violinist and following Formula 1 racing.

In 1999 she joined the Sign Design Society.

Clive Chizlett is aged 67, a retired typesetter, proofreader, sub-editor and typographic designer. He has worked in the printing and publishing industries and as a practitioner and lecturer in graphic design.

In 1992 he delivered a paper on interlingual message-exchange to the Monotype Conference in Cambridge. His paper proposes a system for interlingual transactions, a system in which the encoding procedures are centred on a core-lexicon of pictographs and ideographs. The outputs might be messages in the typographies which relate to the administratively privileged languages of the EEC.

He has published articles and conference papers on the grammar of wayfinding; on structured report-writing; and the link between the abacus and pictographic records in Bronze Age Mesopotamia. He has lately circulated papers on the Chinese concept-script and on a Chinese system in which ideographic characters are used as rebuses with which to convey the pronunciation of Anglo-American English words and phrases. Having retired from full-time lecturing in 1989, Chizlett is occupied with generic and theoretical aspects of design rather than specific projects.

He is becoming partially-blind and partially-deaf. He notes that his general learning ability is deteriorating too and says that he expects to be three parts ga-ga within the next few years. If he were to survive until the year AD 2006, he would be among the 60 per cent of the UK population who will then be aged between 65 and 95 years.

In 1999 he too joined the Sign Design Society.

Shared Concerns

The Sign Design Society was founded in 1991 to raise awareness of signing and to raise standards of design and installation of signs. Membership of the London-based SDS is currently about 60 and includes design practitioners, manufacturers and installers of signs, academics and wayfinding planners and managers. There are overseas members (Holland, Italy and Japan). And there is a quarterly journal, *Directions*.

One evening each month, a score or so of SDS members and guests meet in London for an illustrated talk and discussion. The topics range from heraldry to iconic safety-signs; from inkjet-printed banner production to the testing of pictographic signs for the Dutch rail network; and from split-flap message-display systems to photoluminescent signs for emergency evacuation of public buildings.

Following their first meeting at an SDS evening dedicated to design management, Chizlett and Gausman exchanged copies of their papers on wayfinding. She mailed to him her research dissertation titled Disorientation, and he mailed to her his paper 'Navigator: Strategic Planning of Wayfinding Guidance Systems'.

Chizlett writes, 'My own enquiries into wayfinding are objective, theoretical, narrow and impersonal. Hers, on the other hand, are subjective, practical, research-based, real world, and always, always, centred on the needs of the wayfinder but particularly the sensorily impaired wayfinder. Added to which, both of us have to live with varieties and degrees of cognitive or sensory impairment. That does not mean, of course, that we are socially inferior in some way. Nor do our respective impairments license us to be critical of those who commission, plan and design audio-visual guidance systems for wayfinders.'

Tunnel Vision Part One: the Problem

Gausman's paper 'Disorientation' examines wayfinding provision in several built environments in London: the Victoria rail and coach terminals; the Barbican complex; and sundry galleries and museums.

Her enquiries led her to consult agencies for persons with disabilities or sensory impairments: the Joint Mobility Unit, the Dyslexia Institute and the Royal National Institute for the Blind, are examples. The RNIB drew her attention to their newly-developed typeface and screenfont Tiresias (Exhibit 1). She also worked with sensorily-impaired individuals by way of questionnaires and by way of reconnoitring built environments in their company. She interviewed operators and managers of particular sites and interviewed designers who specialise in planning and designing audio-visual guidance systems for use by drivers, riders and pedestrians. And she read widely the literature on wayfinding, the psychology of perception, and the designing of iconic and typographic signs.

Gausman developed one of her field-studies of built environments beyond critical review and moved it forward into the domain of detailed, remedial proposals: the

ABCDEFGHIJKLMNOPQRSTUV
WXYZabcdefghijklmnopqrst
uvwxyz1234567890£€$¢¥+
= ÷ # < > @ ! ? & (. , ; :) [ ] { } / \ %
∞ Æ Œ Ø Å ø æ œ å ß * ¼ ½ ¾ « » ‹ ›

Exhibit 1 : Tiresias is the name of a character-set which has been designed to benefit part-sighted readers. The light-on-dark sanserif has been developed by Royal National Institute for the Blind to be used as screenfont, typeface, and wayfinding character-set. Tiresias is an ophthalmological refinement of the Victorian typeface Grot 216. RNIB recommend that Tiresias should be used to compose words in upper-and-lower-case instead of capitals. Words composed of capital letters do not form characteristic word-shapings, unlike words composed of upper-and-lower-case letters. Word-shaping helps part-sighted readers to decode messages and discourse with comparative ease and precision. See also Exhibits 4 and 5.

South Kensington Underpass, a pedestrian tunnel some 600 yards in length which provides a subterranean link between Kensington Road and Cromwell Road (Exhibit 2).

Several national museums, institutes and colleges are served directly or adjacently by the Underpass tunnel. At the southern end is South Kensington Underground Station (Circle, District and Piccadilly Lines) and at the northern end are the Royal Albert Concert Hall, and the Royal College of Art.

Gausman found the Tunnel to be dark, gloomy, grimy and sinister by day, by night, at dusk. On one of her reconnaissances of the Tunnel she was accompanied by a severely part-blind man with his guide-dog. The man drew her attention to the disturbing, even painful effect, of moving from the darkness of the Tunnel into ordinary daylight. The sharpness of the transition is actually intensified for part-blind persons. Similarly, moving from daylight into the dark Tunnel actually intensifies the degree of partial blindness for several minutes. The effect on residual sightedness can be painful and disorienting and arises from the extreme contrast between the light and the dark.

Gausman observed of the Tunnel that much of the wayfinding signage is lofted too high; that ill-lit, gloss-surfaced sign-panels can be unreadable, particularly so when the surfaces reflect whole lengths of neon-tube. She noted a lack of tactile, bas-relief signs for hand-touch or sole-tread; that glare-lit posters and retail displays tend to distract the anxious, confused, time-pressed traveller. And she asks why is there a total absence of reassurance signage, why are there no reassurance-points, to confirm or correct one's wayfinding decisions *en route*?

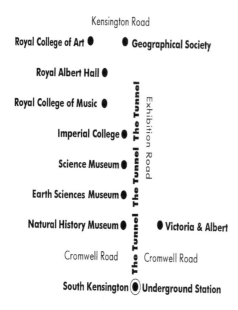

Kensington Road

Royal College of Art ●   ● **Geographical Society**

Royal Albert Hall ●

Royal College of Music ●

Imperial College ●

Science Museum ●

Earth Sciences Museum ●

Natural History Museum ●   ● **Victoria & Albert**

Cromwell Road   Cromwell Road

South Kensington ◉ **Underground Station**

Exhibition Road

The Tunnel The Tunnel The Tunnel

Exhibit 2 : The Tunnel was chosen by one of the authors for a field-study dedicated to wayfinding in built environments. The study comprises an analysis of the problems created for first-time users of the Tunnel, and a set of proposals for alleviating or resolving the identified problems. Other field-studies, limited to problem-analyses, include Heathrow Airport, Victoria Rail Terminus and associated Underground Station Complex, and the heritage town of Rye in East Sussex.

Tunnel Vision Part Two: the Proposal

Gausman began her scheme of remedial recommendations by attending to the ambient lighting and ambient colour. Should there be graduated lighting between the Tunnel and its exits to ease the transitions from dark to light, from light to dark, from artificial light to daylight, from daylight to artificial? Might the glare-effects of the neon-lighting be alleviated by the use of louvred tube-housings? Louvred lighting would also improve the readability of gloss-surfaced signage panels.

Following the recommendations of the American colour-consultant Faber Biren, Gausman suggestsed that the prevailing gloom of the Tunnel might be dispelled by simply but thoroughly cleaning the walls. Might the grey-white wall-tiling be replaced by a fresh colour-scheme: stimulating yellow and/or orange; or relaxing blue and blue-green?

Turning to the typographic signage, she adopted the character-set Tiresias, developed by the RNIB (Exhibit 1). In place of black lettering on a gloss-white field, she recommended white or yellow lettering on a matt-surfaced black or midnight-blue field. Furthermore, she recommends that wording should always be in upper-and-lower-case instead of capital letters only. Words in capital letters tend to form rectangular silhouettes but words in upper and lower case (as in the text you are now reading) tend to form unique and distinctive shapes. Such word-shaping is useful to all wayfinders but particularly so to wayfinders with one or another form of sight-impairment. Word-shaping is particularly important in the context of wayfinding because most sign-panels are viewed from below, or to one side, at more or less fore-shortened angles. And in a hurry. . .

Gausman went on to recommend that the identity-icons already designed for the museums, institutes and colleges served by the Tunnel should be incorporated into the wayfinding signage and should also be used as repeat-pattern motifs and murals along the passages leading to and from specific buildings and complexes.

Eye-level signage might be augmented by Braille and by bas-relief tactile systems which relate to touch or tread. There might also be sensor-triggered or touch-triggered auditory renderings of messages.

She particularly recommended for the benefit of able and disabled wayfinders that reasssurance-points be available at two, perhaps three critical junctions within the Tunnel. Such points would help the lost or anxious wayfinder to find or to confirm location and orientation. The *You Are Here* maps might need to be complemented by a simplified compass-rose.

Six or seven colour-coded route-lines might be set into the Tunnel floor to guide wayfinders passing northwards and southwards through the Tunnel. Such route-lines would be dedicated to specific museums, colleges and institutes. However, one needs to remember that one male in twelve has defective colour-vision and thus has difficulty in distinguishing between reds, greens and browns. Chequering or parallel bandings of colours might be desirable when planning the allocation of route-lines so that each route-line has distinctive configuration in addition to its one or paired colours. Furthermore, each route-line might be formed from laid bricks or tiles so that there is distinctive tread-tactility. Surfacing might be studded and/or ridged or criss-cross textured. 'Science Museum, sir? Certainly. Just follow the yellow brick road. That's right, sir: the ones with the diamond-shaped studs'.

It is noteworthy that Gausman's training as a graphic designer has directed her attention towards auditory and tactile signage as systems that are complementary to visual and audio-visual signage.

Boundaries and Barriers

It is clear that wayfinding, whether it be first-time or reiterated, whether real-world or cyberspace, needs to rely upon acquired familiarity with the given environment. Furthermore, the wayfinding process is coloured by our cognitive experience of environments generally. For example, we expect to model each new environment in terms of its prominent features and landmarks. We expect to model and record in our minds the spatial relations between the landmarks. Left at the traffic-lights; onwards to the second roundabout; turn right, keeping The Feathers pub on your left; and straight on to the clock-tower, about half a mile; at the clock-tower, pick up the A259; turn north and follow the signs to Dover. . .

However, our acquired wayfinding models are broken, or chaotically dispersed, when our cognitive experience is literally baffled by novelty or by change. A first-time encounter with an environment might be discouraging: no prominent landmark by which to steer and to maintain one's direction; no memorable feature to use for purposes of reassurance. And a familiar environment might baffle a wayfinder when some familiar landmark is destroyed or obscured or some novel and unfamiliar feature is installed.

We draw attention to major causes of bafflement among first-time and experienced wayfinders. We propose to classify such causes under two broad categories: *boundaries* (relating to the wayfinder) and *barriers* (relating to the environment).

Varying in their nature and degree, there are cognitive and perceptual boundaries to the navigational powers of individual wayfinders.

Varying in their nature and strength, there are situational barriers within the environment which effectually delay or obstruct all wayfinders as they attempt to move fluently, confidently and reliably through the environment towards their overall goal by way of their interim objectives. Such barriers are to be found among natural, built, and cyberspace environments.

Perceptual boundaries include sensory impairments. From birth, or from some point in our lives, many of us are afflicted by poor or absent hearing. Many of us have, or will develop with age, impairments of sight as short- or long-sightedness (astigmatism), cataract, glaucoma, corneal scarring, retinal and foveal degeneration, defective colour-vision, nystagmus (juddering eye-movement) or strabismus (double vision).

All such afflictions of hearing and sight make it difficult, even impossible, to cope with barriers created, deliberately and inadvertently, by poor design management and unimaginative provision of wayfinding guidance. For example, how many of us could easily read a text printed in pale blue on a glossy, mid-blue surface? Yes, blue on blue, work by an award-winning design group.

With or without the use of one's deaf-aid, many of us have been effectually barred from understanding a loudspeaker announcement because of booming echoes, faulty equipment and incoherent diction.

Turning to cognitive boundaries, we need to note that half of the general population has, by definition, below-average intelligence.

Non-culpably, and unfortunately, some 30 millions of us in the United Kingdom might have difficulty in coping with the urban environments and civic complexes that are designed for us by some very intelligent and well-trained people: architects, engineers, computer-scientists, systems analysts and information designers.

In addition to the range and variety of physical, sensory and cognitive impairments and disabilities throughout the population, there are emotional disorders and personality dysfunctions. These many and various afflictions blight the day-to-day life of millions of people of all ages.

As each of us moves towards and into old age, our cognitive and perceptual boundaries tend to shrink, to tighten. In particular, our sight and hearing, our quickness of wit, tend to degenerate. And we are moving towards a time, around the year 2006, when 60 per cent of the UK population will be aged between 65 and 95 years. Sooner or later, all of us will need all the help and facility we can get, particularly when trying to find our ways through built and cyberspace complexes.

Confused States

There are barriers to efficient wayfinding which affect all wayfinders. Such barriers occur everywhere. We suggest that there are at least three primary causes of the wayfinding barriers.

Firstly, there are disordered priorities.

Secondly, there are inept or weakened design managements.

Thirdly, there is widespread ineptitude in the analysis and design of interactive guidance systems for day-to-day use by first-time and experienced wayfinders.

The major airports of the UK supply case-studies of barriers to wayfinding that are caused by disordered priorities. The anxious and weary wayfinder, possibly unable to read English or to comprehend announcements in English, will be distracted by retail display and its associated glare-lighting, by giant back-lit posters and by the icons, graphics and colour-liveries presented by hundreds of corporate airlines. The wayfinding system is placed about fourth or fifth in the order of priorities.

At Heathrow terminals one will find that a critical junction of four footways and two staircases is the site for large back-lit advertisements at the expense of necessary wayfinding cues. The wayfinding passenger is not a customer of the British Airports Authority which manages Heathrow and other UK airport terminals. BAA's customers include the retail and fast-food outlets, the display advertisers and the hundreds of airlines. The wayfinding traveller, therefore, can get lost.

Disordered priorities engender wayfinding barriers in many shopping malls, city centres and large public buildings such as hospitals. Among the sub-systems of wayfinding guidance there is the iconic scheme of communication dedicated to emergency evacuation of sites. It seems to us reasonable that the disposition of the iconic scheme should always have first priority, over-riding priority relative to the wayfinding guidance system as a whole. It seems reasonable to us that wayfinding should always have over-riding priority relative to retail display and advertisement sites. Alternatively, get lost. Alternatively, get killed. . .

We believe that there are widespread failures among practitioners, teachers and students of architecture, surveying, civic planning and information design to address the subject of wayfinding with the necessary degrees of attention, insight and knowledge required by the subject. However, we also believe that there is a growing consciousness of the significance of guidance systems for users of complex networks.

If it Looks Like a Duck. . .

Many hazard-signs, safety-signs, are given form as graphic icons. Such signs, particularly pictographic icons, notionally transcend the barriers created by language differences. (Pictorial icons do not necessarily transcend the barriers between cultures. There are cultures in which the women wear the trousers and at least one culture in which men wear skirts, sorry, kilts).

A ban on cycles; a need to be aware of cyclists; a high hazard of black fire? beware medieval knights?

The sets of icons which relate to traffic-management and to hazard-warning are normally developed and licensed by international or governmental agencies for enforcement in law by national governments. Traffic-management icons include signs with banning (interdictory) functions and signs with hazard-warning functions. In effect, the signs comprise an ideographic field and a pictographic icon placed on that field. The fields are white, bordered with red: a circular disc for banning signs and a triangular plate for hazard-warnings. Such a simple grammar and lexicon enables us to ban uses of bicycles and, using the same pictograph, to warn of the possible presence of cyclists further along our way.

Within the internationally established system of safety signs, hazard-warnings are, again, triangular in field. The edge-bordering and pictographic icon are always black, the field-colour yellow. The black on yellow regime gives rise to numerous instances of ambiguous signification. The fire-hazard sign has an icon of black flames which resemble a clump of weeds; the laser-hazard sign has an icon which comprises a laser-beam and burn-focus but it appears to signify a black cartoon-spider impaled on a black knitting-needle; and the radiation-hazard sign looks like the lugubrious face of a giant panda.

It seems to us very odd that safety-signs include pictographic icons which are effectually baffling, dangerously obscure. In this matter, we have signs which constitute barriers, opaque barriers. Why?

Given the recent developments in touch-triggered and sensor-triggered *auditory* signs, we touch upon the concept of auditory equivalents of pictographs: onomatopoeia. Thus the auditory icon for fire-hazard might be a series of five-second sound-plays comprising the crackle of flames accompanied by fire-engine bells. . . Information design curricula should not be limited to purely visual channels of communication.

A Little Knowledge. . .

Access to the Internet and to the designing of websites is open to everybody. We have the means to compile and generate texts, tabulations, images, colours, textures and icons onto batteries of on-screen pages. The icons might be off-the-peg or bought-in bespoke designs or user-generated. But most of us are not trained as audio-visual communicators, designers, publishers, typesetters, proofreaders or sub-editors, nor as iconographers. Our worldwide poverty as multi-skilled website-operators gives rise to websites which have the substance and appearance of parish magazines produced by chirpily enthusiastic but incompetent amateurs.

We must expect that inept, or totally absent, quality-control will produce incorrect spelling and grammar and slovenly styles of language. We will have to live with commonplace insensitivity to design considerations. Fuzzy and confusing embellishments. Clumsy and oafish uses of type. Designs of pictographic icons which are densely intricate and thus inscrutable. Designs of icons which are semantically clear to nobody other than the little mutual admiration society which operates the website.

Inscrutable and meaningless icons are frequently construed as though they were *simulacra*. (A double-rooted parsnip might form a simulacrum of a grotesque human being; a stain on the wall might form the simulacrum of the map of India). If and when the icon resembles a clump of weeds instead of a blazing fire, that icon is a barrier to effective communication. The formation of simulacra is an incorrigible phenomenon in human beings: we are so powerfully equipped to signify and infer that we cannot avoid doing so when the visual stimulus is supplied to us. And where some icon inadvertently forms a simulacrum which is inappropriately comical, or offensively gross, then nothing can prevent us from regarding the whole website as ill-conceived and ill-operated.

We end our discussion of boundaries and barriers in the context of wayfinding with two observations. Firstly, all of us, even the youngest and ablest, can be situationally afflicted by cognitive and perceptual boundaries (stressed, hurrying to an appointment, unwell, tired) or situationally delayed or obstructed by some barrier (lighting that is weak or glaring, confusing messages, an ambiguous icon). Secondly, we observe that when environmental guidance-systems provide for visual, auditory and tactile signs by way of thoughtful and imaginative planning and design, there are benefits for all of us, able and disabled alike.

Signs of Meaning

Since 1989, Chizlett has been free to follow a range and variety of research studies under the generic title Signs of Meaning. Several of the studies within the Signs of Meaning programme relate directly or indirectly to iconic communication.

The Navigator study has delivered a concise but comprehensive grammar with which to describe wayfinding environments (built or cyberspace). The grammar can also be used as an instrumental means with which to prescribe wayfinding guidance systems within given environments. Guidance systems accommodate media or channels which are visual, auditory, audio-visual and tactile. Visual and audio-visual media (static and dynamic) exploit typography icons (pictographic and ideographic), pictures (drawn, photographed, filmed) and colour-combination. Tactile guidance relates to touch and tread.

Throughout Navigator, the message-functions of guidance systems comprise directional and orientational functions; site-labelling and route-labelling; commands, authorisations, and bans; hazard-warnings and prescriptive advice; instructive and evaluative functions; emergency. The emergency functions within guidance systems need to be modelled and prescribed before any other function so that an ideal and proper site for an emergency sign is not requisitioned for some other purpose. The various message-functions are derived from the field of linguistics rather than semiotics. A notation used within Navigator is illustrated in Exhibit 3.

Associated with Navigator is the Turnstile project which models traffic-movement through built environments, on foot or in vehicles, and in relation to large-scale all-ticket or at-the-gate events.

Included in the Signs of Meaning programme are two studies which are closely engaged with iconic communication: Prima Facie and Silent Messenger. Prima Facie proposes a scheme for a system of context-governed interlingual message-exchange. Silent Messenger is a review of the Chinese concept-script and its significance to discussions of iconic communication, and to discussions of interlingual exchange of messages and discourse.

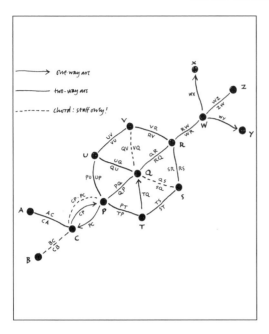

Exhibit 3 : Using a notation borrowed from
mathematical net-theory, a built environment or a
cyberspace might be modelled or prescribed as a
compound set of one-way and two-way links [arcs]
which connect the set of junction-points and goal-
locations [nodes]. Such net-sketching need not be to
scale and drawing need not be refined, but there
must always be accurate and comprehensive
indication of relations between nodes by way of the
arcs. Each node, each arc, will need to be initial-
lettered and thus labelled for purposes of overall
planning and eventual design. Each first-time
wayfinder is usually looking for the exact and
minimal sequence of arcs which will lead them
through the system to their goal with speed, ease,
assurance, reassurance, economy of movement, and
moment-by-moment precision. Wayfinders will
apply the same criteria when they make their
sequential return-pass through the system. Nodes
are decision- points for which undistracted
directional guidance is frequently essential. Goal-
locations often need distinctive, confirmatory site-
labelling such as Accounts or John Doe or
Radiography et cetera.

Prima Facie has been presented to the international Monotype Conference at Cambridge (1992) in a paper titled 'The Dream of Leibniz'. Prima Facie is also described in 'The Token Woman', a paper presented to the Second Workshop on Iconic Communication at Bristol (1999).

Encoding regimes within Prima Facie data-processing are based on uses of pictographic icons with a *semantic* function combined with ideographic icons with *inflectional* functions (systemic and grammatical).

Transcoding and decoding processes generate outputs expressed as messages in one or more of the natural languages. Note that the emphasis here is on messages within contexts and conventions (bookings, purchases, invoices, appointments, etc). Prima Facie is not directed towards discourse and is not part of the domain of machine-translation from a given source-language to one or more target-languages.

The Dottiness research-schemes (illustrated in Exhibits 4 and 5) arose from the observation that the alpha-mosaic character-sets used on many online message-display machines are difficult to read, whether or not one is able-sighted. Messages can be particularly difficult to read when viewed from below or to one side. Message-display machines are widely used: motorway gantries, railway concourses, airports, busblinds.

Many message-display systems use standard character-sets that are limited to capital letters plus numerals and a few punctuation icons. As indicated earlier, messages expressed in upper-and-lower-case are very much easier to read than messages expressed in capital letters only. Words printed in upper and lower case form distinctive, even unique, word-

Exhibit 4 : Many public-information systems employ message-display machines which use standard-width characters. Each of the letters and numerals is fitted into a British Standard cell-matrix of 35 on/off light-diodes in a 7 x 5 array. Wide letters such as M are squashed into their cells but slim letters such as I are artificially expanded to fit into their cells [topmost row]. Only capital letters and numerals are normally generated by such systems. The authors propose single-column component-cells in place of the BS whole-assembly cells. When combined with improved control logic, the component-cells give access to lower-case characters; natural widths to wide and slim letters; stylised user-generated icons; combinations of double-height and single-height messages within one display; easily readable word-shaping at distance and at fore-shortened angles; and on-line messages in any of the eleven EEC typographies, including greek and, by extension, cyrillic. See also Exhibit 1 and Exhibit 5.

shapes. Characteristic word-shapes are useful to all wayfinders, able-sighted or partial-sighted, particularly when wayfinders see such word-shapes at steeply foreshortened angles.

To achieve upper and lower case character-sets, it is vital to achieve width-variants of the characters: wide for W and w but slim for i and j, for example. The Dottiness research required the re-examination of control logic within the message-display systems. Such re-examination led to a simplified circuitry but also to extraordinary opportunities to incorporate pi-sorts and user-generated icons within the set of accessible characters. Furthermore, it becomes possible to generate double-height character-sets, together with all the characters needed to represent the typographies of, say, the eleven administratively privileged languages of the EEC (to include Greek and the extensive requirements of Portuguese language-notation).

The Signs of Meaning programme, as a series of enquiries, relates to generic and recurring problems within information design and iconic communication.

What Next?

Gausman's approach to research is richer and deeper than Chizlett's but certainly complements his. Her Disorientation paper and his Signs of Meaning programme are steps towards joint exercises in research and development, theory and operations.

They believe that curriculum and practice of wayfinding design need to accommodate iconic communication in a range and variety of forms: ideographic, pictographic and ideomorphic; auditory, audio-visual and tactile.

Among the disciplines to which wayfinding is a material concern we identify architecture and planning, government and administration, computer science and systems analysis, and information design (with particular attention to cultural aspects of iconography and the uses of auditory and tactile channels of message-exchange).

Chizlett and Gausman are not alone in sharing an overall, strategic objective: to contribute towards improved guidance systems within built and cyberspace networks for the benefit and well-being of wayfinders who might be able or disabled, cognitively or sensorily impaired, to include, of course, children.

Exhibit 5: Instrumental message-displays often use liquid crystal technology with which to form alphanumeric character-sets. Daimler-Benz Aerospace have developed a system for assembling characters, and messages, based on a single-column, ten-level component-cell (shown extreme left). Within each level, square or triangular elements can be switched on or off. There are 29 elements distributed among the ten levels of each component-cell. Note here that the g h k letters need four single-column cells each: three cells for the letter plus one (with all of its 29 elements switched off) for the inter-character spacing. Similarly, the i and j letters require two single-column cells each. The whole project is devised to improve comprehension of on-board instrumental displays throughout long flights.

References

Biren, F. (1969). *Light, Colour and Environment*. Reinhold, New York.

Chizlett, C. (1995). 'Ariadne's Thread: the Strategic Planning of Signposting Networks.' *Directions* no 8: The Sign Design Society.

Chizlett, C. (1997). 'Assisting with Enquiries: Scheme to Improve Alpha-Mosaic Message-Display Systems'. *Typographic* no 51: International Society of Typographic Designers.

Follis, J. and Hammer, D. (1979). *Architectural Signing and Graphics*, Whitney Library of Design, USA.

Garland, K. (1994). *Mr Beck's Underground Map*. Pineland Press.

Gausman, M. (1998). *Disorientation*. Dissertation for research degree. University of Middlesex.

Miller, C. and Information Design Unit. (1999). *Wayfinding: Guidance for Healthcare Facilities*. The Stationery Office.

Nolan, G. (1997). *Designing Exhibitions: To Include People with Disabilities*. NMS Publishing, Edinburgh.

RNIB Royal National Institute for the Blind. (1998). *A Design Guide for the Use of Colour and Contrast to Improve the Built Environment for Visually Impaired Persons*. RNIB.

Sassoon, R. and Gaur, A. (1997). *Signs, Symbols and Icons: Pre-history to the Computer Age*, Intellect.

Sign Design Society. (1998/9). 'Terminal Disorder: Wayfinding at Heathrow'. *Directions* no 15: Sign Design Society.

Sign Design Society. (1998). 'Tiresias Screenfont for Visually Impaired Persons Using Monitor-Screens'. Directions no 17: Sign Design Society. (The screenfont Tiresias is available from Bitstream UK, Atrium Court, Apex Place, Reading, Berks, RG1 1AX, UK.)

6. Communication through Icons

Masoud Yazdani

How could two people who do not know each other's language communicate with each other? Koji Kobayashi chairman of Japan's Nippon Electric Co. (NEC) foresees 'a situation that would make it possible for any person in the world to communicate with any other person at any place and any time'.

Kobayashi (1986) aims to exploit future developments in machine translation, speech synthesis and recognition. An English speaker may pick up the telephone and speak with a Japanese person in English. It would be the task of the telecommunication system to recognize the sounds and translate them into Japanese and later translate the reply into English. This proposal is still far from becoming a real possibility.

As an intermediate solution Yazdani (1987) proposed to the EU's DELTA project an environment which could assist users of electronic mail systems to compose and understand messages. As a result of this proposal we were asked if we could investigate the possibility of producing a multi-lingual 'Welcome Pack' which could describe a computer system (EPOS) to the users as they saw the system for the first time. In order to do this we decided to use iconic presentation methods instead of a series of presentations in different languages. We produced a rapid prototype to show the concept of an iconic presentation as seen in Figure 1.

The work that we produced offered interesting proof of concept for our ideas without having the potential to be scaled up to commercial applications. Nevertheless, many examples of the use of icons as replacements for text have begun to appear on the market in niche topic areas (with various levels of success) including *The Wordless Travel Book* (Meader, 1995), which uses pictures to illustrate the traveller's needs rather than providing phrases.

Mealing and Yazdani (1991) presented design consideration for a visual language and how it could be developed to a level that would enable presentation of factual information in a way that most people without much difficulty and without training could understand the meaning of the message. Figure 2 shows an example of this concept's application to the domain of booking a hotel room.

This communication system uses icons, which represent units of meaning greater than single concepts. In return the icons can explain themselves (if the need arises) in order to clarify the meaning and provide the context. Such 'self explaining icons' use simple animations to help the user understand the meaning of the message clearly and thus avoid the problem of ambiguity associated with static icons.

This work represents an enthusiastic case for a pictorial system, which could take over from text for person-to-person communication using cartoon-like animations.

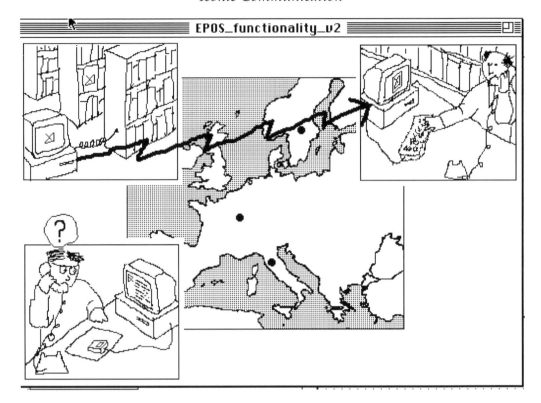

Figure 1. A sample screen from the EPOS HyperCard stack

However, the diversity of the cultural backgrounds of users of such systems has so far made it difficult to design a pictorial language.

I aim to continue to explore the potential of cross-language communication systems that avoid the use of words and rely solely upon pictorial symbols. However, most papers in the present volume deal with cross-cultural communication systems that use pictorial symbols to complement text, using icons as a way of adding value to textual information.

Cruickshank and Hughes (1999) and Cruickshank and Barfield (in this volume) offer a more recent development of the original e-mail proposal with users being given the chance to design their own icons in order to add an emotional dimension to their e-mail messages. Figure 3 gives an example of a user-designed icon using the base elements offered by this system.

Despite this change of objective from icons as a replacement for text (the pre-millennium work) to their being an adjunct to text (post-millennium work reported in this volume,) there are a number of issues that remain of concern to graphic designers and computer people in our community of researchers. We need to consider how to read, write and learn icons in addition to how to design new ones. The role of metaphor as a background to all of this is critical in the success of any development, as

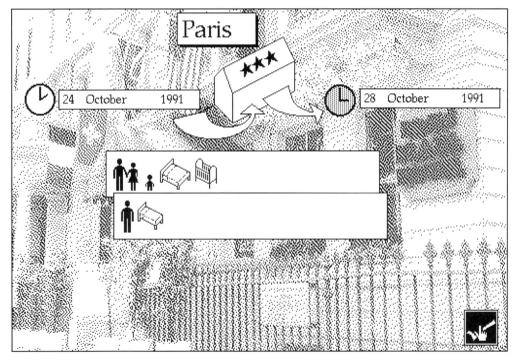

Figure 2. A sample screen from Hotel booking system

is the cultural reference. And as with all design, 'fitness to purpose' brings with it the need to consider the users' objectives.

The argument that we should consider the combination of text and icon as a solution to our communicative objective may be a positive step forward. Is it not true that we see in our everyday life people combining spoken language with gestures, hand and eye movements, intonational variations?

Figure 3. Talk (Cruikshank and Hughes, 1999)

If we move away from purely iconic to an 'icon and text' solution we can leave behind some of the problems that have slowed the progress of the development of the earlier work. However, combining a typographic system and an ideographic system brings with it new problems to solve. For example Figure 4 shows a case where adding picture to the text adds ambiguity rather than more clarity.

There are serious doubts about the conventional wisdom that multiple media will improve communication! In fact, Krause (1993) in a series of experiments has shown that integration of text and graphics encourages high error-rates in users of word processing packages.

We need to be aware that some information is communicated better by one kind of medium than another as each medium has both constraining and enabling features, while some other information is communicated better by a combination of media. The problems we face are how we should select and apportion content to different media and how we coordinate media. How can we ensure that given communicative goals are achieved by any resulting artifact?

Some of the key choices are

• What media or combination of media would suit that information best?
• How to design the presentation of information in the chosen media.
• How to maintain presentation consistency.

These issues are mostly being ignored at present as pictorial material seems to act as decoration on most World Wide Web pages! However, there are signs that the

Figure 4. An example of mismatch between text and picture

need for a systematic approach is being appreciated in the more popular uses of icons – both within conventional computer applications (Sassoon and Gaur, 1997) and in systems intended for use on the Web (Honeywill, 1999).

In addition, mobile video phones will soon be available. These devices will allow transmission of visual images along with sound (and, possibly, textual annotation via their keypads). It will be interesting to see how more effective these 'multimedia' video phones will be for communication purposes. It will not be unrealistic to assume that the screens on these devices may be capable of emulating the display properties of conventional paper. This will enable us to communicate using icons and free-hand sketches that we generate using some form of stylus. Indeed, we may also have libraries of our own personal icons stored within the phones themselves which we can use to build iconic communication sequences.

References

Cruickshank, L. and Hughes, B. (1999). 'Facilitating the Evolution of a User Driven 'Icontextual' Internet Patois' *Digital Creativity*, vol. 10, no. 2, pp. 79-89.

Honeywill, P. (1999).*Visual Language for the World Wide Web*, Intellect, Exeter.

Kobayashi, K. (1986).*Computers and Communications*, MIT Press.

Krause, J. (1993). 'A Multilayered Empirical Approach to Multimodality' Mark (ed.) *Intelligent Multimedia Interfaces* Maybury, The MIT Press, Cambridge, MA, pp 328-52.

Meader, J. (1995). *The Wordless Travel Book* Berkeley, Ten Speed Press.

Mealing, S and Yazdani, M (1991). 'Computer-based Iconic Communication', *Intelligent Tutoring Media,* vol.1, no. 3, pp. 133-36.

Sassoon, R. and Gaur, A. (1997). *Signs, Symbols and Icons,* Intellect, Exeter.

Yazdani M. (1987). 'Artificial Intelligence for Tutoring' in Whiting and D.A. Bell (eds.) *Tutoring and Monitoring Facilities for European Open Learning,* Elsevier Science Publishers, pp. 239-48.

Proposals

7. Do You See What I'm Saying?

Stuart Mealing

Introduction

In direct communication between humans, the words spoken are supplemented by a range of accessories such as body language, expression, gesture, intonation, volume, etc. which serve to qualify the bare bones of the message. Indeed, these paralinguistic features can often communicate more than the words themselves and can even provide sufficient clues to transcend the barriers of foreign language. This rich layer of meaning is stripped off in the transposition of a message to naked text, although punctuation marks can provide symbolic representation of some elements !?*! The layer is also largely lost in verbal communication that lacks visual support, for example in a telephone conversation (and it is interesting to note that extra verbal feedback from the receiver, such as a periodic grunt of acknowledgement, is required in this context to sustain the transmission). VAT (Value Added Text) provides visual mappings for these features, mappings which can then be combined with raw text to restore some of the lost semantic support.

These mappings can be abstract, symbolic, representational, mimetic, static or kinetic. They can offer clues, hints, intimations, implications, insinuations, context or warnings and their relationship to the text can be as prologue, background, coda, costume, choreographer or perhaps even as enveloping environment. Their application can vary according to the medium in which they appear and they can readily borrow from the grammar, syntax and vocabularies of art, design, film, theatre and existing sign languages. In many instances they draw on the ubiquitous skills of the graphic designer, formalising intuitive matches between form and content that occur in printed and screen media.

Interaction between the form of the high level language in a message and the form of the visual support devices proposed herein might often be subtle and potentially fragile, a fairground of gratuitously dynamic material being likely to lead to semantic overload. A matrix of visual elements could be constructed which stretches on one axis from pictorial to symbolic and on another from static to dynamic. Within such a schema one could intuitively label as 'hot' those that are both kinetic and pictorial and as 'cold' those that are both static and symbolic but it would be presumptuous to think that high 'temperature' necessarily corresponded to speed or ease of information access (See Figure 1).

On Being Understood

When I first visited France I used monotonic schoolboy French and elicited little understanding. My wife, however, made no effort to speak the language but gestured, grimaced, used English with heavy intonation and was universally comprehended. I now speak only slightly better French but wave my arms about, try (on advice) to impersonate Maurice Chevalier and come closer to matching the level of understanding she achieves. It is clear that words are only one element of the information that enables communication between humans.

Gesticulating is instinctive and an integral part of the speech process that may even help shape the thoughts underlying speech (Hall, 1998), a gesture being conveniently defined as a significant movement of a limb or the body and also the use of such movements, especially to convey feeling or as a rhetorical device (Concise Oxford Dictionary). It has become elaborated and formalised into a number of sign languages, for example British, American and Amerind, all of which have both symbolic and mimetic elements, the latter of which are often accessible internationally. There is also spontaneous signing which, when used by my wife, is likely to accompany a single word or phrase and communicate a single semantic unit but when used by deaf children can be constructed, untaught, into sentences. (Goldin-Meadows and Mylander, 1998).

Semiotics and Syntax

A semiotic division can be made of the major signs and signals of communication into verbal and non-verbal, the latter dividing again into visual and tactile. Within the category of 'verbal', the linguistic element of speech, which converts words into sounds, can be distinguished from the expressive, non-linguistic, vocal elements of

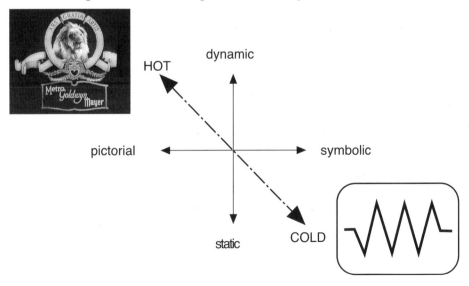

Figure 1. Classification of visual signifiers

language known as suprasegmentals. The three key prosodic features of language are pitch, loudness and tempo, which together contribute to its rhythm, and it is helpful to note that they are readily measurable – this is significant because it potentially offers data as input for automatic mapping. The need for students of language to accurately record spoken language has resulted in many previous attempts to find visual transcriptions for these nuances that can serve as a phonetic shorthand.

Suprasegmentals also include other voice qualities such as timbre and intonation which can give clues about the emotional state and social group (indexical) of the utterer as well as about the information structure of the utterance. For example, whispering can tell of secrecy or conspiracy and emphasis on one word can indicate that it has acquired significance earlier in a conversation (as in Dame Edith Evan's famous rendering of 'A handbag?') (Evans, 1932). Unfortunately for the attempt to find international mappings, few of these effects have a universal interpretation – a husky voice can mean either sexual desire or respect according to the language in which it is used, and in a number of languages the meaning of a word can be altered by changing pitch level.

The visual element which is of most obvious interest in the context of VAT is kinesics, which is the systematic use of facial expression and body gestures and movements to communicate meaning (Crystal, 1989). Other visual constituents worthy of study are sign language and writing – particularly punctuation. (Reverse mapping from punctuation to speech was famously practised by Victor Borge in comedic performances where he supplemented read text with instinctively onomatopoeic sounds that stood for punctuation symbols.) Possibly also worth consideration is the subtle tactile element of proxemics, which studies posture and body distance and was devised by Rudolf Steiner (1861–1925), who advocated body movement as a synchronous adjunct to speech in eurythmy, which he said created 'visible speech'.

Any direct mapping of spoken text would necessarily reflect the syntax of the verbal message. It is not the case, however, that English syntax represents the only available model and different languages organise the grammatical elements of subject, verb and object into different word orders. Whilst the order SVO is common to 75 per cent of the world's languages (Crystal, 1989), it is not always the case. Sign language, for instance, often starts with the object and Spanish precedes questions with a question mark. Yoda 'Strong am I with the force', (a Jedi master in the film The Emperor Strikes Back) a character from the Star Wars series of films, uses an OSV construction and the contextual clarity of opening with an object is tempting for an iconic language.

Presentation of Text

The textual message is intended to be presented on screen with VAT features added but the manner in which the text, whether typographic or iconic, arrives on screen will determine which methods of attaching visual supplements are appropriate. A spoken message arrives over time with only a single point of the sound wave being received at any one moment. A literal conversion of a spoken message to visual text might therefore have the text passing (at speaking pace) behind an opaque medium with a vertical slit in it. Understanding of a spoken message requires, however, that memory has held preceding sounds and converted them first into words and then, singly or in groups, into meaning. To match this extended model the slit could be replaced by a window graded, right to left, from transparent through translucent to opaque. In this way the recent text would be visible but would fade as it moved away from the 'now' slot (see Figure 2).

Whilst it is important to consider how speech functions, it is not the purpose of VAT to try to imitate spoken language but to add meaning to the text which is its visual incarnation and we can therefore make our own decisions about how the text is best presented. This freedom would, of course, be limited if we chose to design VAT for application in a pre-existing textual context, such as e-mail.

An e-mail message, when opened, arrives (effectively) as a complete block. A ticker tape machine or teleprinter delivers the message character by character at the typing speed of the operator. Applications designed for authoring multimedia presentation allow bullet points to slide into place in letter-, word- or sentence-sized chunks. Scrolling allows a message to be run through at a user's own pace. Subtitled films present text in units roughly matched to a short period of speech, usually semantically coherent and with punctuation used to improve comprehension. These presentations could perhaps be categorised as either frozen or fluid, each mode having a different chunk refresh times.

It might even be viable to use more adventurous animation techniques to bring text onto the screen. Behavioural 'gaits' could allow words (or other units of text) to run, sidle or mope from the wings onto the stage as appropriate. With the word treated as an independent, animateable form, it could 'jump' up and down in excitement or become sufficiently anthropomorphised to make its own gestures.

The mapping process might be driven by the referent or by the target, probably determined by whether the source was speech or text. Also, since paralinguistic features do not necessarily map neatly to text units (as, for instance, when intonation changes during a word or a gesture is made in silence) it is necessary to accommodate the notion of fuzzy mapping.

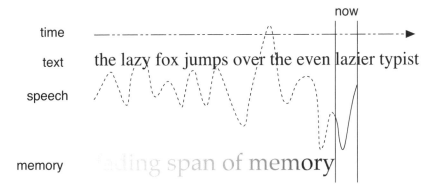

Figure 2. Comparative presence of text, speech and memory

Some specific options suggest themselves. Text could be presented in big, sentence- or paragraph-sized, chunks but VAT features then applied over time at a rate approximately matching speech. (Remember the ball bouncing over the words to a song at the cinema or in a TV programme and the 'Mexican wave' beloved of sports crowds?) New text chunks could be substituted en bloc, added to en bloc or scrolled into place. If VAT features were to be applied over time, the effects could either be locked onto text and held in place or removed as later text was similarly supplemented. An example of such a rolling application would be if words were individually coloured or refonted in succession. It is interesting to conceive of a system at an advanced stage of development in which the text was behavioural; in which the text 'understood' its own meaning and responded with self-applied VAT features.

Units of Mapping

It is necessary to decide the granularity of meaning at which the message elements will find a visual match. A 'top down' approach to language would theoretically attempt a single mapping for the message in its entirety whilst a 'bottom up' approach would seek to separately match every meaningful item. It might be tempting to start with word-level mapping but a word is not necessarily a satisfactory semantic unit, as the expression 'kick the bucket' clearly shows. Gestural communication also maps only intermittently to individual words, typically when the form of an object is mimed. Some possible units are defined by Crystal (1989)

Chereme –	the smallest contrastive unit in a sign language
Grapheme –	the smallest contrastive unit in the writing system of a language
Lexeme –	the smallest contrastive unit in a semantic system
Morpheme –	the smallest contrastive unit of grammar
Phoneme –	the smallest contrastive unit in the sound system of a language
(Even *Mytheme –*	the smallest contrastive unit of structure found in mythical narratives)

I now also propose the picteme as the smallest contrastive unit of pictorial or visual meaning, though, like the quark, it is hypothetical and still being sought. A one to one mapping of morpheme to picteme would be convenient though unlikely but mapping to a lexeme is a more reasonable aim.

At this early stage the project is open to any mapping possibility and there is no good reason why several mapping levels should not coexist. For example, a background mapping 'which set the scene' for the whole message could lie beneath text which incorporated a change of scale mapped to volume on which was superimposed a dynamic colour change mapped to an emotional state.

Visual Signifiers

There is a range of existing visual representations that can be used, in whole or part, to communicate (or in this case, amplify) a message. They are often close in meaning and poorly differentiated, the following attempt at defining some being largely based on the Concise Oxford Dictionary.

Sign –	a feature of language or behaviour that conveys meaning
Symbol –	a mark or character taken as the conventional sign of some object, idea, function or process
Icon –	a sign which has a characteristic in common with the thing it signifies
Pictogram/pictograph –	a pictorial symbol for a word or phrase
Emoticon –	a pictogram used to add emotional context to computer-based text :-)
Ideogram –	a character symbolising the idea of a thing without indicating the sequence of sounds in its name
Hieroglyph –	a picture of an object representing a word, syllable, or sound; an element of a pictorial writing system
Logogram –	a sign or character representing a word
Rebus –	an enigmatic representation of a word by pictures, etc. suggesting its parts
Image –	a representation of the external form of an object(s)
Picture –	a visual representation of some object(s) or idea

Some signifiers that may be used, such as changes of scale or overlaid colours, do not comfortably fit any of the above definitions and are classified here as 'transformations' though, since they are symbolic in effect, they could be considered as a subset of symbol. Others, such as cartoons, are a special case of an image, of particular interest because they are often designed to illustrate subtle ideas without recourse to words.

The key to the useability of any of these signifiers is that they are easily understood or, if they are new to the viewer, that they do not inhibit understanding of the underlying text. Anything introduced by VAT must add to understanding of the message or, at worst, be neutral to it until learnt. Another caveat is that whilst it is theoretically acceptable to mix signifiers, note must be taken of the intellectual strain on the viewer of having to move between the different translation modes this implies. It might be like having a piece of text which randomly uses mots from a versheidenheid of diverso linguas.

Mapping Options

Given that we can identify and quantify salient features of language and have suitable visual targets to which they can be mapped, then we need to establish the semantic and presentational relationship between the two. There are a number of possible options.

The relationship of referent to target could be abstract, as, for example, with a simple colour coding of volume in which the red pole represents maximum volume and the blue pole minimum volume. Alternatively, the relationship could utilise existing symbolic notations, such as a diagonal band to represent negation or a change of font to represent different emotions. It could also have a representational relationship which could range from photographically realistic to stylised, perhaps as a background image illustrating the context of the message. If typographic then the font itself could be the mapping agent, its style being matched to message using the same professional intuition which graphic designers use in the production of printed and screen material.

The graphic symbolism in Figure 3 is the province of the typographic designer and includes consideration both of layout issues and graphetics (Crystal, 1989) (a term coined on analogy with phonetics to mean the study of the physical properties that constitute writing systems). It is evident in a very pure sense in griphi (shaped poems) and concrete poetry, where the form is so powerful as to becomes the content. 'Typocollage' by John Heartfield (Heartfield, 1917) combines words and symbols in a layout that conveys meaning beyond that of the elements alone, whilst the poem *Lautgedicht* by Man Ray (Ray, 1924) merely uses fat, word-length dashes, arranged into verses, in the place of words to convey all the rhythm of a conventional piece. This principle can also be seen in transcripts of computer programs where, in the high level language Pascal for instance, layout features such as the indenting of nested loops provides a visual picture of the program's flow.

The visual signifier could be static, (both spatially and/or temporally), for instance, if a word was attributed a colour which remained unchanged whilst it was displayed, or it could be dynamic. If dynamic then its change over time (scale, position, orientation, colour, etc.) could be synchronous with a linguistic referent or independently animated. In the latter case it might, for example, be mimetic in the same way as elements of sign language.

The appearance of visual clues could be as prologue, setting the mood or context by way of introduction to the text and/or as coda concluding the message. It could be as background to the text or as 'costume', wrapping or dressing the text in colour or pattern. Perhaps the visual mapping could be environmental, creating a complete stage for the message, or could assume the role of director or choreographer and determine the form of the whole message performance. Indeed, metaphors of theatre such as these might come to shape the whole mapping production.

Television and film also offer a visual grammar which is sufficiently well assimilated, in the Western world at least, to be appropriated for VAT. The techniques of freeze, flashback, slow and speeded motion to reorganise time and place, of fades and wipes to move between sequences and of asynchronous cuts between vision and sound (so that sounds from one visual sequence overlap into the next) to achieve semantic continuity are all commonplace. Techniques such as these could be called on as an aid to narrative structure, perhaps applied to a dynamic background image or to the text block. It is also noted that multimedia has opened the floodgates to non-linear presentation of information, although it is not currently intended to depart from linear mapping.

Once a paralinguistic feature has been found a suitable visual mapping it could be applied to the message scene in a number of ways. If volume was mapped to colour, for instance, and the text was typographic then the colour at any

ROMANTIC

neutral?

mechanical

Figure 3. Expressive typeface

moment could be applied either to the whole body of text visible, to the whole of the background, to the current text element (letter, word, phoneme, morpheme, etc.), to the background local to that text element or to a discrete area of screen set aside to display such mappings. In general terms, therefore, it could be applied locally or globally to text element, background or reserved space and applied either statically or dynamically.

With kinesic features the mapping is visual to visual – from one form, usually animated such as in a gesture, to another which might well be static. It is easy to conceive of a number of pictographic icons which could stand for gestures but the idea carries with it the burden of having to be learnt. A likely alternative is an animated icon (Mealing and Yazdani, 1993) which could enact a stylised and possibly caricatural mime, the animation appearing either on every appearance or on request. The integration of an iconic sub-language with the main text is more problematic than that of the text and background transformations largely mooted up to this point. Icons could be integral with the text, which is likely to impair its reading, or adjacent to the text. In either case any animation is likely to be constrained to the current text element for fear of the screen being awash with simultaneous, kinetic distractions. An alternative presentation is to have the animation appearing in a discrete window – much like the signer added for deaf viewers to some television programmes – in which case the animations would necessarily be consecutive.

Dimensions of Mapping

The mapping process can be enacted across a number of dimensions. Volume (high/low), for instance, could be mapped on a single axis to colour (red/blue) or on twin, parallel axes of both colour and scale (big/small). Three dimensional prosodic space (tempo, pitch, loudness) could be mapped to three dimensional colour space (red, green, blue – RGB). This last example has the advantage of matching screen display technology in which pixels are set by their RGB values, though it still leaves the choice of which of the variables is mapped to which. In RGB space each of the prosodic dimensions would be mapped to a different colour: perhaps loudness to red, pitch to blue and tempo to green. Each combination of prosodic values would therefore produce a different colour mixture – on a scale from 0 to 256 the combination quiet, slow and high pitched (50,50,200) produces deep blue; loud, fast and low pitched (200, 200, 50) produces a lightish greeny yellow; very loud, fast and high pitched (250, 200, 200) produces a light, warm grey; three maximum values produces white and three zero values (or silence) produces black.

Closer consideration, however, suggests that the convenience of RGB colour space might be less appropriate than some other options. It is likely to be clearer to use the axes of HSV (hue, saturation and value) colour space, in which loudness could be mapped to value, pitch to hue and tempo to saturation, for example, because these three dimensions are more obviously differentiated by the human eye/brain. The four dimensional colour space of CMYK (cyan, magenta, yellow, black) which is used in printing is easily mapped to RGB space for display purposes and offers another axis if needed (See Figure 4).

Spatial position (on XYZ axes) of text elements could also be employed, so that if loudness was matched to the Z-axis a loud element would be displayed closer and a quiet element further away. Of course, on a two dimensional screen depth is virtual, the result of a viewing transform, and it might be desirable to enhance depth cueing with other devices such as distance-fogging or shadow-casting. Alternatively, since a three dimensional message space does not have to be seen frontally (i.e. 'down' the Z-axis), a viewing position could be used which provided a sight-line at an angle to all the axes. Other options are to make some or all of the text elements three dimensional, to uses changes of scale as well as, or instead of, spatial depth, to take elements in or out of (virtual) focus and to use degrees of pixelation to regulate emphasis.

Emotional Elements

Rather than map to clearly measurable paralinguistic features such as volume, it would also be possible to map to the emotional states that the individual features combine to indicate. It would be convenient, for instance, to be able to directly recognise underlying anger or apathy in a message. The VAT elements which stand individually for the demonstrable signals of an emotional state may, of themselves, combine to simulate understanding of that state but a single signifier is another option.

Whilst an intelligent system which identified the emotion could be envisaged, application of such an indicator in the short term is more likely to be applied by a human being who recognises the symptoms. That person could theoretically be the transmitter but it would usually be incongruous to self-consciously imprint one's emotional state onto a transmission. More likely is that the person indicating the emotional side would be an observer of the transmitter, either acting 'live' in the case

Figure 4. Some mapping options for 3D prosodic space

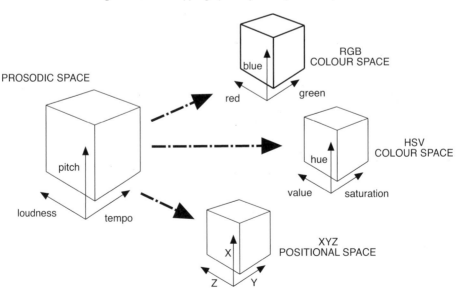

of instant transmission or retrospectively if transmission of the message was to be delayed. Thus could excitement, boredom, involvement, calmness, friendliness, surprise and other contextual features be specifically transmitted.

Comprehension, Control and Context

Since text on its own is comprehensible it is not essential that the value added features of a message are clearly interpreted by the receiver. Repetition over the course of a number of communications is, however, likely to build up or reinforce associations which will be instinctively called on in future. It is not, therefore, necessary to learn VAT, merely to experience it and let its meaning accrue. Even if no value is added, all that is sacrificed is bandwidth.

As has already been suggested, a fully automatic mapping system would be ideal but must remain a long term aim. It is relatively straight forward, however, to extract suitable data from spoken text in order to allow the mapping of prosodic features to visual transformations such as changes of colour or scale. This could be realistically expected to be carried out in real time. If, however, the system is not to automatically provide intelligent translation in the short term then VAT must be implemented by human hand, either that of the originator of the message or of an intermediary. A message that does not need to be transmitted live could have VAT added as a post-production process, in which case automatic mapping becomes optional and compromise is likely – perhaps automatic prosodic mapping composited with user selected elements.

It might be appropriate to pre-select a visual background for a message in order to establish its context but, as has been pointed out, it is less likely that a conscious decision would be made to display anger or apathy. If a message were to pass through a third party – a secretary or translator – these emotional colourers could be added by the intermediary before transmission. Also a medium such as e-mail, though usually transmitted directly between the principals of a communication, is composed before transmission and therefore allows time for value added editing. E-mail, if we exclude the option of sending a message as an attachment, would have to be re-designed to permit VAT additions but we plan here for e+mail!

The language mode to be addressed by VAT also needs consideration. Is it appropriate to design to supplement a message created in a formal, written style as well as one which is casual and conversational? The informality of typical person-to-person e-mail is closer to that of spoken language than most written styles and the use of the screen as a delivery medium offers a very different dynamic to that of paper. The level of interaction between users of internet chat rooms, however, is much greater than that of e-mail users – a difference between conversation and correspondence. One important consideration of computer mediated communication (CMC) is the way in which the medium changes the message.

Conclusion

Since VAT is to be derived from natural language with all its paralinguistic accessories then crude application of this new accessory will lean towards a hot, expressive communication mode. It will, however, be open to levels of refinement, perhaps as it cools, and a variety of delivery methods will be amenable to supplementation with VAT applied at different temperatures. Even a translation from screen, its natural home, to paper would be possible if dynamic elements were removed or found symbolic equivalents.

A large range of options has been suggested for implementing the principles of VAT and all will be prototyped before a working selection is made. With information communication technology (ICT) developing at a rapid pace, it is likely that limitations which might restrict the initial choice of workable VAT features will vanish over time and the full, prototyped vocabulary will be available as an extended resource for future access. One early ambition of VAT is to capitalise on the speech recognition technology that is now readily available. It will aim to overlay the text automatically derived from the spoken word with visual supplementation that maps accompanying prosodic variations, so that speaking into a microphone directly generates typographic VAT on screen.

And what of naked VAT? What sense, if any, might VAT features make if stripped from the text they are designed to accompany? Watching television with the sound turned off does not remove all understanding and VAT is offering to find visual form for those missing sound clues as well as mapping kinesic features. It is at this point that the possibility of providing an additional level of understanding to groups with limited language ability arises. Perhaps even a pet animal, already sensitive to the paralinguistics of humans, might prove to have some response!

Initial experiments with VAT are being conducted using English alone but in the knowledge that to realise its potential it must address international issues and different cultural contexts. Issues of transmission medium and application interface are also deferred until it is clear which VAT elements are most effective and are therefore to be the focus of development. A full range of features, meanwhile, is being prototyped and tested, further background research is being undertaken and a hunting party has been sent out to search for the elusive picteme.

References

Concise Oxford Dictionary. (1992). The Electronic edition, Oxford University Press. (adapted)

Crystal, David. (1989). The Cambridge Encyclopedia of Language (2nd ed.), Cambridge University Press. Ibid. (adapted)

Evans, Edith. (1932). As Lady Bracknell in the film The *Importance of Being Ernest*.

Goldin-Meadows, Susan and Mylander, Carolyn. (1998). 'Spontaneous sign systems created by deaf children in two cultures'. *Nature,* vol. 391, pp 279-81.

Hall, Sarah. (1998). 'The instinctive gesture', *The Guardian,* 19th Nov.

Heartfield, John. (1917). Reproduced in Ades, Dawn. (1993). Photomontage, Thames and Hudson Ltd.

Mealing, Stuart and Yazdani, Masoud. (1993). 'A computer-based iconic language', *Multilingual multimedia*, Intellect.

Mealing, Stuart. (1994). 'A computer HINTerface', *Intelligent Tutoring Media*, vol. 5 no. 2, Intellect.

Ray, Man. (1924). Reproduced in Reichardt, Jasia. (1965). Between Poetry and Painting, Institute of Contemporary Arts, London

Yoda (1983) a Jedi master in the film *The Empire Strikes Back*.

8. IconText: An Exploration of the Limitations of Iconic Languages

Colin Beardon

Introduction

When icons first appeared on our computer screens they were very attractive. They were a good way of referring to the objects 'inside' our computers and possessed a clear operational semantics. The actions of clicking, dragging and dropping mapped onto the set of things we normally wanted to do with our machines. Together, the representational form and operational semantics replaced the language of operating systems and provided us with a model for understanding a technology that had previously been almost incomprehensible. They soon became so popular that different application programs adopted them and they emerged as one of the four pillars of the modern WIMP environment.

A merchant of doom might have warned of the great danger in proliferating such systems: a virtual Tower of Babel as iconic systems grew without direction or control. In the event there has not been any such effect or, at least, it is not a serious problem as yet. Users seem able to manage the growing arrays of iconic toolboxes and, though clearly some difficulties are encountered, I have heard no one advocate a general return to text-based command languages.

On the other hand, it is possible that we are not maximising the potential of this novel technology. We tend to see these uses of icons as pragmatic solutions to usability problems ('iconic interfaces') whereas we could perhaps see them more fruitfully as complex languages involving the equivalents of nouns, verbs, etc. (i.e. as natural 'iconic languages'). The study of iconic systems as languages is, I would argue, a field worthy of much study and may lead to significantly new fields of computer use.

In this article I will describe IconText, an iconic language developed by the author in the mid-1990s. It embodied many ideas from both the philosophy of language and the field of computational linguistics but, rather than seeking to analyse (or generate) particular sentences in a language, it provided a computer-based environment in which a wide range of iconic messages could be written and read. Being computer-based, this environment was able to exploit the interactive capability of multimedia computing and, in particular, to use hypertextual structures to help convey linguistic concepts.

IconText is loosely based upon Roger Schank's Conceptual Dependency (CD) (Schank, 1973). This was chosen because of its inherently diagrammatic nature and because it had proved of practical use in a number of projects (e.g. Schank, 1975;

Wilensky, 1981). Schank's Conceptual Dependency claims to be a well-defined notation for representing the meaning of sentences in 'an unambiguous language-free manner' (Schank, 1973). This representation is through CD-diagrams which consist of words laid out in a 2D arrangement and connected by various types of arrow (Figure 1). CD-diagrams are not iconic, in that the objects that fill the various locations at the end of arrows are traditionally words, though it would take very little effort to replace the words in a CD-diagram by icons. One would then have a kind of pictorial map of the sentence, displaying both the referents of the individual words and the structure that binds them together.

CD-diagrams explicitly separate out the representation of form (the spatial arrangement and the arrows) from the content (the words) and in doing so they situate themselves within a particularly modernist tradition, the roots of which can be found in many related fields concerned with communication.

Form and Content

The philosophy of logical positivism, much of computational linguistics and the design of iconic language systems have all sought clarity in language through the division of messages into elements (that directly relate to the world) and structures (that determine how these elements combine to form complex meanings).

For example, Otto Neurath (a graphic designer who subscribed to logical postivism) described his ISOTYPE system as a picture language and said of it, '. . . the picture language is an education in clear thought.' (Neurath, p. 22)

In the philosophical treatise called the Tractatus, Wittgenstein was also primarily concerned with achieving clarity.

> Everything that can be thought of at all can be thought clearly. Everything that can be put into words can be put clearly.
>
> (4.116, Wittgenstein, 1961)

To achieve such clarity Wittgenstein forced binary choices onto language. All uses of language must be either 'meaningful' or 'meaningless'. Meaningful uses of language are those that are either 'true' or 'false' (2.21; 4.023). All other uses of language are marginalised as either meaningless riddles or things about which we cannot speak.

Figure 1. 'While going home I saw a frog.' An example of CD representation (Schank, 1973)

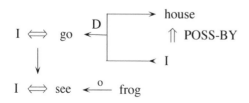

Neurath was also concerned with the use of communications systems for the expression of scientific or factual information, though in his case he related this to addressing social issues such as housing, education and health.

The Vienna Circle of logical positivist philosophers provides the link between Neurath (who was a member) and Wittgenstein whose work was appreciated by members of the group and who had many ideas in common with them (Lupton, 1986). One of the fundamental tenets of logical positivism was that the truth relationship between any natural language expression and the world depends upon a set of fundamental physical observations that, at some level, can be mapped onto the parts of the language. In other words, there are atomic acts of observation that correspond to atomic elements of language. The complex statements of language (insofar as they are true or false) are seen as complex constructions of such atomic elements.

Wittgenstein argued for the isomorphism of language, pictures and reality.

> The fact that the elements of a picture are related to one another in a determinate way represents that things are related to one another in the same way.
>
> (2.15, ibid)

This is a clear invitation to see pictures in terms of a visual syntax which, in some sense, mirrors the semantic relations between the constituents of the picture.

> Every statement about complexes can be resolved into a statement about their constituents and into the propositions that describe the complexes completely.
>
> (2.0201, ibid)

Thus we arrive at a compositional semantics in which the meaning of a complex phrase is derived from the meaning of the individual components through the application of general compositional rules which are based upon the syntactic relations between the parts (Charniak, 1981).

While both Neurath and Wittgenstein believed in such compositionality, what makes them especially interesting for us is that they both saw this as operating primarily pictorially. Neurath said that in ISOTYPE 'the effect is a language picture' and he referred to ISOTYPE diagrams as 'fact-pictures'. Wittgenstein also saw linguistic statements pictorially. He argued that every meaningful statement was, in some sense, a picture.

> A picture is a fact.
>
> (2.141, ibid)
>
> A picture is a model of reality.
>
> (2.12, ibid)

The elements of the picture are assumed to directly indicate the objects they represent.

> In a picture the elements of the picture are the representatives of objects.
>
> (2.131, ibid)

(The word 'picture' may nowadays seem slightly inappropriate as it has the connotation of a photo-realistic reproduction of nature. It might help our comprehension if we were to substitute the term 'diagram'. In a diagram we are less likely to assume that the arrangement of objects is determined by physics and accept that it could equally be determined by some symbolic principle, such as temporal relationship.)

Wittgenstein says that both written and spoken languages can be usefully thought of as a picture in that both are composed of elements in a particular configuration. Indeed, what is common to the written and spoken forms, or to the same idea as expressed in two different natural languages, is that they share the same underlying 'picture'.

Neurath also saw his picture language as providing the common underlying form for statements in other natural languages.

> We have made one international picture language (as a helping language) into which statements may be put from all the natural languages of the earth.
>
> (Neurath, p.17)

The view that there could be a common underlying form to all language, and that this could be made explicit, was shared by many computational linguists in the 1970s and 1980s. They sought to devise representations with the expressive power of natural language but which avoid its ambiguity or diversity of forms. In Chomsky's case (1957) the canonical representation was syntactic ('kernel sentences' or 'deep structure'), in Winograd (1972) it was procedures in Planner, in Schank (1973) it was Conceptual Dependency diagrams, in Montague (1974) it was Intensional Logic, while others have used first-order logic, frame notations, messages and many more besides.

The intention of these approaches is that the meaning of a natural language sentence is fully described in terms of some canonical system. Woods (1978) referred to such canonical systems as Meaning Representation Languages (MRLs). The aim of each MRL is two-fold. Firstly it aims to represent unambiguously the true meaning of a sentence. Secondly, it enables a semantic representation that serves some other purpose. An MRL, for example, may provide the means for translation into another natural language, or provide a reformulation of a sentence that can directly access a database.

Within CD, which is the particular MRL chosen to form the basis of IconText, the simplest symbol is a lexical entry which refers to an object and which Schank calls either a 'Picture Producer' or a 'Picture Aider'. These are the conceptual equivalents of 'noun' and 'adjective'. In CD these simple symbols contain sufficient semantic information to implement any later semantic constraints (e.g. only animate objects can be the subject of an action). Simple lexical entries can be combined with specific relations (e.g. LOCATION or POSSESSED-BY) to produce more complex Pictures.

Referring to Objects
Traditionally it has been held that there are three main ways of referring to an object. These involve:

a) names, in which there is a direct and atomic learned relationship between word and object;
b) descriptions, in which a noun phrase is used to describe the object in question; and
c) ostensive definitions, such as saying 'This!' or 'That!' accompanied by a pointing gesture.

We will consider each in turn.

Icons and Names

For Wittgenstein, as many other philosophers of the time, a name is the simplest unit within a language both syntactically and semantically. That is to say, it is a word (or part of a word) that cannot be decomposed further and it refers directly to a part of reality.

> The simple signs employed in propositions are called names.
>
> (3.202, Wittgenstein, 1961)
>
> A name means an object. The object is its meaning. . .
>
> (3.203, ibid)

We have seen that, according to the picture theory of meaning, a sentence (be it spoken, textual or iconic) is ultimately composed of atoms that refer directly to objects. If we replace the linguistic atoms of language by atomic pictures (in our case, icons) then various new considerations raise. Figure 2 contains various iconic atoms that refer to the object 'men' and the way they do this varies from the arbitrary (Figure 2a), through the iconic (Figures 2b – 2d), to the pictorial (Figure 2e).

While it is fair to say that naming words are essentially arbitrary in the way they refer and that therefore there is no alternative but to learn their meaning, with pictures there is arguably no need to learn because the relationship to the referent is based upon prior observation – Figure 2(e) for example is clearly a man. It would be quite wrong, however, to see pictures as an ideal method of reference. There are a number of things pictures are not good at expressing (for example, 'the game of poker' or 'the class of all mammals'). For the purpose of communication, pictures can also reveal too much information. Figure 2(e) might equally well stand for 'grown men', 'male teachers' or 'office worker' or have a number of other interpretations.

Neurath developed ISOTYPE to convey general rules and so had a natural bias towards referring to classes rather than particulars. He said that:

Figure 2. Five different ways of referring to men

> The sign 'man' has not to give the idea of a special person with the name XY, but to be representative of the animal 'man'.
>
> (Neurath, p.33)

He also adds that this is not a universal rule,

men

Figure 3a. Fourteen compound icons (cursors used in Photoshop 4.0)

Figure 3b. Seven atomic elements within the fourteen compound icons of Figure 3a.

for it may be necessary to give the picture of a special person in a teaching-picture – that is not at all out of harmony with the rules of picture language.

(ibid)

Just as a name is not necessarily a whole word in a written language, so it is the case that a whole icon is not necessarily the simplest unit of meaning within an iconic language. Individual icons are usually quite discrete, taking up a fixed size of, say, 16 x 16 pixels; but as icon systems have become more complex, so we have seen the development of compound icons (Figure 3a). Within these there are two or more elements which, relative to the set to which they belong, are the smallest unit of meaning (Figure 3b). These are not absolute semantic primitives: it is always open to a designer to decompose any 'smallest unit' into further sub-parts but that does not mean that any particular set does not have its atomic elements.

An example might help to explain some of the issues involved. A particular person may be referred to by means of

- a name (e.g. 'John Smith' or just 'John');
- a full description (e.g. 'the tall man, aged 30, who is standing next to David Davies');
- a head noun used as a shortened description and relying heavily upon context (e.g. 'the man');
- an ostensive definition (e.g. 'You!' accompanied by a pointing gesture).

IconText tries to tread a careful path through these philosophical niceties. Its general position with regard to the problems of naming and describing can be summarised as follows. Just as with natural language, there is both a dictionary of general terms and a means of dynamically creating structures that describe objects. These structures are such that they have within them a designated single space for a 'head term' (or 'head icon') which is the equivalent of a 'head noun' in a noun phrase. It is also possible to refer to iconic structures by means of a single term which I will refer to as the 'direct term' or 'direct icon'. This direct term does not refer directly to the (real world) object but

Figure 4. Twelve icons in a dictionary (representing perhaps black, white, house, city, woman, man, telephone, dog, tree, book, car, aeroplane)

rather to the description. By default the direct term will be the same icon as the head term but it may be replaced or stylised. Finally, linguistic naming (e.g. 'John') is represented in Quinean fashion as simply another descriptive property. That is to say, it is the equivalent of 'I have the property "John"', where the property in question is the 'name-label' property.

The most fundamental part of IconText is the dictionary (Figure 4). Authors can access a set of icons shared between users but there is no problem if a user wishes to define a new icon or define a local meaning to some existing icon.

Interactivity is employed to provide explanations of the semantics of any icon. If the user clicks on an icon, a picture dictionary is accessed and an animated explanation shown of the normal reference of the icon. The possible techniques one may adopt in constructing such animated dictionary explanations is a complex subject that is beyond the scope of this chapter. Any author-generated changes to the dictionary will be transmitted as part of the message. Icons have no properties and are not typed, so any icon can appear anywhere in any window.

There are some icons that do not refer to physical things. These include icons that refer to a type of event (e.g. change_location, change_state), icons that refer to a type of relation (e.g. ownership, equality, causality) and icons such as the question mark (used to indicate the focus of a question).

Pictures that Describe Objects

Within IconText an object is represented by a window that shows an icon for the head term and icons for its modifiers. For example, the phrase 'the black car' will be represented by a Picture-Producer icon for 'car' in the top left corner and a Picture-Aider icon for black elsewhere within its frame (Figure 5). Any number of Picture Aider icons can appear within the frame so that we could represent, for example, the phrase 'old, large, dirty, black car'. If there is no head term then the whole might represent 'something black'. If the black icon appears as the head term, then the whole might represent 'blackness'.

A person called 'John' is also represented as an object. We create an object window for a (male) person with the name-label 'John' (proper names are one of the few places where text is allowed). The default direct icon is the head icon but Figure 6 shows a possible new icon that might be deliberately created for the purpose of referring to this description of John.

Figure 5. Object windows for: 'the black car', 'something black' and 'blackness'

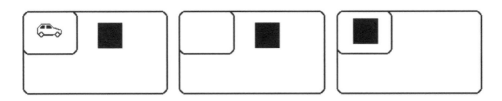

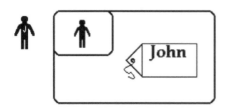 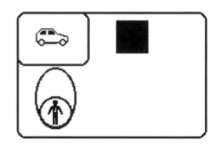

Figure 6. An object with a linguistic name ('a man named John') and a direct term

Figure 7. Linked object windows: 'a black car owned by John' (linked to Figure 6).

The phrase 'John's black car' introduces a relationship (ownership) between the two objects. We add an ownership icon to the window for the car (Figure 7). The object within this ownership icon is the direct term for the object screen for John. Clicking on it will take the user directly to that window.

The stylised symbol of a circle within an ellipse was initially developed to indicate property ownership but it seems possible to use it more abstractly. In context, it can express a wide range of related concepts such as parenthood, nationality and physical inclusion without too great a risk of ambiguity. It seems likely that a limited set of abstract relational icons might generate a large number of different interpretations in different contexts.

Before we leave the issue of referring to objects, we should consider ostensive definitions which are often assumed to be the ideal way to unambiguously denote an object. In many respects they are similar to the use of the 'point-and-click' facility we are familiar with when using a mouse but ambiguity can still be a problem as there is no guaranteed consistency in the type of thing that is selected. (For example, within GUIs we normally use 'click' to select an object but when using the 'eye-dropper' tool we use it to select the colour of a pixel.) Within IconText the only ostensive definitions are declared within the envelope (see below).

Propositions that Refer

Referring to Events

Within his picture theory of meaning, Wittgenstein did not make a clear distinction between objects and events except through the choice of the term 'proposition' or 'state of affairs'.

> In order to understand the essential nature of a proposition, we should consider hieroglyphic script, which depicts the facts that it describes.
>
> (4.016, Wittgenstein, 1961)

Wittgenstein saw events as simply static (i.e. atemporal) representations. Neither was Neurath particularly interested in the distinction, mainly because his diagrams aimed to show universal relationships rather than particular events.

Schank, by contrast, is very interested in events. His cognitive equivalent of a 'proposition' is a 'conceptualisation'. The structure of a conceptualisation is that it is typically based around one of fourteen primitive ACTs (e.g. MOVE where an agent is involved in moving something, INGEST where an object is taken into a body and PTRANS where an object changes its physical location). Particular verbs may be represented by an ACT with particular restrictions on its related case structures (e.g. 'object', 'direction', 'instrument'). Conceptualisations may also describe a static state of affairs or a change of state.

In IconText active events are represented by a special window which may be animated. The case structures defined by CD (object, direction-from, direction-to, etc.) are the equivalents of specified positions within the event window. Direct icons can fill any of these slots but not all slots have to be filled. For example, in Figure 8 the slot for the place where the man came from remains unfilled.

We can get an impression of the meaning of this event window from its static representation - Figure 8 is about a man going to a city, but we do not know which man, which city or where the man came from. We can interrogate the objects to discover, say, that the person is John and the city is London. We can also interrogate the event by clicking on the arrow to start an animation: in this case the icon for John starts on the left and moves rightwards across the screen ending next to the icon for London. The implementation of each event window has both a static 2D representation (the juxtaposition of the icons and the arrow) and an animated representation.

Where there is an INSTRUMENT case, as in 'John drove to London', we adopt Schank's approach which restricts the instrument case to further events (i.e. 'John went to London' has an instrument slot that is filled by 'a car went to London'). IconText does not show the instrument event as an explicit icon but places it on a stack of events immediately behind the current event. The deeper the user goes into the stack, the more instrumental detail is provided about the action. Schank insisted that a conceptualisation can have at most one instrument case and this must be a further conceptualisation (that is, not a Picture).

As with objects, each event has a single icon which can be used to refer to it in other windows and the user has the power to choose a new icon to name the event if desired.

Figure 8. An event window which superficially says that a man went to a city. The stacked window reveals the INSTRUMENT case (i.e. how the event was carried out)

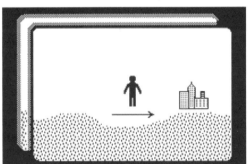

Referring to Relations

By means of object and event windows it is possible to make iconic statements that are roughly equivalent to simple present

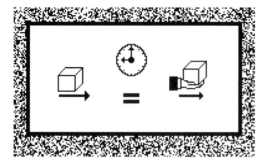

Figure 9. A relation window indicating that a PTRANS took place at the same time as a MOVE

tense sentences in a natural language. That is to say, we have little difficulty representing sentences such as 'Mary drives to Manchester.' or 'The big brown dog is eating a bone.'

To build more complex sentences, IconText provides the capability of representing two fundamentally different types of discourse relation: ideational and interpersonal (Grosz and Sidner, 1986; Maier and Hovy, 1991). Ideational relations express different kinds of relation between objects, events and relationships while textual relations refer to the author's relationship to the reader.

The basic structure of all relationships is that the two related entities are shown on the left and right and the relationship is shown in the middle. Where the relationship is of the form of attribute and value, then the attribute type is shown at the top and the attribute value is shown at the bottom. Figure 9 indicates that a 'PTRANS' (left) and a 'MOVE' (right) are connected by a relation whose type is 'TIME' (top) the value of which is 'EQUAL' (bottom). It is therefore equivalent to saying that the two events take place at the same time.

Interpersonal meaning is 'writer-and-reader oriented'. This is information that an author can provide concerning the discourse structure of the message. Tonfoni (1994) suggests a set of iconic symbols for expressing such structure. In IconText such information is not only declarative but is used in the creation of the animation from the static message structure that the author has created.

Neurath claimed that a benefit of pictorial languages is that,

At the first look you see the most important points. . .

(Neurath, p.27)

IconText provides an even more powerful implementation of this ordering. For example, consider the author's assumption as to what the reader already knows (the given/new distinction in linguistics). If we allow the given part of the discourse to be identified by the author, then during the animation these parts of the message can be presented first so that the reader is oriented before new information is provided.

A second example is the focus of the message. An active link is made between the message in the envelope (see Figure 10) and that part of the message that the author chooses as the main focus. This, in turn, indicates a preference for the starting point of the animation.

For example, a declarative message that is expressed by the English sentence, 'Mary drove to Manchester in her black car' will be presented in three consecutive animations:

1 an animation involving only Mary going to Manchester,

2 an animation explaining the instrument case involving a car going to Manchester,
3 an explanation that the car was owned by Mary and was black in colour.

If we transform this sentence into a question such as , 'What colour car did Mary drive to Manchester?' we must do more than replace the icon for 'black' by the question-mark icon. We also need to reverse the order in which the stages are shown (i.e. 3, 2 and 1).

The envelope window always appears first and always looks the same (Figure 10). It has standard slots representing the author ('me'), the reader ('you'), the message and the time of writing ('now'). The author and reader slots are linked to object windows which, typically, give the name and address of the person but may also show a naming icon. The time of writing may be linked to a window which represents a specific time. There is not yet a sophisticated representation for time, which may require a specific notation or even a separate window (see Ludlow, 1992). As indicated, the message icon is linked to the 'focus' – the relationship or event that is most central to the message.

Issues

In this chapter I have tried to show the underlying principles of an iconic language that operates within some very strict limitations. Principally these are:
a) that all meaningful language use is factual,
b) that 'picture languages' convey meaning through their form,
c) that meaning can be derived irrespective of context and function.

These limitations may apply to many of the limited iconic systems that have been developed but they do not apply within a more general communication medium that is comparable to natural language.

Extensions can be made to the underlying assumption that all meaningful language use is factual to allow for questions and imperatives but the real issue is that this assumption ignores the 'colour' of language – the connotations rather than the denotations. In the Tractatus Wittgenstein tried to avoid the connotations, deliberately isolating language so that it was 'colourless' (i.e. purely denotational). This is made clear when he talks about the relationship of a musical performance to a musical score,

Figure 10. The envelope window

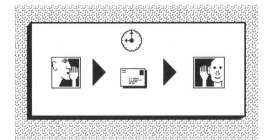

There is a general rule by means of which the musician can obtain the symphony from the score. . .

(4.0141, Wittgenstein, 1961)

The uniqueness of each musical performance is denied. There is a sense in which all performances of, say, Schubert's Great C Major Symphony are identical but there is another important sense in which they are all different. The Tractatus

89

chooses to highlight the similarity and sideline the difference and we are left with a poorer language because of it.

Wittgenstein's concept of a 'picture' seems very metaphorical. He writes:

> The fact that the elements of a picture are related to one another in a determinate way represents that things are related to one another in the same way.
>
> (2.15, ibid)

There is a tendency to read this as referring to physical relations but this is not the intention. Non-physical arrangements are specifically allowed for in which the form of the picture is referred to as 'logical form'.

> A picture whose pictorial form is logical form is called a logical picture.
>
> (2.181, ibid)

Such a 'logical picture' is, however, often based upon simile (or what is often incorrectly called "metaphor"). For example, if I say, 'My love is like a red, red rose', then in terms of the Tractatus, I am simply expressing a commonality of 'logical form' between my love and the rose. Once this door is opened, the possibility of totally reliable communication retreats and we are left with all the ambiguity and richness inherent in simile, metaphor, hyperbole and the whole semiotic bag of tricks.

The Tractatus first appeared in print in 1921. Twelve years later, Wittgenstein was giving the lectures which became the Blue and Brown Books and these argued a very different approach to understanding language. Right at the beginning we are told,

> We are up against one of the great sources of philosophical bewilderment: a substantive makes us look for a thing that corresponds to it.
>
> (Wittgenstein, 1960, p.1)

There is the acceptance that words, as elements of a language, do not necessarily have meanings outside their contexts of use. On being puzzled by a particular use of a word, he says, 'I know what a word means in certain contexts.' (p.88?). An alternative view of language emerges that places language within the context of use. A word or expression is explained if we can describe the successful actions that follow from the use of the word.

Though written nearly 70 years ago, the Tractatus is an attempt to describe theoretically a particularly formal type of language use and, by driving it to its logical conclusion, to show where it will break down and how it might need to be transcended.

The particular type of language it presents can be described as follows:
(a) We are only interested in the truth or falsity of what is said.
(b) There are atomic elements.
(c) Atomic elements refer unambiguously to an object.
(d) Elements can combine pictorially to produce (more) complex elements.

(e) The meaning of a picture is compositionally derived from the meaning of its elements by means of a function representing the logical form of the picture.

(f) The pictures thus produced refer unambiguously to the real world.

Even in situations in which condition (a) applies, conditions (c) and (e) remain problematic. We can never practically know that the denotation of any symbol is unambiguously understood and we can never know that the 'logical form' that one person derives from a picture is the same as that derived by another. We can be aware of these problems, however, and use our graphic and design skills to minimise them.

If we want to use icons and move away from such a literal use of language (that is, relax criterion (a) then the concept of iconicity may no longer be appropriate. Pictures, in all their complexity, can begin to participate in a language (or 'language-game') in their own right and not just as pointers to some linguistically presupposed object. That, however, is the topic of yet another paper.

References

Chomsky, N. (1957). Syntactic Structures. Mouton, The Hague.

Charniak, E. (1981). 'The case-slot identity theory', *Cognitive Science*, 5, 285-92.

Grosz, B. J. and Sidner, C. L. (1986). 'Attention, Intentions, and the Structure of Discourse', *Computational Linguistics* 12(3), 175-204.

Ludlow, N. D. (1992). *Pictorial Representation of Text: Converting Text to Pictures*. PhD thesis, Dept. of Artificial Intelligence, University of Edinburgh.

Lupton, E. (1986). 'Reading Isotype'. *Design Issues*, III(2), 47-58.

Maier, E. & Hovy, E. H. (1991). *Organizing Discourse Structure Relations Using Metafunctions.* Paper presented to the European Natural Language Generation Workshop: GMD-IPSI, Darmstadt.

Montague, R. (1974). *Formal Philosophy*, Yale University Press, New Haven.

Neurath, O. (1978). *ISOTYPE: International picture language*. Reading, UK: University of Reading, Department of Typography and Graphic Communication.

Schank. R.C. (1973). Identification of conceptualisations underlying natural language. In R.C. Schank & M.C. Colby (eds.) *Computer models of thought and language*, W H Freeman, San Francisco, pp. 187-247.

Schank, R.C. (1975). *Conceptual information processing*. North-Holland, New York,.

Tonfoni, G. (1994). *Writing as a visual art*, Intellect Books, Oxford.

Wilensky, R. (1981). 'PAM' In: R. Schank and C. Reisbeck (eds.) *Inside computer understanding* (pp.136-79). Lawrence Erlbaum, Hillsdale, NJ.

Winograd, T. (1972) Understanding Natural Language. Edinburgh University Press, Edinburgh.

Wittgenstein, L. (1960). *The Blue and Brown Books*. Harper and Row, New York.

Wittgenstein, L. (1961). *Tractatus logico-philosophicus*. trans. D.F.Pears & B.F.McGuiness. Routledge and Kegan Paul, London.

Woods, W. (1978) Semantics and Quantification in Natural Language Question Answering. in M.Yovits (ed.) *Advances in Computers, vol. 17*. Academic Press, New York, pp. 2-64.

9. Visualisation of Textual Structures[1]

Graziella Tonfoni

Visualisation is a powerful mean for both understanding and sharing knowledge. Knowledge today is being built both locally and globally, and effective exchange of textual information, which is culturally bound, requires an enhanced competence and encompassing vision. Possible misunderstanding and misinterpretation due to multicultural diversity and the inherent complexity of day-to-day communication, occurring throughout different media, may in some cases cause tremendous confusion if such complexity is not properly acknowledged and handled consistently.

Global management of information, which is mostly coming in the form of texts, requires a complex competence, a skilled ability, and high sensitivity to allow readers to actually understand and interpret texts the way they were meant to be interpreted when they were first generated.

CPP-TRS (Tonfoni, 1996) is a metalanguage and a markup language meant to visually convey through a set of icons interpretive cues regarding the communicative context of a certain document to a very high level of precision. It is based upon a combination of ten signs meant to convey the communicative function of each text, eleven symbols meant to indicate the communicative intention varying throughout sentences and paragraphs, and four turn-taking symbols indicating the role the reader is expected to play. The visual system is also meant to promote qualitative reasoning upon the nature of information which is textually displayed.

The overall system is also meant to cover those operations which are performed upon text in many and various ways and in different cultural settings.

Introduction

In the present chapter strong analogies are drawn between visual perception and natural language based textual perception, and a comprehensive system for integrating research in natural language and in vision is presented. The aim is to provide an interpretive model for textual visualisation as well as a set of conceptual tools, which may consistently describe and define those specific aspects of natural language that best represent structure, function and intention in sentences and paragraphs. Qualitative reasoning about communication occurring via natural language in the form of text is proposed and a visual representation system and a highly specific terminology are introduced and illustrated in order to define close relationships and analogies existing between visual perception and language perception phenomena. Terminology coming from vision is therefore transported and adapted to language problems at various levels of complexity.

The model presented here is grounded upon a theoretical framework for text preprocessing (Tonfoni, 1996) which leads towards the planning of a new way of conceiving text processing, here defined as style sensitive processing.

The aim of the present research has been to support a consistent metalanguage for visualizing different stylistic resolutions, based upon a basic terminology, meant to define those aspects of a text which would not be visible or recognisable without a consolidated and a consistent conceptual framework.

Multiple Viewing and Complex Textual Visualisation

A mental model for representing a variety of phenomena which involve knowledge representation and information processing (Hegarty, et al., 1988; Johnson-Laird, 1983) may become a very useful device for information-seeking (Marchionini, 1995).

Visualisation of information has attracted a wide population of researchers coming from computer science, cognitive science and linguistics.

Visualisation is a broad term which covers a whole range of representation structures of diverse nature and complexity, such as, for instance, icons and diagrams.

More precisely, diagrams are abstract graphic portrayals of the subject matter they represent (Lowe, 1993). Along those lines, texts may be conceived in terms of portrayals of the knowledge they represent.

To represent basic entities, which need then to be analysed as to be productively used, some of the current terminology in Textlinguistics is useful.

Text was initially conceived in terms of deep structure and surface structure of meaningful relationships, and differences between basic semantic entities and final output were originally conceived and defined in terms of text transformations (Van Dijk, 1972) to cover a new entity named 'text', which was considered to be different in nature and complexity from the recently defined linguistic entity 'sentence' (Chomsky, 1957, 1965). Visual representations of different kinds meant to describe specific features and explain relevant relationships were consistently produced.

Along these lines, a consistent and more complex reformulation of a new textual paradigm was made available (Ballmer, 1981) and text was conceived and visually represented as a complex entity resulting from a dynamic procedure of understanding evolving progressively in time (De Beaugrande and Dressler, 1981). Time in text understanding representation has to do with the progressive and asynchronous process of interpretation by text receivers, which happens at different stages and at various levels.

Correspondence between text receivers, who we may now also define as textual diagram observers, and perceptors reacting towards the text producer, whom we may also define as the diagram author, represents an interesting topic for exploration and further research which may productively be linked to observation of different types of individuals dealing with different kinds of textual problem-solving tasks and reacting in a variety of ways (Chi, Glaser and Farr, 1988).

A text may be productively envisioned as a diagram, where diagram means a highly articulated drawing and a visual structure which outlines and explains the partitioning of the text and the cognitive operations which are behind and beyond text itself and represent the stages in the progressive layout of meaning. All those operations which may be observed and have to be named and categorised consistently refer back to the so-called process of comprehension and interpretation of a given text. A mental model for enlightening interpretation complexity may profitably entail dynamic viewing of text, where by text a basic linguistic entity is considered together with its own originating communicative context, which may then, according to a multiple viewing and complex information visualisation, be conceived in terms of a textual holographic representation.

By referring widely to terminology, which is well-known in vision, we may build a complex model, which may consistently represent multiple contexts explosion of interpretation, generated by multiple context attribution. We may also proceed towards accurate definition of just one specific context, whenever possible attribution of many contexts at the same time may result in an undesirable condition.

Communicative context is the combination of communicative function, communicative intention and communicative turn-taking, controlling each single text or paragraph of a text, here defined as text unit. An appropriate definition to be attached to text is actually 'textual hologram'. A textual hologram is a three dimensional representation meant to be perceived and processed according to a highly context sensitive set of cognitive processes.

Only a high level of accuracy and precision in the processing of each textual unit, which has first been identified, will ensure the possibility of visualising multiple and complex text interpretation processes according to the text perceiver's point of view and perspective.

Two kinds of textual holograms are illustrated: transmission textual holograms and reflection textual holograms.

Three dimensional visualisation of different communicative positioning stages within the same text would in fact explode interpretation processes if larger interpretative patterns were not first identified and clarified to guarantee that consistent text perception occurs at each given stage and time of observation on the text perceiver's side. Text understanding is in fact a dynamical and not only linearly evolving process.

Communicative positioning patterns may be found (Tonfoni, 1996) which reflect upon text. They are generated by consistently triggered communicative positioning attitudes, as will be more extensively illustrated further on.

We will now show how differentiated stages of meaning creation may be derived from a progressively shifting and dynamically changing text visualisation process. Three dimensional representation of complex interpretation in a given text may well serve both to represent meaning potential and to eliminate undesired ambiguity. It is important to visualise complexity in the first place, since a text is in itself a complex entity.

Communicative context, which is communicative function, intention and turn-taking, may in fact be missing or ambiguous in texts exchange, given the gap existing in time and space between the production process and the understanding process, which occur asynchronously.

Texts are also likely to undergo loss of context or context shift, which may result in possible ambiguity or multiple interpretation.

The concept of textual hologram is meant to represent multiple meaning reflection and refraction phenomena in communication. Textual holograms processing is meant to visualise in accurate and reliable ways communicative context, which would jeopardise interpretation and understanding if missing or left invisible.

Transmission textual holograms are organised by text producers who want to make sure that the message is received, meaning perceived, charged by those very kinds of communicative function, intention and turn-taking, which they specifically want to assign to the message, both globally and locally.

If the textual hologram producer's main concern is to ensure that a stabilised and clearly-defined context is conveyed together with text, such text will have to be turned into a three dimensional representation of each textual unit, charged with a precisely defined set of contexts, which is locally assigned to each textual unit.

Reading and understanding of a textual hologram will therefore imply progressively shifting time and context so as to adopt a different perception, perspective and point of view, which may vary at each given stage of the interpretation process. Transmission textual holograms may also serve a quite opposite purpose: text producers may decide to explode the context potential and leave multiple interpretation possibilities open, stage by stage, by attributing to each textual unit a whole variety of plausible and possible contexts. If such process is to be undertaken, a whole interpretation explosion will come out of it, allowing text receivers, here also called text perceivers, to react in multiple ways, as opposed to directing them towards a pre-planned comprehension process, as in the previous case.

Transmission textual hologram is a productive concept meant to indicate stage by stage how the interpretation dynamics may be monitored.

The concept of reflection textual hologram is also a productive one. Reflection textual holograms are organised by the text perceiver out of the perception of a certain text, to which a specific context is assigned, permitting consistent comprehension so as to be able to reply accordingly and consistently.

Reflection textual holograms derive from the need perceivers have to define a certain context for their own interpretation of a received text to be sent back to the original producers. By adding context themselves, perceivers indicate what they are reacting to so as to allow the original text producer to add a new context or modify the indicated one, thus trying to optimise communication as much as possible by reducing the bandwidth and gap existing between text producer and text perceiver (Tonfoni, 1996). If ambiguity or exceedingly high complexity of the original text is perceived, a reflection textual hologram represents such complexity and may be sent back to request the original producer to select and identify the most appropriate context to be attached to it for most accurate and consistent interpretation.

A reflection textual hologram in the form of a reply may, in this specific case, represent the originating text together with one or many possible contexts for interpretation attached to it, then checked and confirmed or disconfirmed and deleted by the original producer permitting proper interpretation by the text perceiver according to the most suitable context attribution, which is the result of a meaning negotiation.

The whole concept of textual hologram is based upon effective recognition of intrinsic complexity of each text and textual unit. Especially when space and time variables play a significant role in text production and perception and when a temporary vacuum of context or context redundancy occur, visual techniques assume an extremely relevant role.

Identification of most accurate context for consistent interpretation is in fact made possible. Keeping multiple contexts open may in some cases result in added value to the text itself, as we were taught to think about literary and poetic texts.

On the other hand, it may constitute a major problem for accurate interpretation of an extended set of texts, like strategic documents, upon which decision-making is based or intercultural exchange of opinions on strategic matters.

Multiple possible context attribution may in fact result in noise and redundancy if not properly handled, thereby slowing down or even blocking out a whole chain of textual units, which may be productively linked together to produce meaning.

A 'snowball-like effect' may actually alter the intended meaning of a single text unit, reflecting on a following text unit or set of text units, thereby jeopardising consistent interpretation in global exchange of information and knowledge. A textual hologram is a high visibility device meant to be both descriptive and explanatory.

A New Framework for Viewing Natural Language and for Visualizing Text

'Communicative positioning attitudes' reflect upon text in its various stylistic variations, which may be defined as stylistic textual resolutions in various cultural settings.

The basic communicative positioned entity is text, whereas various text segments may show an alternation of different communicative positioning attitudes so that text really embodies more than just the sum of its segments. There is both competence and capacity on the individual's side to represent and perceive an infinite number of texts and text segments and to evaluate them consistently with their respective communicative positioning within a certain culture and communicative situation. The output result of a certain communicative positioning attitude or set of attitudes needs to be consistent; if some discrepancy were to occur between the communicative positioning attitude intended and its reflection upon style in text, then problems in interpretation would arise.

Discrepancy may be generated by an intentional uncooperative attitude during the communicative intercourse. Discrepancy between a communicative positioning attitude and its reflection upon the style of a text or text segment may in this case be viewed just like a syntactic rule and its violation in a certain sentence, resulting in distortion of meaning, which is quite obvious and easy to fix.

There are a whole variety of reasons why this should happen, most of which are actually unintentional.

Consistency between the communicative positioning and the respective stylistic output in text, which we may call final textual resolution, may be missing due to context-shift and stylistic drift which have occurred and passed almost unnoticed. Consistency is the output result of actual matching of a communicative positioning attitude and its most appropriate stylistic textual resolution.

In such a case, a textual segment turns naturally into a fully cohesive textual unit. The issue of consistency and inconsistency between language final output and intentionality has been raised in linguistics and in philosophy of language (Austin, 1962).

The speech acts theory (Searle, 1969) identifies a set of intentionality categories represented and carried on by specific verbs.

The context and style sensitive model here illustrated is meant to make qualitative reasoning upon the nature of information and the way information is packaged possible in the first place by supporting both text producer and text receiver with a visual metalanguage meant to raise visibility of stylistic choices made within a text.

The acronym CPP-TRS (Tonfoni, 1991, 1994i, 1994ii) stands for Communicative Positioning Program–Text Representation Systems.[2] CPP-TRS is a highly articulated metalanguage based upon a set of icons meant to represent progressive stylistic decision-making in text by supporting a whole set of icons, which represent the various aspects of the communicative context. Stylistic final resolution for each single textual unit is brought to light and visually conveyed by means of combinations of a variety of icons.

Visualising, defining, and creating articulated metaphors so as to explain complex phenomena or processes, which cannot be seen because they are actually invisible, is something which is very much used and practised in science. In order to be considered as scientifically grounded, a theory of language and of context and style sensitive text processing should entail observation, explanation, description and definition in order to produce prediction and evaluation at the end. CPP-TRS icons and, more precisely, textual signs, textual symbols and textual turn-taking symbols are progressively indicated from Figure 1 to Figure 4.

Text Visual Processing and Context and Style Sensitive Parsing

In order to describe a metalanguage for context and style sensitive text processing such as CPP-TRS, it is most appropriate to underline that what comes out as a result is both a new scientific framework for analyzing natural language and a visual text programming language.

The CPP component works as an interpretative device, whereas the TRS component is the metalanguage, which is meant to assign consistent interpretation to texts and text segments, which are in this way turned into textual units, both statically and dynamically.

If vision reflects the information processing task of understanding a scene from its projected image, in the same way a theory of visual text processing may have a parsing component performing the task of assigning interpretation values to a text from its projected positioning.

The task of a visual text processing language is to specifically proceed towards assigning signs and symbols to text segments in order to make communicative pattern recognition and context sensitive processing possible at the end.

A context and style sensitive programming language may produce a solid description not only of text itself and of those knowledge domains which are involved (text-image), but also of the communicative positioning attitudes, which are reflected (text-scene).

A context and style sensitive approach is meant to specifically address the issue of obtaining a three-dimensional analysis of 'text-scenes', by attaching a specific context to each textual unit: just like in vision, optimal textual resolution may entail a whole set of enhancement procedures.

Just as there are a few levels of information processing in computer vision, there are many levels in text to be first recognised to be properly and separately handled. Early syntactic processing and knowledge representation models have primarily addressed sentences and paragraphs, which may here be defined in terms of 'lines' and 'regions'. Context and style sensitive processing (Tonfoni, 1996) may be considered as some kind of high-level text processing because it is meant to enhance textual information visibility by attaching descriptions of text scenes, which means that it makes three-dimensional text analysis possible.

Understanding an image in vision requires a priori knowledge and the same is true for a text image, bound also and dependent upon expectations. Knowledge representation structures are most relevant for allocating consistent expectations, such as frames (Minsky, 1975), scripts (Schank, 1981), plans (Wilensky, 1983) and plot units (Lehnert, 1981). There exist also communicative positioning expectations, which allow a text-scene to be understood in its full complexity.

In the early years of research in vision, numerous techniques were developed for extracting lines and edges from images: Winston (1970) has started thinking of extracting concepts out of narrative texts, drawing significant analogies between vision and natural language. Just as after edge elements are detected and then grouped into meaningful lines, so text fragments may be grouped into meaningful textual units.

Another aspect of image analysis found to be most relevant is 'region identification': segmenting an image into regions is a complex and not at all intuitive process and is the exactly complementary process to edge detection.

Regions may be over-divided or under-divided; a region may correspond to more than one surface and surface variations may split a whole surface into several regions. A whole variety of possible resolutions shows in various types of texts, some of which are very different to process. Based on careful analysis of various types of texts, we may derive that text segmentation is a different process altogether: paragraphs and sentences may also be over-divided or under-divided and a conceptual territory may correspond to more than just a sentence or paragraph.

It may also reflect different contextual assumptions deriving from a diversified perception of the same situation at different times or under different cultural boundaries.

Square

For general information and general story.

Frame

For a story analogous to another previous story.

Square within a Square

For summary and reduced information out of a previously given general information or story.

Grouped Semicircles

For concepts that emerge from previously given general information or story.

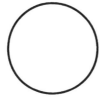

Circle

For a global or general concept that emerge from a previously given general information or story.

Triangle

For a memory text and subjective experience triggered by a previously given general information or story.

Semicircle

For a particular concept extracted out of a previously given general information or story.

Inscribed Arcs

For adding an alternative development to a story or a previously given general information.

Right Triangle

For comment deriving from a previously given general information or story.

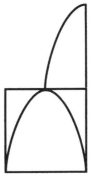

Opened Text Space

For opening up a new text segment in a text for a new alternative to a story or a previously given general information.

Figure 1

Marr (1978) underlines the need for choosing appropriate kinds of representation systems for different levels in the vision process. In natural language processing research as well, it is most important to underline the need for differentiating among different levels of understanding, in accordance with Minsky (1975), Schank (1981), Wilensky (1983).

The role of a certain kind of representation is to make certain information explicit at an appropriate level and time. Specific selection of a certain kind of representation will therefore deeply affect the kind of analysis which a text may consistently undergo and the kind of data and evidence we may derive from that. When specific image understanding programmes were started, adequate conceptual tools were also developed in the field of vision, which could be consistently adapted and productively transferred into research in natural language processing aimed toward organisation of a complex and natural model for automatic extraction of relevant information out of texts. Along those lines, we may think of developing context and style sensitive systems, which may be conceived and designed in order to allow for different levels of interpretation and conceptual extraction out of texts to actually occur, so as to enhance the level of transparency that some communicative intercourse and activities strictly require.

A three-dimensional text-scene analysis corresponds to a process of complete description and recognition of text complexity and a context and style sensitive analysis of text will also make it possible to capture the inherent complexity of a text when transported from one culture into another and from one setting into a different one.

The present approach is meant to augment already existing models of two-dimensional text processing by obtaining three-dimensional text processing, which is a tremendously powerful enhancement, both for text generation and for text understanding. Context and style sensitive text processing indicates the fundamental role of each specific communicative environment.

To be accurately checked, detection and reconstruction of the originating communicative positioning of a given text are to be derived either from direct observation and accurate analysis of the variety of positioning attitudes shown by individuals participating to the process or by accurate projection of estimated attitudes based upon culture-bound and context-dependent assumptions. If context and style sensitive systems are designed to handle information which comes out of a noisy communicative environment, as the one we live in today, they obviously have to allow for readjustment at different degrees. Visual preprocessing is a first step for enhancement and is already a very common practice in visual data processing. Context and style sensitive techniques are aimed towards monitoring different kinds of operations which may be performed upon text by supporting consistent interpretive tools and specific techniques for text modification at different levels of complexity, which would otherwise be unmanageable.

Describe

From Latin" describo", write around. It means giving as much information as you want with no need to follow any logical-chronological order.

Define

From Latin "definio", put limits. It means giving just some information, the relevant one, about a certain topic: there is a need to select and choose just relevant information.

Narrate

It means presenting facts and events by following a logical and chronological order.

Point out

It means getting a point, specific event or fact, out of a narrative, focusing on that, adding more information, therefore expanding it.

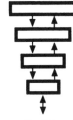

Explain

From Latin "explano" - unwrap, open up. It means representing facts in a cause-and-effect order; it is possible to start from the original cause and get down progressively to a set of effects, or proceed from effects going back to the original cause.

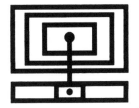

Regress

From Latin "regredior", go back. Regression means here giving more information about a certain item within a chain of information.

Reformulate

From Latin "reformo/reformulo" - change shape and shape again. It means changing attitude toward information packaging: from explaining into describing, or defining, or informing, etc.

Figure 2

Textual Visual Processing

If a text contains a satisfactory set of control elements, such as CPP-TRS icons, less ambiguity or meaning distortion is likely to occur. If distortion still occurs, each element becomes as easy to recognise as to identify the nature of the problem of interpretation, which led to distortion in the first place. Meaning allocation by visual means allows meaning reallocation as well. Visual remodelling of a text requires previous information about the original modelling of a text, whereas indirect remodelling of a text based upon pure guessing and without previous access to context dependent assumptions and culturally bound knowledge is not an adequate procedure, even if performed upon an evidently highly distorted text sample. It may in fact result in a temporary solution but not a complete one.

Meaning distortion and inconsistencies as well as uncontrolled collateral effects in interpretation may in fact continue and expand.

Resampling of a text implies step by step repositioning: it therefore requires the construction of an ideal text image by determining for each textual segment the corresponding one in the distorted text. It also implies accurate search for causes of distortion, which may vary in radical ways. Communicative redundancy as well as noise may play a fundamental role.

A very effective way to reduce noise in text without losing relevant details is to proceed toward producing different copies of the same text, through progressive adjustment stages. Through the use of textual signs we may easily recognise and group together text segments sharing the same communicative functions: a text region may in fact be defined as a set of text segments which share communicative function. In context and style sensitive text processing it is evident that in order to have appropriate text region segmentation it is necessary to incorporate knowledge about the context in which a text was generated at a certain time. This means that the communicative context, which is communicative function, intention, and turn-taking must be attached consistently to each textual unit.

A textual space which is fully charged with communicative context is a text region.

Further problems in text region segmentation may arise when there is no content uniformity. Therefore noisy regions may result at the end as a consequence of dishomogeneous distribution of context charge, given the instability of content.

There are two solutions to such a problem:

1) Text region growing: starting with many text segments, then merging them into similar regions until the only regions that remain are uniform.
2) Text region splitting: starting with a single and large text region, such as the entire text, then dividing it into different parts and then splitting until uniform text regions result.

In order to proceed towards accurate text region segmentation, an accurate search and analysis of the originating context as well of progressive context shifts is imperative.

In strategic documentation management, loss of crucial information may be due to the difficulties occurring in text region segmentation, where some content which is of major relevance may be lost in the process of both text region growing and text region splitting.

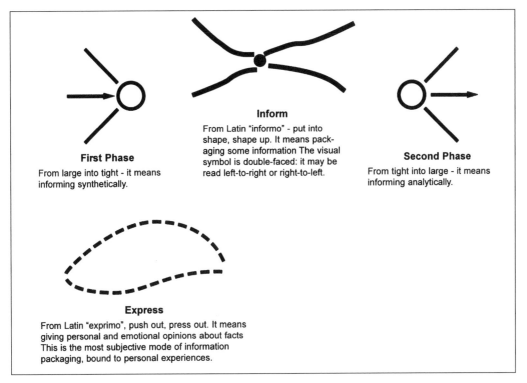

First Phase

From large into tight - it means informing synthetically.

Inform

From Latin "informo" - put into shape, shape up. It means packaging some information The visual symbol is double-faced: it may be read left-to-right or right-to-left.

Second Phase

From tight into large - it means informing analytically.

Express

From Latin "exprimo", push out, press out. It means giving personal and emotional opinions about facts This is the most subjective mode of information packaging, bound to personal experiences.

Figure 3

Consistent text region segmentation is strictly bound to specific contextual and cultural features identification and capacity of discriminating among different kinds of textual units, which may have been packaged according to different priorities and in different circumstances.

The amount of information carried by texts and text units may also deeply influence the process of text segmentation.

Discriminating among different kinds of textual units, which may have been packaged according to different priorities and in different circumstances, is therefore of substancial help in text region segmentation.

A different combination and alternation of communicative positioning attitudes found by projection will evidently reflect upon text region identification in a microscopic analysis of textual units. By tracing back each of the single contexts attributed to each textual unit, we may reconstruct entire text regions and verify if such reconstruction is appropriate or if some adjustments are still necessary. Different communicative contexts attributed to textual units will result in different stylistic resolutions affecting text interpretation at a global level, as it will be possible to have emerged from an overall text survey.

Qualitative reasoning upon information turns out to be a valid element of discrimination among qualitatively and quantitatively different kinds of information. A radical distinction obviously exists between information quality discrimination in unprocessed texts and in preprocessed texts. It is one thing to attribute meaning to a culturally bound and highly context dependent conversational interaction between partners coming from diverse backgrounds and negotiating for a common solution, with time gaps, and a completely different thing to label an interaction based upon a controlled vocabulary which is consensually shared.

Accurate text understanding involves accurate text units analysis: as we have seen, text segmentation techniques are intended to organise text regions, showing some sharing of relevant characteristics like uniformity or intensity. Uniformity means a common sharing of a more global function, whereas intensity means sharing communicative intention and communicative turn-taking. We have seen that the most powerful approach to text processing is the text-scene approach, where the overall communicative positioning of a certain text is taken into account before proceeding to any further text or text segment analysis. Intrinsic features of a three-dimensional analysis of text are:

1) textual orientation, the preliminary identification of global communicative function of a text, which is then represented and visually conveyed by textual signs;
2) textual intercourse distance, the consistent identification of local communicative intention, which is then represented and visually conveyed by textual symbols;
3) textual reflectance, the final identification of local communicative turn-taking, which is then represented and visually conveyed by textual turn-taking symbols;
4) interpretive incident illumination, the global impact of turn-taking, still represented and visually conveyed by textual turn-taking symbols.

Such inherent complexity is carried out through a set of icons and the various intrinsic values attributed to each sign and symbol may be computed for each text and text unit with some approximation first, and with higher precision after accurate text preprocessing has indeed occurred. Given the cost of such enhancement, it is quite clear that texts which should undergo the process are ones where misunderstanding and confusion are a major problem. Once again we may consider strategic communication first of all, both in its conversational format and in its written format, which is documents and reports.

Static vs Dynamic Visualisation.

Conversion of verbal sequences into written sequences in all of its consequences is another relevant factor which must considered in analysing context varying throughout a sequence of text units. The more unstable and volatile the context, the more inconsistencies may be easily generated and transported throughout the whole text and further text adaptations, such as summaries, commentaries, abstracts and excerpts.

If redundancy is of help to eliminate noise, it is not solving the problem: sudden context shifts, resulting in misleading ramifications, are frequent phenomena that are not easy to identify, at first glance. Text shifting and meaning motion, which means that radical changes occur and reflect upon the interpretation process by and large, are not intuitively found. Discrimination capabilities between and among different causes

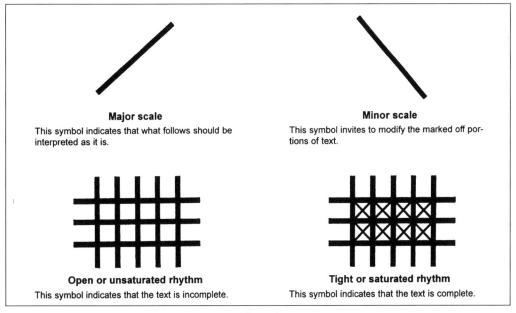

Figure 4

of sudden shifts up to radical changes are necessary. It is important to be able to recognise and deal with inconsistencies and overlaps, which may temporarily occur and be fixed at the end.

Let us now briefly mention a few basic problems occurring in analysing meaning motion caused by context shift and style drift, where by drift we mean a deviation resulting from progressive shift of both context and style having progressed so far as to affect significantly the so-called conditions of satisfaction for previous interpretation to still be acceptable. It is once again productive and useful to access terminology coming from vision and motion, which can here be easily adapted to textual matters.

1) The interpretation reflection problem: motion and context shift occur prior to text images identification and as a consequence of such delay. In order to be able to distinguish text images within a sequence which is already subject to drifting, it is most important to establish which lexical elements are causing the context shift in the first place. If lexical items are not found, then textual segments should be carefully analysed, because stylistic resolution inaccurate attribution may be where the problem resides. Determining the correspondence of lexical elements from one text segment reflecting into another one is called the interpretation reflection problem.

2) Three-dimensional meaning motion analysis: motion and context shift analysis provides specific cues for fixing the problems derived from drifting. This is due to the capacity to perceive differences occurring between context bound communicative intercourse and context controlled interaction. Recovering the three-dimensional text-scene out of a purely bi-dimensional text image is possible and

105

feasible if the fixing occurs when the context drift is first noticed. Delays in taking action may cause the problem to become too difficult to solve given the rising expansion of inconsistent assumptions and collateral side effects and ramifications leading towards multiple directions and becoming therefore difficult to control. Further research should be done on such capacity, which may be defined in terms of text perception capacity.

3) Reallocation of context derived interpretation cues: the final step in text repositioning is the recovery of consistent interpretation cues, which becomes possible through availability of valid descriptive and explanatory models and theories.

Each of the three problems here indicated may be studied at three levels, which are:

1) Text segment level: if there is no prior knowledge about the structure of the specific context and culture, then any analysis must rely upon information distribution intensity within the text.

2) Text region level: there is some previous knowledge available about the specific context, so that search for more details may be extended immediately throughout various text-regions.

3) Text-scene level: there exist knowledge which is widely available throughout text regions, and traces of context shift are also well identified as well as changes continuing to take place if not stopped by appropriate text repositioning. Accurate analysis of context shift needs to follow.

Text producers show their level of sensitivity and their capacity of perception if exposed to various problems of text repositioning within their own culture.

Another major issue now addressed is how much changes occurring in cultures and in organizational structures affect understanding of texts and communicative intercourse.

Though text producers are encouraged to think of change as an opportunity and as a challenge to cooperatively reshape their own culture, instability of content deriving from context shift is perceived as a threat. As a consequence of instability in context attribution due to continuous change, the following effects may be observed:

- increasing quantity of texts coming in fuzzy, both synchronously and asynchronously;
- increasingly contradictory and inconsistent texts units which need to be checked, updated and upgraded continuously;
- increasingly frequent change of interpretation cues which are often contradictory, depending on continuously occurring context shift.

If individuals, such as decision-makers, needing accuracy in seeking, accessing and using information coming in textual form cannot be supported with a set of effective conceptual tools as well as with technology, they will encounter many difficulties of different kinds in making reasonable projections and predictions out of the enormous quantity information which is now available. Daily events, current interactions, occasional conversations as well as planned meetings establish the conditions for information to flow throughout different media and in many ways.

Information may therefore be viewed as coming in various flows and waves to be filtered, categorised and organised to be accessible and reusable for different purposes at different times. As soon as some information is found to be of relevance and becomes stabilised and turned into a text, then the need to organise text units in ways which may be made fully transparent becomes a major issue. Information packaging based upon both topic continuity and context consistency is a most fundamental process upon which accurate and timely decision making resides. Availability and accessibility of contextualised packages of information in the form of texts and text units may be significantly supported by an enhanced visual labelling system, which may help speed up effective retrieval too.

Each text unit, which is a consistent topic and context completed section of a text, may be recognised as an entity by itself ready to be linked to other text units according to topic continuity and context consistency and will be labelled according to qualitative reasoning criteria upon the nature of the information.

Not only is it important to suggest statistical methods for identifying topical words in the form of keywords but also to supply interpretive clues for adding qualitative reasoning on top as well. By showing and illustrating visually which kinds of progressive revisions have produced which textual transitional states and by indicating explicitly those upgrading and updating operations and various modifications which have been performed, it will also be possible to trace back an individual's contributions in text reshaping all through the different context shifts which have occurred at various times.

Reshuffling pieces of information coming in textual and other forms, entails a very specific context sensitivity.

A consensually shared framework for interpretation needs to be available to be referred to in order to classify texts consistently, based upon a common understanding and naming of the different operations performed.

According to such perspective, each text may carry its own history attached while undergoing changes of various kinds and may therefore be visualised progressively as transitioning throughout different states of information, which affect its originating communicative value more or less radically.

Transitional states in a text are therefore to be considered those temporarily defined and stabilised states of information which provide evidence and support for a certain set of decision-making processes which have occurred or are going to occur next. Change applies to the conditions of satisfaction any communicative occurrence entails as well as to priorities and roles played by single individuals involved.

Temporarily stabilised textual states will therefore provide evidence and visibility for each individual, who is actively involved in the process of interpretation. Texts organised and built up according to such a view also constitute a tremendously rich repository for collective memories within a certain culture and organisational structure. This way context for accessing further more culturally bound information and for proceeding towards an in-depth understanding is also provided.

Conclusions

Visual text preprocessing is an effective way to help eliminate ambiguity, and context and style sensitive processing has been defined as a kind of slowdown process for accurate detection of the most relevant information in text images and text images sequences meant to then allow for correct identification of original text-scene and text-scenes. As has been illustrated in this chapter, such a model incorporates both analysis of text images, their respective projection onto text-scenes and control on the overall system at different levels of detail.

What has also been demonstrated is that the non-linear dimension of natural language communication occurring both verbally and textually is a source of difficulty for correct projection at different levels of complexity. Discriminating among qualitatively different aspects, just as in vision, is a complex task which may nevertheless be handled consistently. Uniqueness and continuity are important qualities of any representation system active upon text, especially when applied to text-scenes recognition. This is why an iconic language may provide users with a variety of representation models meant to cover the complexity of the issue at stake.

A variety of schemes, visuals and icons are proposed for each definition based upon qualitative reasoning communication. Another important process which has been analyzed is text image and text-scene detection and, as a follow-up, the decision-making process necessary to establish an appropriate level of detail to be chosen for accurate representation.

A context and style sensitive visual language for processing text, such as the one here described, may be of tremendous assistance in assembly, handling and inspection of information packages by supporting a wholly consistent methodology for recognition and identification of textual units, respective positioning and orientation within a certain context and culture. Without context and style sensitive capabilities, information may in fact be gathered and processed in unreliable ways. Incorporating context through visual devices such as icons presented here are means lowering significantly the costs of inspection.

Visibility and reliability of a commonly shared set of operations, which are visible and fully accessible, allows in fact further checking to take place. In order to achieve a highly reliable performance, careful attention must be paid to each one of the stages here described.

Appropriate textual images production devices as well as text-scenes detection equipment, complemented by consistent planning of appropriate procedures, will allow us to proceed towards designing text recognition algorithms, which may be harmoniously merged with already existing statistically based methodologies of current use. Capabilities of the kinds here illustrated may significantly increase both speed and accuracy in information-seeking.

Notes

1. I wrote this paper while I was Visiting Professor at the College of Library and Information Services (CLIS) at University of Maryland, College Park, US.

A synthetical version of 'On Merging Vision and Natural Language Processing within an Artificial Intelligence Framework and Beyond' has been presented by the author at the American Association for Artificial Intelligence 1996 Fall Symposium, held at the Massachusetts Institute of Technology, November 9 – 11, 1996, on 'Knowledge Representation Systems based on Natural Language', M.I.T., Cambridge, U.S.A. with the title: 'High Performance in Text Processing: a CPP-TRS Environment'.

2. An illustration of the CPP-TRS system as well as a specific bibliography by the author is available at: http://www.intellect-net.com (search for /authors/ and then search for /tonfoni/).
    I would also like to thank James Richardson, Technical Communicator, for having supported his expertise in producing an English summarised version of my three previously published Italian books on CPP-TRS which was published by Intellect, UK as the first English abridgement, with the title 'Writing as a visual art', reprinted in 2000.

Acknowledgements

I am grateful to Dean Ann Prentice at CLIS for having made this expansion of my research possible.

I am grateful to Dr Pete Daniel, Curator in the Division of the History of Technology at the Smithsonian Institution in Washington DC, for commenting on the present paper and for his constant encouragement.

I am grateful to Prof. Masoud Yazdani, also the president of Intellect, for allowing reproduction of CPP-TRS figures and visuals the way they appear here, as previously published in my book: Tonfoni, G., *Communicative Patterns and Textual Forms*, 1996, Intellect.

I am grateful to Michele Semenza, a student of mine at the University of Bologna, CIRFID, for help in final formatting and insertion of figures.

References

Austin, J. L. (1962). *How to do Things with Words*, Oxford University Press, Oxford.

Ballmer, T. (1981). 'Words, Sentences, Texts and All That', in *Text*, vols. 1-2, pp. 163-89.

Chi, M. T. H., Glaser, R., Farr, H. J. (1988). *The nature of expertise*, Lawrence Erlbaum, Hillsdale, N. J..

Chomsky, N. (1957). *Syntactic Structures*, Mouton, The Hague.

Chomsky, N. (1965). *Aspects of the Theory of Syntax*, MIT Press, Cambridge, Mass.

De Beaugrande, R. A. and Dressler, W. (1981). *Einfuhrung in die Textlinguistik*, Max Niemeyer Verlag, Tubingen.

Dijk Van T. A. (1972). *Some Aspects of Text Grammars – A Study in Theoretical Linguistics and Poetics*, Mouton, The Hague-Paris.

Johnson-Laird, P. N. (1983). *Mental models: toward a cognitive science of language, inference and consciousness*, Cambridge University Press, Cambridge.

Hegarty, M., Just, M. A., Morrison, I. R.,(1988). 'Mental models of mechanical systems: individual differences in qualitative and quantitative reasoning', in *Cognitive Psychology*, vol. 20, pp. 191-236.

Lehnert, W. G. (1981). 'Plot Units and Narrative Summarization', in *Cognitive Science*, no. 2, pp. 293-331.

Lowe, R. K. (1993). 'Diagrammatic information: techniques for exploring its mental representation and processing', in *Information Design Journal*, vol. 7, no. 1, pp. 3-17.

Marchionini, G. (1995). *Information seeking in electronic environments*, Cambridge University Press, Cambridge.

Marr, D. (1978). 'Representing visual information', in *Computer vision systems*, (eds.) A. R. Hanson and E. M. Riseman, Academic Press, New York, pp. 61-80.

Minsky, M. (1975). 'A Framework for Representing Knowledge', in *The Psychology of Computer Vision*, ed. P H. Winston, Mc Graw Hill, New York, pp. 217-77.

Roberts, L. (1965). 'Machine perception of three-dimensional solids', in *Optical and electrooptical information processing*, J. Tippett (ed.), MIT Press, Cambridge: Mass., pp. 159-97.

Schank, R. C. (1981). *Inside Computer Understanding*, Lawrence Erlbaum, Hillsdale, NJ.

Searle, J. (1969). *Speech Acts: An Essay in the Philosophy of Language*, Cambridge University Press, Cambridge.

Tonfoni, G. (1991). 'Communicative cooperative interaction models: gapfilling processes by reformulation', in *Referate der Dritten Arbeitstagung Dialoganalyse III*, S. Stati et al. (eds.), Tubingen, Max Niemeyer Verlag, pp. 405-14

Tonfoni, G. (1994 i). 'CPP-TRS: on Using Visual Cognitive Symbols to Enhance Communication Effectiveness', in ISMCR-94: Topical Workshop on Virtual Reality, Proceedings of the Fourth International Symposium on Measurement and Control in Robotics, NASA, Houston, USA, Nov. 30-Dec. 3, Library of Congress, 94-69310.

Tonfoni, G. (1994 ii). *Writing as a Visual Art*, Intellect, Oxford (first English abridged version with J. Richardson and with a Foreword by Marvin Minsky).

Tonfoni, G. (1996). *Communicative Patterns and Textual Forms*, Intellect, Exeter.

Wilensky, R. (1983). *Planning and Understanding*, Addison Wesley, Reading.

Winston, P. H. (1970). *Learning structural descriptions from examples*. Rep. no. TR-231, AI Laboratory, M. I. T., Reprinted in P. H. Winston (ed.) (1975) The psychology of computer vision, Mc Graw Hill, New York, pp. 157-209.

Development of Prototypes

10. The Augmentation of Textual Communication with User-created Icons

Leon Cruickshank and Lon Barfield

Introduction

This composition describes an ongoing project at the Digital Media Laboratory. This research facility within the University of the West of England, Bristol, has brought together a team of designers, theorists and programmers to investigate the potential for icons to be used within electronic text communication. The team working on the Icon project consists of L. Barfield, L. Cruickshank, S. Slocombe and Prof. M. Yazdani.

The Icon project is looking specifically at the increasing use of electronic media for conversational communication either in open forua (e.g. Chat Rooms, intranets and Muds) or via e-mail. It is important to note that we are not concerned with fact-intensive information like timetables or company catalogues; this type of information has its own distinct set of developmental issues to explore.

Our premise is that conversation using text-based digital media is hampered by an inability to express the nuances of meaning (emotional, cultural, physical, sensory) that enrich most other forms of communication.

It will be argued that the user-led development and application of iconic elements within a text can help enrich the communication process. This will enable user groups to develop their own way of augmenting texts in a similar way to other aspects of their communication: spoken language, dress, music and so on.

This hypothesis has been investigated in both theoretical and practical modes. This paper will document these processes and conclude with a discussion of the problems in the Icon project that have yet to be solved, the future direction of the Icon project and areas of activity that remain to be explored.

There are many ways to investigate the opinions articulated briefly above. The most direct route to many of these problems is to re-assess the title of this work.

Does textural communication need to be augmented at all?

Exactly what does user-centred mean and why should text be augmented in this way rather than in any other way?

Text Augmentation

Network-based text systems predominately communicate text using an encoding called ASCII. This encoding assigns each character a number and transmits strings of these numbers between computers. This has the advantage that it allows text to be transmitted and received very quickly as a string of numbers. Although increased bandwidth now means that more complex representations of text can be transmitted, there are few universal standards and ASCII remains a universal standard and is still the main way that text is communicated.

The disadvantage of this encoding is that an author of a document cannot determine the visual properties of characters and of the document as a whole. The text sent to the target computer is displayed in a typeface and layout determined by the recipient. The user has only limited control of the layout by means of creative use of punctuation and simple layout (line breaks, new paragraphs). This lack of control compounds the problems inherent within a text-based conversational system.

The richest form of communication is the physical interaction of people. This predominantly uses words but these are supplemented by other factors. These can include facial expression, body language, dress, context, smell, complexion, fashion and a myriad of other factors that all govern our understanding of the conversation's meaning. Christian Metz[1] calls these factors non-specific codes of meaning and argues that these codes have a significant role to play in the formation of meaning.

The nuances of meaning that are not part of the overt specific meaning of the communication are present in all forms of communication. In a hand-written letter we have the script employed, the colour of the ink, the type of pen (e.g. crayon, cheap biro or fountain), the paper, the scent if you are lucky (or the smell of a tax demand). With mass-produced communication books you have the typeface, the paper, the illustrations, the layout. All these factors modify our appreciation of the words that carry the core meaning of the communication. It is these non-specific codes of meaning that allow us to communicate nuances and undercurrents in conversations and it is precisely these non-specific codes of meaning that are absent from plain-text, e-mail communication.

The assertion here is not that text is not a powerful communication tool; it patently is. For textual communication to be used most effectively, where it can convey nuances of meaning, it requires skilled senders, receivers and time to compose messages. We encourage and applaud the sophisticated use of language; we are also offering an additional option or layer of meaning to help users express ideas in different ways. To a certain extent, Internet Service Providers (ISPs) are taking a similar approach. AOL's (America On-Line) latest portal software allows users to embed images within text messages as long as the receiver is using the same version of their software. Although these icons are a limited set and cannot be added to by the users, it is nonetheless a good indication of the demand that these icons are used in on-line conversations.

The facility to add illustrations to e-mail documents can be seen as evidence of an appreciation on the part of the ISP that increased bandwidth can be used to give their portal added value. A further drawback is of dedicated Internet Service Provider solutions is the fact that any additions to the text can only take place between people that are also clients of that particular ISP. This is compounded by the fact that Internet access is fragmenting into a myriad of companies all offering free Internet access, the end result being that most text is still seen in plain format.

The restrictions placed on the communication of non-specific as well as specific codes of meaning have implications both for the meanings that can be read from a piece of electronic text. The lack of depth of textural communication removes many of the clues we use to verify the information received by us. Face-to-face communication allows us to gauge the truthfulness of statements. This can be achieved both directly (is the person talking to you really wearing a yellow angora cardigan) and indirectly (is the person's body language confident or do they look like they are hiding something). Letters have postmarks, signatures, and letterheads. Books have the reputation of the publisher and author and the material investment in production, and all of these things help to substantiate their content. Conversational communication lacks many of these checks and balances.

Although lack of verification is an issue for academic use of electronic media, for conversational communication this is not necessarily problematic. The creation of Avatars or online personas can be a liberating experience that builds on the narratives we weave around any conversational interchange. Digital communication takes this narrative weaving to new heights; the most basic traits like gender or height become variables to be determined by the sender.

Verification is not a central concern of the Icon Project; however it is a potent demonstration of the impact that stripping away levels of meaning can have on a text. The problems inherent in the communication of nuances of meaning in electronic conversations are put into context when one cannot tell the gender of the person one is talking with. The communication of nuances like emotional modifiers (I am joking, I am serious) and other cultural values such as those carried in a person's clothing or handwriting are more important in conversations than bald facts.

There have been attempts to address the issue of communication of nuances of meaning in textual communication. There are a number of graphic languages that claim to have advantages over text languages[2]. Generally, psychologists or behavioural psychologists have developed these languages to replace text communication and have a self-contained vocabulary and syntax. The most significant of these approaches will be examined in more detail below.

There are also a number of examples of spontaneous attempts to add layers of meaning to plain text. This vernacular activity is characterised by building on textual communication rather than trying to replace it. This building or augmentation approach results in the development of a flexible evolving system with local variants and connections.

A common way of making textural communication more spontaneous is to use acronyms. These make for faster communication allowing conversations to be faster paced; some of these go further than 'straight' descriptive examples of acronyms like LOL (Laughing Out Loud). Some acronyms invoke humour and a vocabulary that show a move away from simply aping conventional communication. It would be a very confrontational person who says GLB4UGH (Get lost before you get hurt)[3] in a physical conversation; there is sense of fraternity, an almost subversive exclusion from conversations with acronyms like POS (Parents Over Shoulder).[4] This sense of local grouping, in terms of web communication rather than geographical location, can be seen in variations of acronym. In one listing of acronyms (America Online`s list), both ROFL and ROTF[5] can be used to denote rolling on the floor laughing.

The use of acronyms is evidence that people are not happy with using the same conventions used in spoken conversation when typing. New conventions are being developed spontaneously to accommodate this new form of communication.

It is unsurprising that along with the use of acronyms the most prevalent forms of vernacular augmentation have evolved using common punctuation as a source. Contemporary punctuation has a dual role: it is concerned with the structure of texts to enable us to distinguish coherent parts of a text. The structural role of punctuation is relatively new, as Ellen Lupton explains in Period Styles: A History of Punctuation[6]; punctuation is also used to give an indication of the emotional emphasis placed on a selected piece of text. In today's texts, this includes the exclamation mark, the question mark and the use of capitals. The use of punctuation to give emphasis rather than structure was much more important in the past when text was often read aloud.

Punctuation was very regional in its application and interpretation well after Guttenburg invented the movable type printing press. It was only with the truly mass production of printed material that conventions started to be widely accepted. The application of punctuation before the unification through mass production is analogous to today's electronic communication; production is not centralised and the medium is still in its infancy, new conventions are emerging. In the 16th century, individual printers were free to set words completely in CAPITALS or to put s p a c e s between individual letters of words for added emphasis and italic scripts were developed.[7]

Today new conventions are developing in an adhoc way to augment textual communication, particularly in a conversational context. Some of these conventions include a return to a medieval strategy: to use all capitals is considered to be shouting. Another approach is that a word or words with stars (*) before and after them should be seen as being bold or underlined. This last example is established to such an extent that when this arrangement of words and stars is used in the word processor Word 98, the program automatically converts the words into bold type.

These widely applied conventions are examples of an extensive set of punctuation modifiers. Some of these aspire to be widely used while others are very specific in their application and are relevant to a particular group.

Emoticons or more colloquially smilies are a vernacular system of creating representational icons within a text using punctuation as the source. These started off being quite simple expressions of emotion, hence the smiley tag (:-) . This system has been built upon by individuals with many personal pages devoted to putting forward suggestions of different emoticons. There are 50 to 60 different emoticons being widely published but the fluid, open system of use and dissemination results in the constant suggestion, adoption or rejection of new emoticons by some groups and not others, making absolute categorisation impossible and redundant.

Several aspects of emoticon construction and usage are indicative of the vernacular attempts to augment textural conversation. There are many variations on some basic elements of meaning, (e.g. grin :) :D :o) :-|) This is evidence of an identification of a similar need from several different sources; many people are making suggestions for emoticons. There is also evidence that emoticons are produced for specific groups whether social, cultural or geographic. For example, we have emoticons for Princess Leia (from Star Wars) @(-_-)@ , Homer Simpson (_8(|) and Tony Blair :~] . These examples are dependent on specific knowledge for their significance to be recognised. This was clearly illustrated during the empirical investigation of the Icon Project when icons were spontaneously developed for 'Blair Witch Project', 'keeping it real' and 'Aunt Lynn'. These could not be fully understood by the researchers, as we did not have a compatible framework of understanding. 'Keeping it real' remains a mystery even when it was explained to us at length. The evolution of sophisticated and interconnected emotions can be seen in the development of the icon[8] for Yuppie $-) in one source and I love money[9] in an unrelated source $). Both of these icons communicate connotations of money, colouring the way the individual perceives the world in a way that is not easy to communicate succinctly in words alone.

The final observation of the development of emoticons is that as the possibilities for the combinations of punctuation are used up, emoticons are becoming increasingly tenuous. Examples of this feeble generation of meaning can be seen in the icon[10] for spider (/\(00)/\). This emoticon uses more characters than writing the word itself; similarly the utility value of this emoticon #####@##### (a centipede in a sombrero) has to be questioned.

The Icon Project – A User-Led Approach

From our initial investigation, we determined that purely textual communication could be enriched with the ability to add nuances of meaning in a graphic way. We also decided to build on working systems of augmentation rather than trying to initiate a radical change in the way we communicate electronically and then trying to convince electronic users to adopt this new system. The Internet does allow minority communication systems to survive: there are many Esperanto language sites[11] on the Internet and over 50 fora for communicating in Klingon[12] and, as we shall see, there are interesting graphic languages that fill this niche.

The decision to be inclusive and to augment textural communication rather than trying to replace it directly relates to the second core issue surrounding the Icon Project: why should the project be user-centred?

The qualities of an open, evolutionary project constrained as little as possible by the preconceptions of its originators and developed in such a way that the project grows, mutates and is developed in ways beyond the designer's control or prediction has been categorised here as user-centred. This transcends the 'taking the users needs into account' approach of Jeorge Frascara's User Centred Graphic Design[13] It is also important to note that we do not take the explicitly anti-design approach to the Icon Project seen in Deboard, Vangem et al.[14] (This can also be seen in the work of Radical Italian design groups like Archizoom and Superstudio.[15])

Our user-centred approach seeks the establishment of a symbiotic relationship between user and designer that allows the innate skills, abilities and understanding of both groups to achieve a balance of expression. In this instance, we are proposing a designed framework in which users can create their own icons and embed them in textual conversations. Fundamentally, we are facilitating the production of emoticons using primitive graphic elements that can be composed flexibly, rather than punctuation with very limited compositional ability.

There are compelling reasons for the development of a user-centred approach rather than a more traditionally hierarchical 'design' solution. These theoretical and practical rationales are underpinned by the political assertion that it is better to include rather than to exclude.

There is a groundswell of theoretical activity that is causing problems in the hierarchical position traditionally assumed by the designer epitomised in the stance taken by Norman Potter in the book What is a Designer?[16] One of the many strands of this debate can be traced back to Ferdinand de Sassure`s rejection of a single, unambiguous meaning [17]. Arguing that the meanings given to words (and signs in general) were not fixed but negotiated within specific cultural contexts set the scene for the development of a move towards authorship being a process of mediation between reader and writer. The existence of national languages is the most direct proof of this assertion; the difference between cat and 'chat' is a regional convention that is not related to the furry animal with claws and big ears. Building on and subsequently, superseding Saussure, Roland Barthes cultivated the notion of 'the death of the author, birth of the reader.'[18]

Strands of thought including those proposed by Foucault[19], Derrida[20] and Leyotard[21] and Deleuze and Guatari[22] all advance this idea from strongly contrasting directions. Grossly simplifying, the common strand that runs through their writings is that the meaning of a text is as much dependent on the reader as the writer.

In terms of the Icon Project, it is counterproductive to attempt the Modernist scheme of producing a universal set of icons that would be appropriate for the masses to augment textural conversation. This task has already been attempted by the Isotype system[23]. If one accepts that the reader and author fix meaning together, then any attempt by a designer to predetermine nuances of meaning could cause problems.

It is not possible from a linguistic/philosophical perspective to develop signs that are universal in their meaning; further, we question the very validity of this aim. Building on the work of Boudure[24] it is a politically dubious act to attempt to dominate a user by attempting to impose a fixed meaning on the user.

The adoption of a user-centred approach for the Icon Project is part of the rejection of a centrally imposed system of communication already evident within digital textual conversation. This rejection is seen strategically in a move away from plain text itself and in the development of systems that allow users to create their own systems of augmentation with the help of designers. In essence, we are accepting that in conversational electronic communication, design does not have the right or the ability to dictate how plain text is augmented. We are promoting an open, evolutionary process that is already in operation despite the restrictions placed on it by current infrastructures.

This approach differs radically from textual alternatives like Elephants Memory, Rebus or Bliss (for details see Cruickshank and Hughes)[25]. These languages have a fixed vocabulary and usually attempt to replace textual communication. This is shown, in its extreme form, with Elephants Memory. This language developed by Timothy Ingen Housz is proposed as an experimental language for children enabled by the Internet. It consists of 50 graphic elements along with a grammar and syntax to guide their composition. In some ways, this contemporary language echoes the aims of Blissymbolics. Developed by C.K. Bliss, this symbolic visual language initially aimed at children with learning difficulties had a rigid visual vocabulary. Bliss saw this language as something fixed and as a replacement for conventional textual communication. His strident views on the use of Bliss can be seen in the text accompanying his letterhead.

> The Blissymbolics and the books are copyright recorded under the Berne Convention, the Copyright act of the USA and the universal Copyright convention. ALL RIGHTS RESERVED. Infringes and perverters have been and will be prosecuted anywhere to ensure uniformity as ONE WRITING FOR ONE WORLD.
>
> (Bliss capitals – C. Bliss)[26]

This modernist approach is problematic in theoretical terms that are reflected in practice. Bliss faltered and ultimately failed because people are generally not prepared to learn and communicate with a rigid new language, syntax and grammar; the required investment in time and understanding outweighs the potential benefits. As Rosemary Sassoon says, 'Bliss has created a dead language a dead language does not allow for evolution. To be effective a modern symbol system must be able to grow.' In this respect, Bliss is the antithesis of the aims of the Icon Project.

Semantic Compaction is an approach to graphic communication that has a much more flexible approach. The language was designed to allow people with very restricted movement to use a very small number of graphic elements to communicate complex ideas. This is achieved by assigning each icon with several different possible meanings. The particular meaning is determined by the context in which the icon is placed, e.g. an apple shape placed next to a tree denotes the fruit apple while if the apple is placed next to a rainbow it denotes the colour red. The meanings assigned to icons and the contexts which determine which particular meaning is relevant is controlled by the user, allowing the graphic language to become more sophisticated as the user's language skills become more developed and more complex concepts need to be communicated. Although this system is interesting, there is still a considerable investment needed in the definition of terms and the learning of both vocabulary and syntax, which would be beyond most users.

The Icon Project Prototype

After the research phase of the project was complete, a prototype system that allows users to develop their own codes and conventions in conjunction with the people with whom they directly communicate was developed. This system would provide a range of primitive graphic components. These components could be arranged to form icons by the user. These icons could then be inserted into textual conversation.

The prototyping for this project consisted of two aspects, a paper simulation of how people would use icons to augment textual conversation and the development of a software prototype to examine the technical problems of textural augmentation.

Paper Prototyping

Before discussing this aspect of the Icon Project it must be clearly stated that this series of practical workshops was not intended to be a full-blown piece of action research. This very small preliminary exercise should be seen as a preparation for the development of a pilot project, being used as a diagnostic tool for the development of future, more rigorous and extensive studies.

Future studies will have to address issues including sample size, the lack of multiple conversations, the reliance on drawing to communicate, the number and composition of basic primitives used (more complex but still ambiguous shapes will be included in the next study). Despite this, there are some tentative conclusions to draw from the sessions described below.

The workshops consisted of a series of three groups, each with a different composition.
- Group 1 had three students (2 computer science students and 1 graphic design student) and a researcher (Lon Barfield)
- Group 2 had 2 computer science students and a researcher (Leon Cruickshank)
- Group 3 had two nurses who had no prior knowledge of the project.

Each member of the group was given a printed sheet (see appendix 1). Taken from this sheet, group members followed these instructions:

> No talking or looking at each other
> Have a conversation on any topic using the roll of paper to write on.
> This conversation must use handwriten capitals; you can also make up pictures using shapes from the sheet provided
> These picture/icons can use any shape on the sheet any number of times but it must include the large box shown in the left-hand corner of the sheet.
> Please put a circle around any of the shapes that you use; if you use a shape twice, put two circles around it.
> If there are icons that you want to use again, please record them in the boxes provided on your printed sheet.

These groups were then given long rolls of paper, stickers and pens and left to their own devices to have a textual conversation. An element of ambiguity was woven into the process to facilitate the intuitive development of textual augmentation rather than measuring the degree to which groups conformed to our expectations.

The initial reaction was one of puzzlement; researchers adhered to the instructions given on the sheet, adopting the position analogous to someone introducing this concept to a group online using text and icons to explain the underlying concept. Group 3 did not have any researcher-guided facilitation.

After an initial phase of confusion, conversation became animated. It was notable that all sessions continued well beyond their planned duration. From a strategic standpoint, there do seem to be differences in the ways the different groups used icons. Group 1 tended towards using icons to replace characters, while Group 2 tended towards the substitution of objects with icons (the replacement of nouns). Group 3 used icons to signify specific people.

The authors do not attach significance to these observations beyond the fact that in all cases there was evidence of the building up of an iconic vocabulary whose elements were adopted and applied within the group. There were interesting resonances across groups along age/educational groupings. One of the researchers attempted to signify 'student' with this icon (see Figure 1). The younger students, who did not associate long hair with students at all, did not recognise this. Conversely, all students recognised the icon as signifying 'keeping it real' (see Figure 2) the precise definition of this eludes the researchers to this day.

There is also evidence of competing icons being developed with a consensus being developed consigning the weaker icons to obscurity. Two icons were produced by group 1 to denote the female gender (see Figure 3) The icon on the right was not used by anyone other than its originator and was quickly discontinued.

From the results of the paper study we are confident that it is worth continuing the development of an open system. There is evidence that discrete dialects could develop,

Figure 1. Icon representing 'student'

Figure 2. Icon representing 'keeping it real'

Figure 3. Icons representing 'woman'

be this along cultural, geographic social or a multitude of other factors, and that these dialects will form spontaneously once a network is in place to facilitate this.

The Digital Prototype

Designing the Digital Prototype

Initial plans were to design a system to augment e-mail with user-created icons. As a result of several discussions at the outset of the project, it was decided that there were many drawbacks to this approach. An alternative approach was developed involving creating a web page that hosted one or more discussions; these discussions would then be text augmented with the user-created icons.

The advantages to this approach were:
- The technical scope was more manageable. Recreating an e-mail package or adapting an existing e-mail package is a large-scale undertaking and would require a lot of work that was not directly related to the core of the project.
- The mechanism for icon sharing would be simple. Implementing icon sharing between a large collection of separate e-mail packages would be difficult to implement effectively. Basing the service around a web site would mean that whenever a user created a new icon it could be added to the pool of icons and selected for use by others.
- The use of the service could be followed. One of the key aspects of the project was following the way that users and different user groups made use of the system. Centralising the communication to one web site ensured that the use of the system could be closely monitored and archived.
- A further advantage for the future is that the archives of use themselves could be made accessible on line, enabling other groups researching in this area to analyse the material for their own research.

Building the Digital Prototype

Once the decision had been made to implement the system as a web page, the choice of technology was HTML web pages, while the functional elements would be programmed in the language Java. The first phase was to construct the system as a stand-alone Java application. Using this application, users could add paragraphs to an ongoing discussion and intersperse their text with icons from a palette of icons. This pool of icons could be supplemented by creating new images using a series of primitives. The icons were implemented as GIF formatted black and white images.

The Digital Prototype in Use

An idea of the technology and interaction involved in the prototype can be obtained by looking at the functionality it offers by means of several screens from the interaction.

A good starting point is the web page that embodies the discussion in a digital version of the roll of paper used in the earlier paper-based experiments (see Figure 4).

Users can alternately or asynchronously append messages to the bottom of the page. The boundary between subsequent messages is indicated by the visual design of the page and the fact that each message is followed by the name of the person who posted the message. The text of the message can be interspersed with small graphic icons.

In order to append a message to the discussion a user starts up the message-authoring package (once the system is ported to the web this would be done by a simple click on a button in the web page). This consists of a textual window where the user can click and type the text of the message (see Figure 5).

Below this there is a text fill-in field where the user can enter his/her name to appear below the message in the discussion (in an eventual web-based system where users log-in to different discussions, this appending of the person's name could be done automatically).

The mechanism to augment the text with icons consists of a menu of icons at the bottom of the window. By clicking on an icon the user causes the icon to be included in the text at that point. (Technical restrictions on the display of text and graphics in the text area mean that the icon is seen as a textual HTML reference in this window; although functional, this is not ideal).

In the event that users might wish to augment the text with an icon that is not part of the icon pool, they click on the button 'new icon' and are presented with the window for composing new icons (see Figure 6). Here they start with a blank icon and can introduce primitive graphic elements by clicking on the pictures below the icon composition area. Once such a primitive is introduced, its position can be modified by using the arrow buttons above the icon composition area. At any point users can choose one of the options at the bottom right of the screen to clear the icon composition area, to save the icon into the icon pool or to quit the icon composition and return to the message composition area.

Extensions to the System

This digital prototype confirms the working of the technologies being used; the next stage is to port the Java code to the web in the form of an Applet and to improve some aspects of the usability. Once this is done it would be possible to use the set-up for experiments in much the same form as the paper-based trials.

Further amendments would allow the system to be used over the Web by larger user groups. In particular, the following areas are being considered for amendment.

Icon Composition

A more advanced icon composition tool needs to be developed. However, this should strive to remain simple: the key to icon creation is that users can do it simply and quickly, on-the-fly; creating an icon is not the creation of a precise masterpiece but the creation of a fast aid to communication.

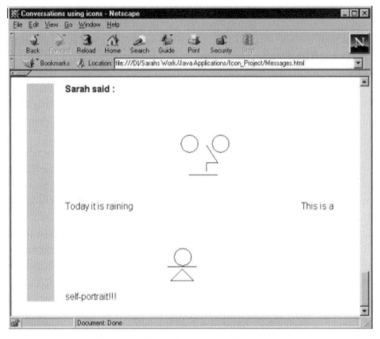

Figure 4. The web page of a discussion

Primitives and Icons

During the paper-based trials it was noted that there were many icons used that involved primitives above and beyond the initial primitive set on offer. In particular, a blank or empty face would be a useful primitive, as would other general forms, such as a cloud (cloud, thought bubble, sheep's body, mop of hair, etc).

It might be useful to allow users to define their own primitives. An even more flexible approach would be to remove the distinction between primitives and icons and bundle everything together in one pool. This would allow users to incorporate icons in their text and to build new icons from simple primitives in the icon pool or augment existing icons (combining a face icon and a line to give a face with a moustache).

Managing Multiple Discussions

Eventually the service should be able to support multiple discussions; a group of users should be able to say 'lets have a text-based discussion with icons' and get their own dedicated discussion area. Such a service would require an extra level of design to manage multiple discussions in this way and to manage the associated pools of icons, answering such questions as how icons are shared between different discussion groups and how users will be supported in dealing with large numbers of icons in the pool.

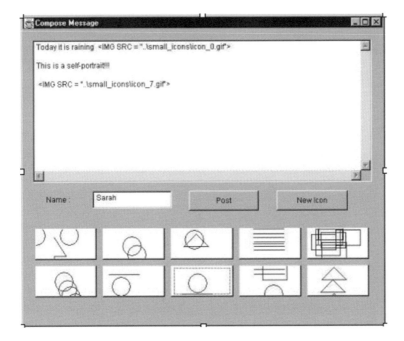

Figure 5. Message composition window

Conclusions

There are many current developments related to the enriching of textual communication. Browser related e-mail packages allow the sending of e-mail messages with HTML mark-up and some web-based e-mail services offer the user ready-made templates for their e-mail, in effect a stationary pack of different sorts of paper. Augmentation with predefined icons has been discussed earlier and with the advances in sound technology, services are starting to be offered augmenting or replacing textual communication with computer-based voice mail.

In commercial terms, these developments in richer computer-mediated communication make the position of iconic augmentation of text unclear. However, even if there is no mainstream place for the technology, we expect that the service will still appeal to, and be used by, a large niche user group.

In future phases of the project an arena where such users have the opportunity to communicate using user-defined icons will enable us to clarify the expectations that arose from the paper-based experiments. Our hope is that such a web-based system, where the use of icons is easier and more fluid through a lowered threshold, will yield results that will support our paper-based observations and even produce other, as yet unexpected, results.

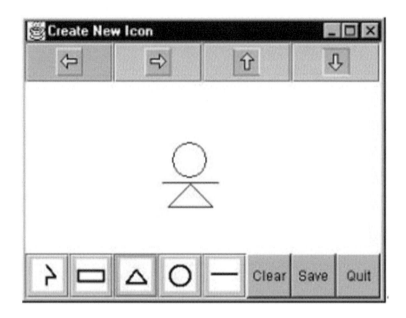

Figure 6. Icon composition window

Notes

1   Metz, C. (1973). 'Methodological Positions of the Analysis of Film,' Screen, Spring / Summer 89 / 101

2   Cruickshank, Hughes. (1999). 'Facilitating the Evolution of a User Driven Iconotextual Internet Patois', Digital Creativity. vol. 10, no.2 pp 79-89

3   Downloaded from the WWW 10 October 1999, AOL Intranet, keyword Acronym

4   ibid.

5   ibid.

6   Lupton, E., Miller, A. (1996). Writing on Graphic Design, Phaidon, London, pp. 33-39

7   ibid.

8   ibid. pp. 39

9   Downloaded from the WWW 10 October 1999, AOL Intranet, keyword Smiley

10 ibid.

11 Esperanto League of Cyberspace (www) downloaded 2 October 1999 from WWW.esperanto.org/elc/.

12 Klingon Language Institute (Internet) downloaded 10 October 1999   www.kli.org

13 Frascara, J. (1997). 'User Centered Graphic Design', Mass Communication and Social Change, Taylor-Francis, UK

14 Knabb, K. (ed. & trans.). (1981). Situationist International Anthology, Bureau of Public Secrets, USA

15 Ambasz, E. (ed.). (1972). Italy: The New Domestic Landscape, New York Museum of Modern Art, USA

16 Potter, N. (1980). 'What is a Designer?' Hyphen Press, UK.

17 Saussure, F. (1966). Course in General Linguistics, McGraw Hill, New York.

18 Barthes, R. (trans. Lavers, A.). (1984). Writing Below Degree Zero, Jonathan Cape, London.

19 Foucault, M. (1980). Power / Knowledge, Harvester Press, London.

20 Derrida, J. (1976). On Gramatology, John Hopkins University Press, Baltimore.

21 Leyotard, J.F. (1984). 'The Postmodern Condition: A report on Knowledge', Minnesota University Press, Manchester.

22 Deleeuze and Guattari. (1994). What is Philosophy? Colombia University Press, USA

23 Meggs, P. (1992). A History of Graphic Design, Van Norstrand Reinhold, USA pp.303-04

24 Bourdieu, P. (1998). Distinction a Social Critique of the Judgement of Taste, Harvard University Press, USA

25 Cruickshank and Hughes, (1999). 'Facilitating the Evolution of a User Driven Iconotextual Patois', Digital Creativity. vol. 10 no. 2

26 ibid.

Appendix 1: Work Sheet Proforma for Iconic Conversation Workshop 1

Exercise - Using icons to help give textural communication depth

Basic Elements

Guidelines for the Iconic Communication Exercise

No talking or looking at each other

Have a conversation on absolutely any topic using the roll of paper to write on, you may want to talk about the idea of using icons to give printed text more emotion.

This conversation must use printed handwriting, you can also make up pictures using shapes from the sheet provided

These picture / icons can use any shape on the sheet, any number of times but it must include the large box shown left.

Please put a circle around any of the shapes that you use, if you use it twice put two circles around it.

If there are icons that you want to use again please record them in the boxes provided on your printed sheet.

This is supposed to be a conversation not a test, so don't think too long about your responses, have fun and try and express your personality.

Make your icons in a box about this size

Icons you want to use again

meaning...

meaning...

meaning...

meaning...

meaning...

meaning...

meaning...

11. VIL: A Visual Inter Lingua

Lee Becker and Paul Leemans

Introduction

As the world becomes smaller through advances in telecommunications, the need for communication between speakers of different languages becomes greater. Concerns about cultural and economic hegemony argue against the use of any natural language and machine translation is not yet perfected and available to speakers of all languages.

With the technological developments of the last decade, such as powerful computers, graphical interfaces and the World Wide Web, an excellent opportunity has been created for a computer-mediated visual inter lingua to meet this need. This iconic language should be designed to take advantage of the technology. People will be able to communicate with an iconic language without the need to draw the pictures themselves, since they can choose these pictures from the screen. This paper describes VIL, an iconic visual inter lingua based on the notion of simplified speech.

Before we describe VIL, we will first give some conditions that a new world language must conform to and mention some earlier iconic languages.

Criteria for a New Language

Richards mentions some conditions that have to be met in order for a world language to be accepted (Richards, 1943):

- Political conditions: These include free adoption, absence of all threats of domination of any type, protection for primary languages and symbolisation of supranational (international) aims. The political considerations seem to argue against any existing national language as a candidate.
- Psychological conditions: The root criticism of any revived or artificial language, however well-designed, is that the immediate incentive, which would make enough people learn and use one is lacking. If one is to go through the trouble of learning a language, then one needs to feel that one will get a return for his/her toil this very year.

Besides the previously mentioned conditions, there are four principles that we consider important when designing a new visual language:

- **Learnability:** The language and the use of its delivery system should be easy to learn.
- **Encodability:** It should be easy to compose messages using the language and its delivery system.
- **Decodability:** Messages composed in the language should be easy to comprehend, i.e. should let the user decode the messages without much effort.

126

- **Extensibility/Evolvability**: The language should have the possibility to be extended and to evolve.

Visual Communication Systems (Pictorial and Iconic)

In visual communication systems there is, just like in written languages, a division in natural and artificial languages. The Chinese writing system was originally pictorial. Furthermore, both the old Egyptians (hieroglyphs) and some North American Indians also communicated through pictures (Gelb, 1963). Both Chinese and hieroglyphs were initially highly ideographic but a fast-function limitation and derivation to phonographic expressions took place and they lost self-explanatory features (Kummel, 1979).

In addition, there are existing signs, symbols and icons that are understood internationally but were not intended as a language. These are, for example, arrows to indicate direction and overlaid diagonals to indicate negation, most of which are found in traffic signs.

In the past, some approaches have been made to come up with an iconic language. Some examples are Semantography (Bliss, 1965) and Isotype (Neurath, 1978). While these languages were not designed to be computer assisted, the most recent attempts in iconic communication are computer-based systems. Two examples are the Hotel Booking System and CD-Icon. The Hotel Booking System was developed by Masoud Yazdani at the University of Exeter and is an initial attempt to create an interactive, iconic dialogue, using hotel booking as its theme (Yazdani et al., 1992). The system allows communication on a restricted domain (that of hotel booking). The purpose of CD-Icon is to explore unrestricted person-to-person communication. It was developed by Colin Beardon at the University of Brighton (Beardon et al., 1993). CD-Icon is an iconic language that is based on Schank's conceptual dependency theory (Schank, 1975). CD-Icon is a means of testing the validity of conceptual dependency directly by using it as the basis of a communication system that uses only icons and no words.

VIL, which stands for Visual Inter Language, is described below. VIL is also a computer-based iconic communication system, designed to allow people to communicate with each other when they share no common language. It allows a user to construct sentences without actually having to type in words, i.e. solely relying on icons. The goal is to make the system language independent so that it can be used universally. Unlike CD-Icon, VIL is not based on Schank's conceptual dependency theory. It has its own grammar and uses larger semantic units corresponding in semantic size to words of natural language. Very important in the design of VIL is the notion of simplified speech.

Simplified Speech

When creating a universal language, the notion of simplified speech is important, since it may be related to theories of language universals and language acquisition. Jacobson and others have assumed that the simpler of two comparable features is likely to be more widespread among languages of the world and also the earlier acquired in child language development (Brown et al., 1964).

Ferguson posed the following hypothesis: 'If a language has an inflectional system, this will tend to be replaced in simplified speech such as baby talk and foreigner talk by uninflected forms (e.g. simple nominative for the noun; infinitive, imperative or third person singular for the verb).' Also, studies of child language development seem to show that children first make sentences without a copula and only later acquire the construction with the copula.

This section describes pidgins, languages arising from the prolonged contact of people speaking two or more languages, and will show that it is very well possible to communicate with a drastically reduced grammatical structure and lexicon. This will support the design of VIL which, much like pidgins, uses the greatest common denominator of languages.

Pidgins

It often happens that, to communicate with each other, two or more people use a language whose grammar and vocabulary are very much reduced and which is native to neither side. This is what constitutes a pidgin.

- A *'pidgin'* is a contact language that is a mixture of linguistic elements of two or more languages. It arises in social and economic transactions between at least two groups, who speak different languages, by a process of restriction and simplification of one of the languages of these groups, usually that in a socially superior position (Foley, 1988).

By definition, a pidgin is no one's native language. The syntactic structure of a pidgin is less complex and less flexible than the structure of the languages that were in contact, and though many pidgin features clearly reflect usages in the contact languages, others are unique to the pidgin. Pidgins have discarded many of the inessential features of the standard variety (see Table 1) (Todd, 1974).

All natural languages have some degree of redundancy. As can be seen from the table, English has less verbal inflection than French, but both pidgins have an invariable form.

Furthermore, in many European languages, plurality is marked in the article, the adjective and the noun, as well as by a numeral (sometimes). Consider for example the sentence 'Les deux grands journaux'. Here there are four overt markers of plurality (in written form, three in spoken form). English is a little less redundant than French but still in 'The two big newspapers' there are two markers of plurality. The pidgins Neo-Melanesian (The pidgin English of Papua New Guinea) and Cameroon pidgin are less redundant still. They only mark plurality by the numeral, tupela bikpela pepa and di tu big pepa (resp. two big newspaper and the two big newspaper).

Some of the simplifications made in pidgins follow here:

- *Number*: no plurals of the 'man/men' or 'computer/computers' type. Instead, in pidgins and creoles nouns are invariable, like 'sheep' (Todd, 1974). Plurality is normally implicit in the context.
- *Gender*: gender distinctions are reduced or eliminated in both nouns and pronouns.

French	English	Neo-Melanesian	Cameroon Pidgin
Je vais	I go	mi go	a go
tu vas	you go	yu go	yu go
il/elle va	he/she/it goes	em go	I go
nous allons	we go	yumi/mipela go	wi go
vous allez		yupela go	wuna go
ils/elles vont	they go	ol go	dem go

Table 1

- *Inflection*: no agreement between subject and predicate. Both noun and verb are invariable, where the singular is used for nouns and the imperative for verbs. Since the verb form is invariable, distinctions relating to time and continuity of action are either understood from the context or are indicated by adverbials or a set of free morphemes, which precede the verb.
- *Questions*: question transformations are absent. Neo-Melanesian interrogatives all maintain the same word order:
  Yu wokim haus? 'Are you building a house?'
  Yu mekim wanem? 'What are you doing?'

  (Schumann, 1978)
- *Negation:* negation is done by having an invariant negation maker.
- *Verbs and tense*: In Haitian Creole all contrasts of number, person and tense have been lost in the verb and every verb has only one form used in inflection (Hall, 1966). In English-Japanese pidgin, adverbs are used to indicate time (Schumann, 1978).

Universals of Contact Situations

Todd poses a hypothesis that there are universal patterns of linguistic behaviour appropriate to contact situations. People of different linguistic backgrounds adjust their language behaviour in similar ways. This suggests that the behaviour is rule-governed and may be the result of linguistic universals. Children, sailors, traders, and Portuguese adventurers might all have been responding to linguistic situations according to an innate behavioural 'blueprint'. He further poses that if it is possible to show that human beings have predetermined propensities for acquiring language, then it may well be that the capacity for linguistic simplification and accommodation – the process that produces pidgins – is also innate and universal. Then it is also likely that there are linguistic universals common to all languages, irrespective of their surface manifestations.

When acquiring language, children produce patterns, which are regular for them but irregular for adults. In such cases children cannot be said to be imitating adults. Studies in unrelated languages like English, Congolese Luo and Finnish suggest that a child's first negatives are regularly 'negator plus sentence', e.g. 'no' plus 'I go'. There is a rule here, and since it is not the adult rule, it would appear to be the child's own contribution.

Furthermore, many parents automatically simplify their language when speaking to very young children. They cut down on sentence subordination, use simple tenses and repeat new words. And they do this without being fully aware of what they are doing and how they accomplish it. In other words, their behaviour seems to respond to a built-in simplification mechanism.

Smith states that both the child in early native language acquisition and the pidgin speaker reduce and simplify language to which they are exposed into a set of primitive categories, which are undoubtedly innate. These primitive categories emerge in speech as utterances relatively unmarked by inflections, permutations and functions (Smith, 1973a).

Corder maintains a similar position but argues that simple codes used in child talk, foreigner talk and pidgins are not simplified. Instead, they represent a basic language, which is expanded and complicated in the process of learning. Simple codes are nearer to the underlying structure or 'inner form' of all languages (Corder, 1975).

Schumann states that the codes may result from regression to a set of universal primitive linguistic categories that were realized in early first language acquisition. Then under conditions of social and/or psychological distance, the pidginised form of speech persists (Schumann, 1978).

Summary

Contrasted with the 'major' languages of Western Europe, pidgins have relatively little morphological variation in their structure. Many grammatical concepts that, in our familiar languages, are expressed by morphological (especially inflection) features, find their expression in syntactical combinations.

From a structural point of view, a pidgin represents the very first stage of rudimentary language learning.

A pidgin serves a function that no other means of communication could duplicate: that of facilitating mutual understanding on a limited range of topics (Hall, 1966).

A pidgin, however, would never be accepted as a universal language because many people believe pidgins are socially inferior. It does, however, show that it is very well possible to communicate with a drastically reduced grammatical structure and vocabulary. Also, an attempt has been made to show that reduced language is closer to our universal roots and more innate than any of the modern languages.

VIL

VIL is, much like pidgins, based on the notion of simplicity. One of VIL's main principles is that it uses the greatest common denominator of many languages to design its grammar. The grammar is then drastically reduced in complexity.

Primary principle: Greatest Common Denominator

VIL adopts a minimal grammar. Every grammatical feature, which is encountered in the vast majority of languages, shall be retained in the grammar of VIL and no grammatical feature shall be so retained if it is missing from any major language. Thus, for instance, the feature of grammatical gender can be dispensed with because it is missing in at least one language, i.e. English (Gode et al., 1955).

We will now give some properties that hold in VIL. Many of these properties are found in pidgins as well.

1. No Linear Word Order

Since VIL was designed as a visual language, rather than the result of transfer to visual modality of spoken language which has evolved in the context of auditory modality, VIL has several advantages over written languages. For one thing, VIL has no linear word order. The icons can be placed in any order since the different cases (e.g. subject, object, indirect object, etc.) are clearly visually distinguished.

Also, sentences composed with VIL are based on deep structure, so there are no different surface structures. Every element is expressed in only one way.

2. Number

There are no plurals of the 'man/men' or 'computer/computers' type. Plurality is normally implicit in the context and can be indicated by a QUANTIFIER or a NUMBER, e.g. 'all book' or 'five book'.

3. Gender

Gender distinctions are reduced or eliminated in both nouns and pronouns.

4. Inflection

Both noun and verb are invariable, i.e. not marked for gender, tense, etc. Since the verb form is invariable, distinctions relating to time and continuity of action are indicated by separate icons (time-when, frequency of occurrence, duration and aktionsarten [1]). Adjectives are invariable as well.

5. Negation

Negation is done by having an invariant way to 'modify' an icon, for example by a diagonal bar through the icon, and will not change any order in a message.

6. Verbs and Tense

All contrasts of number, person and tense have been lost in the verb and every verb has only one form used in inflection. Tense is implicit in the meaning of the sentence when indicated by time demonstratives (last, this, next) or explicit when indicated by time pronouns (long ago, just a moment ago, soon, yesterday, tomorrow, etc.).

7. Auxiliary Verbs

No auxiliary verbs will be used (as in 'I have eaten').

8. Article

VIL does not have a specific article. The definite article ('the') is used in normal speech to refer to something specific that both the speaker and hearer know about. When a speaker says 'did you receive the book?', the hearer knows what book the speaker is referring to. Definiteness may be represented by nominal demonstratives (this, that).

9. Verb Modality: Imperative

Imperative sentences have the same construction as assertive sentences but are distinguished by an exclamation mark icon ('!').

10. Verb Modality: Passive

There is no difference between passive and active sentences as in the following example:

'I kicked the ball to Ilan.'

'The ball was kicked to Ilan by me.'

These sentences have the same deep structure and will be represented in the same way.

11.Yes/No Questions

Yes/No questions, like imperatives, have the same construction as assertive sentences, but are distinguished by a question mark ('?') (See Table 2).

12. Wh-Questions

When the question word is the subject, then in VIL a question mark is also put in place of a noun phrase denoting the particular role/case (See Table 3).

An important distinction is made in VIL between open semantic categories, which have a (possibly) unlimited number of items, such as nouns, adjectives, verbs and adverbs, and closed categories, such as time-when, place-where, quantifier, intensifier, pronoun, demonstrative, auxiliary-modal, aktionsarten, subordinator and coordinator. The open categories have associated lattices of icons from which to choose while the closed categories often may be represented graphically, for example, using a map, calendar or clock.

13. Distinguishing the Major Open Semantic Categories

In VIL, the major categories such as noun, adjective, adverb and verb are distinguished by an invariant visual marker, more specifically by using different borders around an icon. For example, an icon with a square border indicates that the icon is a noun and an icon with a square border with rounded edges indicates that the icon is a verb. This property makes the next property possible.

14. Distinguishing Roles/Cases

In VIL, a visual distinction will be made between nominal constituents that denote particular semantic roles or cases, like subject, direct object and indirect object.

15. Derivational Morphology: Changing a Category

In VIL, the meaning of an icon can be altered by adding to its category marker, for example the border of the icon. This means that categories can be changed. For instance, a noun can now become a verb by adding a verb border to a noun icon. So an icon can have more than one border, where the outermost border determines its category and the innermost border determines which category it is derived from. For example, the icon for the noun '(key)lock' could be transformed into the verb 'to lock' by adding a verb-specific border around the icon. The inner icons will still look exactly the same but the borders determine what the icon stands for. Thus the outer border denotes what part of speech is meant (i.e. a verb) and the inner border denotes what part of speech it is derived from (i.e. a noun). There are several ways a category can change:

- *De-Verbal Nouns and De-Nominal Verbs*

Some verbs will be used as nouns but usually it will be the other way around because it is easier to represent nouns visually, since nouns are more likely to be concrete objects.

Question in English	Question in VIL
Do you like soccer?	You like soccer?

Table 2

Question in English	Question in VIL
What knocks at my window?	'?' knocks at my window (subject)
What did you buy?	You buy '?' (object)
When does the train come in?	The train comes in ('?' in the time-when field)
Where did you buy the sweater?	You buy the sweater ('?' in the place-where field)

Table 3

- *De-Adjectival Nouns and De-Nominal Adjectives*
  Some adjectives will be used as nouns but, for the same reason as mentioned before, usually it will be the other way around. To keep the example of the icon for the noun '(key)lock', this noun can be turned into the adjective 'locked' by adding an adjective-specific border around the icon.
- *De-Verbal Adjectives and De-Adjectival Verbs*
  Adjectives can also be de-verbal as in 'the running man', and the same principle of distinction apply. An example of a de-adjectival verb could be 'to whiten', derived from the adjective 'white'.
- *De-Adjectival Adverbs*
  In VIL an adjective can be used as an adverb too and vice versa. In the sentence 'He solved the problem wisely', the adjective 'wise' is used as basis for the adverb 'wisely' (in a wise manner).

Composing a Message in VIL

VIL is verb centred. The verb determines what are the potential roles of its arguments. As mentioned previously, VIL is non-linear. For consistency and speed of encoding and decoding, the icons will be placed in a predefined (default) location. If wished, they may be moved around, since clear visual elements will specify which icon represents which grammatical entity. The only order involved in VIL is the order of construction of the message. This is a consequence of the fact that VIL is verb-centred. So composing a message consists of a sequence of steps. This also makes VIL easier to learn.

A sentence composed in VIL consists of a verb and some noun phrases, each associated with the verb in a particular semantic (case) relationship. Although there can be compound instances of a single semantic case (through noun phrase conjunction), each semantic case relationship occurs only once in a simple sentence. The semantic cases that are distinguished are agent, theme, source, goal, location, time, instrument, manner, frequency of occurrence, duration and aktionsarten. An explanation of these is beyond the scope of this article. Depending on the verb chosen, some of these semantic cases are mandatory, others are optional.

A program was written implementing the language VIL (in Visual Basic 6). When composing a message in VIL, several steps need to be taken, of which the first three are mandatory and have to be executed in the order specified:
- Select a message type
- Select a verb
- Select NPs with selected verb

- Select a time when the message takes place
- Select a location where the message takes place
- Fill out the remaining parts of the message to finish the message

In the next example the sentence 'I will soon give most of these flies to that spider' will be composed.

By selecting the 'New' icon from the toolbar, a message type iconic dialogue comes up. This dialog asks the user what kind of message will be composed: a declarative, an interrogative or an imperative message (Figure 1). We elect to compose a declarative sentence.

Verbs

Now we need to select the verb. Verbs in VIL are organised according to their shared meaning, since the meaning of verbs is the same across languages (e.g. 'to give' means 'a transfer of possession'). Furthermore, verbs will be decomposed into primitive elements (to a certain extent). This means that more specific verbs will have to be described by their more general version modified by some adverbs of manner or 'aktionsarten' (argue, argue angrily (i.e. quarrel), argue with the intention of reaching an aim (i.e. contest), etc.). VIL's verb hierarchy is a result of research by Levin (1993), Ballmer et al. (1981), Schank, (1975), Walsh (1933), Matsukawa et al.(1991), and Jackendoff (1983).

To facilitate speed of access, the hierarchy will not be deeper than 5 levels. Also, taking short-term memory into account, each category in the hierarchy will hold no more than 9 items (D'Andrade, 1995).

In VIL's verb chooser, the top-level categories of the hierarchy or lattice are 'verbs involving the mind', 'verbs of exchange of possession', 'verbs of physical transfer and location', 'verbs of existence', 'verbs denoting a voluntary activity', 'identity verbs', and 'verbs denoting an involuntary activity'. Selecting a category will bring one down a level in the hierarchy. For instance, double-clicking the 'physical transfer and location' category icon will fill the icon view with its subcategories (Figure 2).

Its children in the icon view represent the categories 'conceal verbs', 'verbs of contact by impact', 'lodge verbs', putting/pouring verbs', 'removing verbs', 'verbs of sending and carrying', 'propel verbs', 'verbs of applying force', and 'physical transfer verbs' (PTRANS).

Figure 1. Selecting the type of message.

To return to our sample sentence, we need to find the verb 'to give'. This verb is not part of the verbs of physical transfer and location, but falls into the top-level category of 'verbs of exchange of possession'. From there we choose 'alienable possession verbs' (ATRANS). This will bring us to the terminals of which some verbs are 'to give', 'to return' and 'to buy' (Figure 3).

Figure 2. VIL's verb chooser, icons in the 'physical transfer and location' category.

VIL's Kernel

After we have selected the verb 'to give' the main screen will load placeholders for the rest of the sentence. The arguments that it will load depend on the type of verb chosen. In this case the verb is of type 'alienable possession' and potentially takes as arguments a source noun phrase, a goal noun phrase, and a theme noun phrase, whose icons are depicted at the bottom of the screen. The other grammatical entities that are put on the screen are 'time-when', 'place-where', 'aktionsarten' (e.g. start, stop continue), 'frequency of occurrence' (e.g. three times a day, sometimes, always), 'duration' (e.g. all day long, for three hours), 'adverb/manner', and 'instrument NP' (Figure 4).

The verb icon is instantiated: it contains the icon for 'to give', and visual elements for grammatical entity, i.e. 'verb' and for category, i.e. 'exchange of possession'. Once it is instantiated, the background colour of an icon changes from grey to white (Figure 5). The tooltips of the icon also help in decoding the icon. These tooltips of the program are language specific textual help and the language is chosen upon login to the system. They serve to help the user in encoding and decoding the message. Another way to help decoding the icon could be to use animation to show the process of something being given.

Figure 3. some verbs denoting alienable possession (give, return and buy).

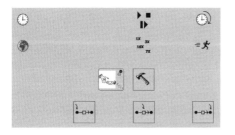

Figure 4. VIL's screen after instantiating the verb with the verb 'to give'

Noun Phrases

Nouns in VIL are organised hierarchically into levels, from generic to specific, with the top-most level being most generic (Smith, 1978b; and Miller et al., 1995). An icon of a noun representing a category (e.g. birds) will ideally be most prototypical for its category (e.g. a robin). Rosch has found that the more prototypical of a category a member is rated, the more attributes it has in common with other members of the category and the fewer attributes it has in common with members of contrasting

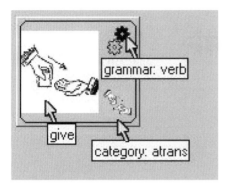

Figure 5. Tooltips help explaining the icon

categories (Rosch et al., 1976). The noun categories and terminals selected to be included in VIL were collected from various visual dictionaries and encyclopedias (MacMillian, 1993, Corbeil, 1986 and Dorling Kindersley, 1995).

Now let's return to our sample sentence. The verb 'to give' takes as its arguments a source, goal and theme noun phrase (Figure 6).

By double clicking on any of these icons, the user is taken to the noun chooser dialogue. This dialogue is the same as the verb chooser dialogue but for nouns. Also, the toolbar has one extra button: 'show pronoun', which allows for the selection of pronouns.

The top-level nominal categories are 'Arts & Entertainment', 'Communication', 'Physical World', 'Science & Technology', 'Beliefs, Custom, and Society', 'Sports', and 'Transportation'.

Let's instantiate our source noun phrase 'I'. We click on the 'show pronoun' button in the toolbar, and the icon view shows all pronouns: 'I', 'You', 'He', 'We', 'You All', and 'They' (Figure 7).

We choose the icon for 'I' by double clicking it. Next we instantiate the goal noun phrase 'spider'. In the noun chooser we select 'Physical World' -> 'Living World' -> 'Animals' -> 'Insects and Crustaceans'. This will fill the icon view with the terminals: 'Praying Mantice', 'Fly', 'Spider', 'Crab', 'Scorpion', and 'Grasshopper'. We select 'Spider' for the goal noun phrase and 'Fly' for the theme noun phrase (Figure 8).

Now that we have chosen icons for our three arguments (source NP, goal NP and theme NP), let's see what the main screen (partly) looks like (Figure 9):

The border for each icon we just instantiated is rectangular, denoting it is a noun. The visual element in the top right corner (for grammatical entity) denotes its semantic case, i.e. source NP, goal NP or theme NP.

Figure 6. Placeholder icons for the source, goal and theme noun phrases

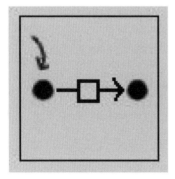
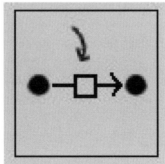
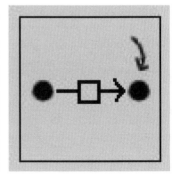

Figure 7. The pronouns I, you, he/she, we, you all, and they

Figure 8. Icons in the insects and crustaceans category

Noun Properties/Modifiers

When a noun phrase has been instantiated (i.e. a noun has been chosen, the background colour turns white), its double-click behaviour changes. Where double-clicking an uninstantiated NP brought up the noun chooser dialogue, double-clicking an instantiated NP will bring up the noun modifier dialogue (Figure 10).

In this dialogue the user can modify properties about the noun like nominal demonstrative (e.g. this, that), quantity, owner noun phrase, comparative noun phrase and one or more adjectives, as indicated at the bottom. The toolbar contains buttons for 'adding an adjective', 'deleting an adjective', 'adding a noun', and 'deleting a noun'. The dialogue contains a tab strip, which contains a tab for each noun in the noun phrase in question.

Now, to indicate 'most of these flies', we select nominal demonstrative 'this' (Figure 11) and quantity 'most' (Figure 12).

In the same way, we selected the nominal demonstrative 'that' for the spider, yielding 'that spider'.

Completing the Message

Let's complete the message by instantiating the rest of the message. The only entity left to specify for the sentence 'I will soon give most of these flies to that spider', is the time-when. The TimeWhen dialogue consists of a 'temporalizer' (e.g. before, while, after) and/or one of the following: a 'time pronoun' (e.g. long time ago, soon), a 'Time Demonstrative' (e.g. last, this, next) plus a 'Time Unit' (e.g. year, week, day, hour,

Figure 9. The main screen after instantiating the noun phrases

Figure 10. The noun modifier dialogue

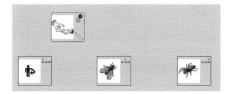

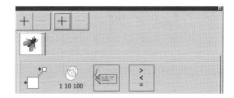

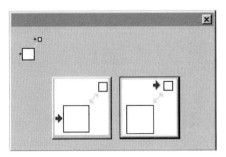

Figure 11. Nominal demonstrative dialogue with icons for 'this' and 'that'.

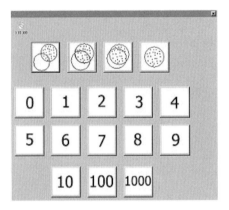

Figure 12. Quantity dialogue with icons for 'some', 'half', 'most', 'all', and numbers.

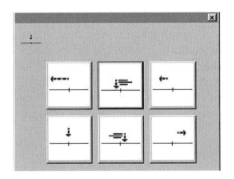

Figure 13. Icons denoting time pronouns like 'long ago', 'just a moment ago', 'past', 'present', 'soon', and 'future'.

season), a 'TimeWhen Sentence', or a 'Time Expression' (e.g. 3 October 1999). For this sentence we need to indicate a time pronoun (Figure 13), i.e. 'soon'.

The message screen now looks like in the next figure (Figure 14).

Now that we have instantiated all the entities for our sample sentence, we need to remove the unneeded icons from the screen. When we click on the 'Update Message' icon in the toolbar (the fifth icon from the left), all uninstantiated icons will be hidden. This way we are only left with the entities we want, i.e. the ones that we need to communicate our message. The following screen shows the completed and updated message 'I will soon give most of these flies to that spider'. The icons for 'aktionsarten', 'frequency of occurrence', 'duration', 'manner/adverb', 'instrument' and 'placewhere' have been made invisible (Figure 15).

The message can be saved to disk but can also be sent anywhere in the world by e-mail. The person receiving the file just double-clicks it and, since the computer recognises the '.vil' extension, it will startup VIL and load the message for him/her. The recipient might decode the message something like this: In the top-right corner he/she sees the 'period' icon, indicating the sentence is declarative. Then he/she might look at the verb, recognise 'to give', and look at the source, goal, and theme NPs. So, far the message 'I give a fly to a spider' is decoded. Then the recipient looks at time-when, and sees that 'soon' is indicated. Now the sentence becomes 'I will soon give a fly to a spider'. Then the recipient looks at each NP in turn to see if any of them has an 'expansion star' (visual element), indicating that the noun has modified properties with it. The recipient sees the

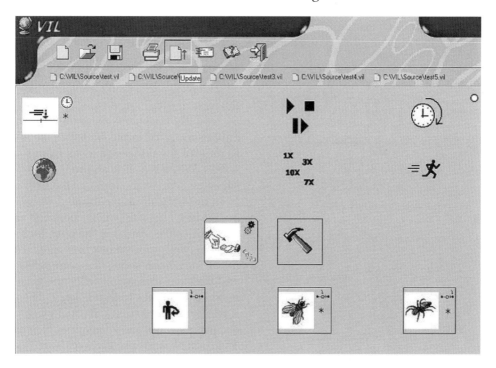

Figure 14. The message after filling in all elements for the sentence 'I will soon give most of these flies to that spider'. Notice that there are still uninstantiated icons on the screen.

expansion stars on two NP icons, double-clicks each of them in turn, and finds that the noun phrases in fact are 'most of these flies' and 'that spider'. Now the recipient is happy to have decoded the message 'I will soon give most of these flies to that spider'.

Evaluating the Design of the Language and Icons

The design of the language and the grammar can best be evaluated when people are actually learning and using the system. But before we can test the system, we must ensure that the icons are developed well. Are the icons truly universal? How many of the icons are conventional and how much time does it take to learn these icons? Are the conventional icons consistent enough so one can predict the meaning of other conventional icons? To answer all these questions we need to test the icons with people from various parts of the world. We are in the process of developing a test plan for both the icons and the VIL system as a whole.

What if the icons are not 100 per cent universal? For an elaborate system like VIL, designing icons that are totally language independent and culturally neutral may prove impossible. Fortunately, users do not require perfect icons, only recognizable ones. One can use images not common to every culture provided that users can still recognize them, e.g. a Chinese user will still recognize an icon of a knife-fork-spoon as

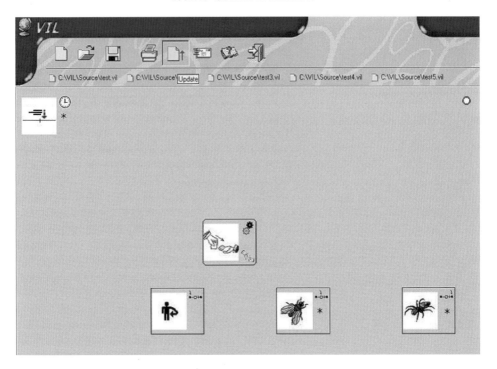

Figure 15. The final message after removing uninstantiated icons. The star in the icon for 'fly' means that this noun has one or more of its properties changed. The user can query the icon to find out about these modifiers.

an icon for silverware (concrete) or food or restaurant (abstract), even though chopsticks and a bowl may be more common in China Horton, (1994).

Summary

We have tried to create a universal language that is easy to learn and use. Remember the psychological aspect, mentioned in the beginning of this paper as a criterion for a world language: if people are to learn a new language, then it should be easy to learn. The root criticism of any revived or artificial written language was that it was too hard to learn. VIL uses a restricted grammar and vocabulary to make the system not only universal but also easy to acquire. Also, the arguments for learnability, encodability and decodability will show that the system is easy to learn and use, so the user should have no fear about learning the system.

Learnability

This means that the system should be easy to learn. We argue that with a visual language the learning process will be much faster than with a written language. This is because it is easier to recognise visual representations than to come up with words for them. Richards and Ogden supported this view. Richards argued that the proportion of

140

the meanings of a language that can be visually presented is an enormously important factor in determining the ease with which it can be learned and retained (Richards, 1943).

Encodability

This means that it should be fairly easy to generate messages. A computer-based iconic language makes this a lot easier by not requiring the user to draw icons but simply letting him or her choose the icons from the screen. The design of the grammar (we take the greatest common denominator of the things to be expressed, i.e. no inflection and no gender, etc.), the design of the hierarchies for our grammatical categories and the design of the program itself all facilitate encoding.

Decodability

This means that the messages that are composed on the system should be easy to comprehend. Our simple grammar and our consistent set of icons and visual elements allow for easy decoding of messages. Possible help features like explanation of the different visual combining features of an icon, possibly animation, could augment decodability.

Extensibility

This means that the system should have the possibility to be extended easily. The design of the hierarchies makes it possible to easily add more icons, without it having to undergo a drastic redesign. Derivational morphology already allows for the language to grow in vocabulary.

Notes

1. 'Aktionsarten', like start, stop and continue, are a means of paraphrasing verbs. They reduce the number of verbs that need to be classified. Specific verbs that can be obtained by paraphrasing a more general verb, need not be classified.

References

Ballmer, Th. and Brennenstuhl, W. (1981). 'Speech Act Classification: A study in the Lexical Analysis of English Speech Activity Verbs,' (ed.) W. Levelt, Spring-Verlag.

Beardon, C., Dormann, C., Mealing, S. and Yazdani, M. (1993). 'Talking with pictures: exploring the possibilities of iconic communication', *Association for Learning Technology Journal*, 1, 1, pp. 26-32.

Bliss, C. K.(1965) *Semantography*, Semantography publications, Australia.

Brown, R. W. and Bellugi, U. (1964)'Three processes in the child's acquisition of syntax.' *Harvard Educ. Rev.* 34, pp. 133-151 (Repr. in 'New directions in the study of language', Lenneberg, E. (ed.), Cambridge, Mass

Corbeil, J. (1986). 'Visual Dictionary'. Fact on File Publications, NY.

Corder, S. P. (1975).'Simple codes' and the source of the second language learner's initial heuristic hypothesis'. Paper presented at the Colloque 'Theoretical Models in Applied Linguistics' IV, Universite de Neuchatel.

D'Andrade, R. (1995).'The development of Cognitive Anthropology', chap. 5: Folk Taxonomies, Cambridge University Press.

Ferguson, C. A. (1971). 'Absence of Copula and the Notion of Simplicity: A study of Normal Speech, Baby

Talk, Foreigner Talk, and Pidgins,' in *Language Structure and Language Use*, Stanford University Press, pp. 277-92.

Fillmore, C. *The Case for Case*. in E. Back and R. Harms (eds.), *Universals in Linguistic Theory*, 1-90, Holt, Rinehart, and Wonston, NY.

Foley, W.A. (1988). 'Language birth: the processes of pidginization and creolization,' In *Linguistics: The Cambridge Survey*, Vol. 4, Language: The Socio-Cultural Context, (ed.) F.J. Newmeyer, Cambridge, NY.

Gelb, I.J. (1988). *A Study of Writing*, Univ. of Chicago Press.

Gode, A. and Blair, H. E. (1955)*Interlingua: a Grammar of the International Language,"* Storm Publishers, New York.

Hall, R. (1966) *Pidgin and Creole Languages*, Cornell University Press.

Horton, W. (1994). *The Icon Book: Visual Symbols for Computer Systems and Documentation*, John Wiley & Sons.

Jackendoff, R. (1983). 'Semantics and Cognition', Chap. 10 *Nonspatial Semantic Fields and the Thematic Relations Hypothesis*, The MIT Press.

Kummel, P. (1979). 'Formalization of Natural Language', Springer-Verlag.

Levin, B. (1993). 'English Verb Classes and Alternations: A Preliminary Investigation,' The University of Chicago Press.

MacMillian, (1993). *The MacMillian Visual Desk Reference*, MacMillian Publishing Group.

Matsukawa, T. and Yokota, E. in Pustejovsky, J. and Bergler, S. (Eds.) (1991). 'Lexical Semantics and Knowledge Representation', Proc. of the First SIGLEX Workshop, Berkeley, CA, June 17, Springer-Verlag, chap. 21 'Development of the Concept Dictionary — Implementation of Lexical Knowledge'.

Miller, G.A. and Fellbaum, C. (1995). 'Semantic Networks of English' in Levin and Pinker (eds.), Lexical & Conceptual Semantics, Blackwell Publishers Ltd.

Neurath, O. (1978). 'International Picture Language,' Department of Typography and Graphic Communication, University of Reading, England, 1978.

Richards, I. A. (1943). *Basic English and Its Uses*, W. W. Norton & Company Inc., New York.

Rosch, E., Mervis, C.B., Gray, W., Johnson, D. and Boyes-Braem, P. (1976). Basic Objects in Natural Categories, Cognitive Psychology, 9, pp. 382-439.

Schank, R. (1975). *Conceptual Information Processing*, North-Holland, New York.

Schumann, J. (1978).*The Pidginization Process: A Model for Second Language Acquisition*, Newbury House Publishers, 1978.

Smith, D. M. (1973a). *Pidginization and language socialization: the role of marking*, Unpublished paper, Georgetown University.

Smith, E.E. (1978b). 'Theories of Semantic Memory', in W.K. Estes (ed.), *Handbook of Learning and Cognitive Processes* (vol. 5), Hillsdale, NJ: Erlbaum.

Todd, L. (1974). 'Pidgins and Creoles', Language and Society Series, Publ: Routledge & Kegan Paul Ltd.

Yazdani, M. and Mealing, S. (1992). 'Communicating Through Pictures,' from the World Wide Web, Department of Computer Science, University of Exeter, England.

'Visual Encyclopedia' (1995), Dorling Kindersley NY.

Walsh, C. (1933). 'The Verb System in Basic English', *American Speech*, 8:137-43, December.

Research Outcomes

12. Icons in the Mind

Philip Barker and Paul van Schaik

Introduction

The term 'icon' is one which has significant history associated with it. Modern day usage of the term regards it as referring to 'an image, picture or representation' of something that exists either in the external world or within the mind of its user. Usually, in the context of referring to objects in the external world, icons are symbols resembling or analogous to the things that they represent. On the dashboard of my car, for example, a 'fuel pump' icon is used to denote the petrol gauge while the 'thermometer' icon signifies which of the other gauges on the instrument panel reflects the engine temperature. Similarly, in many cars, a 'battery' icon is used to indicate the status of the car's battery while an 'oil can' informs the driver that the oil pressure within the engine is (or is not) satisfactory. Other simple icons, similar to those used in this example, are used in many other everyday devices and situations – such as photocopiers, refrigerators, sewing machines, video recorders, microwave cookers, mobile phones, railway stations, airports and so on.

Each of the icons described in the car scenario described above is an example of a static icon. Such icons do not usually change their basic form (in terms of size, shape or position in space). However, some of the properties associated with these icons may change in order to reflect different states of the object, system or process being represented. In the motor car example, the oil can could change its colour from green (indicating a safe oil pressure) to red (indicative of the possible onset of a dangerous situation).

In general, as has been suggested above, within the context of human–machine systems, icons can be used in a variety of different ways and can take on a wide range of visual forms. As well as the static icons referred to above in the motor car example, it is possible to have dynamic icons and animated scenes in order to depict objects and processes (and their states of existence). Dynamic icons may change their shape, size, position and orientation in order to communicate different messages to their users. Naturally, the use of icons of this sort depends critically upon the ability of the host system (in which they are embedded) to make available an appropriate dynamic display medium – for example a computer screen or an LCD display. Of course, within human–computer systems, icons are now widely used in order to facilitate a variety of

143

different functions. This usage is reflected in the well-known WIMP end-user interfaces that are now so popular in many computer systems.

As far as this paper is concerned, we take the 'end-user interface' as our starting point for our discussion of 'icons in the mind'. Our generalised representation of an end-user interface, the effects that it has on its users and the mediating roles that it plays are illustrated schematically in Figure 1.

This diagram depicts the five important functions that an interface performs with respect to facilitating end-user interaction with its host system. These functions are:
- the projection of a *'system image'* to the users of the system;
- the embedding of various *stimuli* and *cues*;
- initiating the recall and/or building of *mental models*;
- using *interface metaphors* to act as *cognitive transfer agents* for shifting knowledge from one *domain of knowledge* to another; and
- providing *interface functionality* to facilitate the *user's intent* in terms of the actions he/she wishes to perform.

In our previous work (Barker et al, 1998ab; Barker and van Schaik, 1999) we have identified the importance of mental models from two critical perspectives. First, the cognitive development of computer users and second, the design of end-user interfaces that support efficient and effective human–computer interaction. An important consideration in our study of mental models was how they are represented both internally (within the mind of the user) and externally (on paper or within a computer system). The relationship between these two different domains (reality and representational space) is illustrated schematically in Figure 2. In this paper we are primarily concerned with iconic representations within the mind of a user.

Bearing in mind what has been said above, it is important to realise that a crucial aspect of all end-user interfaces is the range of 'interface agents' that they embed. An interface agent is an object that is usually embedded within an end-user interface and which performs one or more specific interface functions. Between them the various interface agents that are present in an end-user interface are therefore responsible for

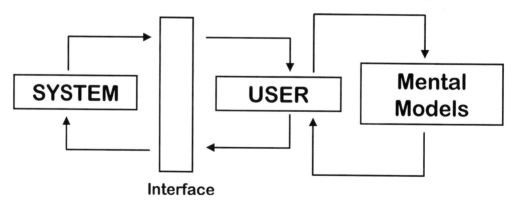

Interface

Figure 1. The role of the end-user interface in human–computer systems

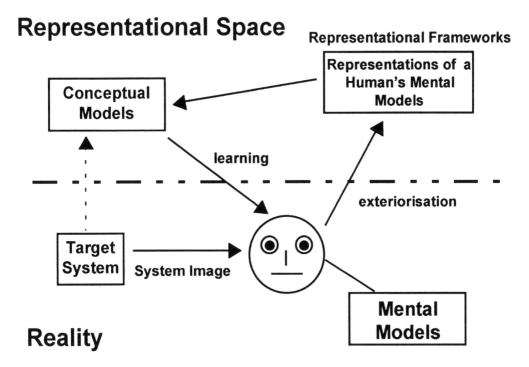

Representational Space

Representational Frameworks

Figure 2. The internalisation and externalisation of knowledge.

providing the functionality associated with that interface. Their main functional roles include: the provision of aesthetic impact; the creation of engagement and motivation within the user; and the provision of appropriate resources to facilitate communication, manipulation and information acquisition.

Figure 3 shows some of the different types of interface agent that are currently widely employed in end-user interfaces to computer systems. As can be seen from this diagram, we regard icons as an important interface agent to facilitate communication with an end-user and/or the expression and facilitation of a user's intent when using a particular interface.

In this paper we consider two important aspects of icons, first, their use as interface agents according to the rationale expressed in Figure 3; second, the use of icons by end-users of a computer system in order to represent and communicate knowledge about that system.

Bearing in mind what has been said above, the remainder of this paper is organised into four main sections. The following section describes and discusses some important issues relating to knowledge representation, mental models and the 'text versus pictures' debate. This is followed by a more detailed discussion of methods for measuring mental models; particular emphasis is given to the analysis of representational styles including pictorial expressions (in relation to the use of teach-back techniques). We then present a case study that outlines some of the findings of

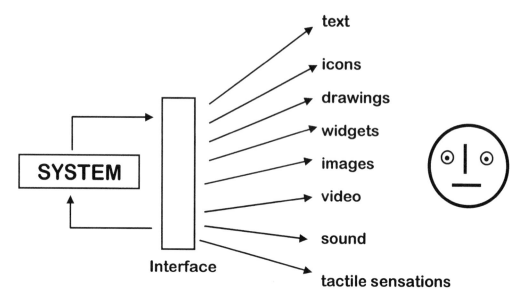

Figure 3. Interface agents responsible for projecting the system image

our research into the use of a teach-back technique for studying mental models and the roles that icons play. Finally, we present some conclusions from this work and outline some ways in which the research might be extended in order to gain further insight into the role that icons play as a component within mental models.

Knowledge Representation

Knowledge is a fundamental commodity that human beings 'accumulate' as a result of their exposure to various experiences. These may involve reading a book, attending a lecture, watching a TV programme, performing a task, talking to a colleague, participating in a debate or reflecting on issues and events. As far as this paper is concerned there are three important aspects of knowledge that we need to review. First, we must consider how knowledge is classified into declarative and procedural types and how these relate to cognitive structures. Then we need to discuss the important relationship between mental models and end-user interfaces. Finally, we must consider the representation of knowledge in terms of 'textual' and 'pictorial' forms. Each of these issues is discussed in the remainder of this section.

Types of Knowledge

Within most organisations, knowledge is now regarded as an important operational resource. Its importance stems from the various ways in which it can be harnessed in order to improve the performance of both individuals and the organisation as a whole. According to Seely Brown and Duguid (1998), within organisations knowledge can take many different forms – for example, social, personal, tacit and explicit. They also suggest that not all knowledge has its origin in individuals. Important knowledge and knowing are often collectively produced and held and can evolve from 'communities of practice'. However, there must be mechanisms to facilitate the common sharing of knowledge. As we have discussed elsewhere (Barker, van Schaik and Hudson, 1998), we believe that the effective transfer of knowledge between groups of individuals depends critically upon the creation of appropriate representational frameworks to facilitate the exteriorisation and ingestion of knowledge in different forms. As we discuss later in the paper, iconic communication is one of many different representational techniques that an individual can use to share his/her knowledge of a topic.

Obviously, knowledge can be classified in many different ways. From a 'classical' psychological perspective, the knowledge that individuals accumulate can be broadly classified into two basic categories: declarative and procedural. Declarative knowledge usually relates to facts and rules whereas procedural knowledge 'tells us' what to do or how to behave in a given situation. 'Paul is male, tall and thin' is an example of some declarative knowledge whereas 'Put it in the top of the oven and cook until golden brown' illustrates an example of a piece of procedural knowledge.

The knowledge that we create as a result of our experiences is stored in a variety of different types of cognitive structure such as associations, lists, scripts, plans, schemata and mental models. Simple items of knowledge might be represented within a single type of structure but more complex knowledge is likely to be distributed across several different structural types. Undoubtedly, mental models are one of the most powerful types of cognitive structure – in terms of their ability to support complex mental processes such as thinking, calculating, predicting, visualising and so on. The way in which we envisage that mental models develop (from simpler cognitive structures) is illustrated schematically in Figure 4.

Owing to the importance of mental models (with respect to the research that is outlined later in the paper) they are described and discussed in more detail in the following section.

Mental Models

A mental model is something we have 'in our heads' that encapsulates the knowledge that we have gained as a result of our experiences. Such models can embed both declarative and procedural knowledge. Carroll and Olsen (1988) define a mental model as a rich and elaborate structure that reflects a user's understanding of what a system contains, how it works and why it works the way it does.

Writing in the context of human-computer interaction, Faulkner (1998) refers to mental models in the following way:

> The human-computer interface. . . protects users from the harsh realities of the system, reflects the system model to them and translates their intentions into appropriate system activity. The user forms a model, known as the user's mental model, of how the application works. This model forms the basis of future interactions with the system and enables users to predict system performance . . . the human-computer interface must help users to acquire an accurate model of the computer system.

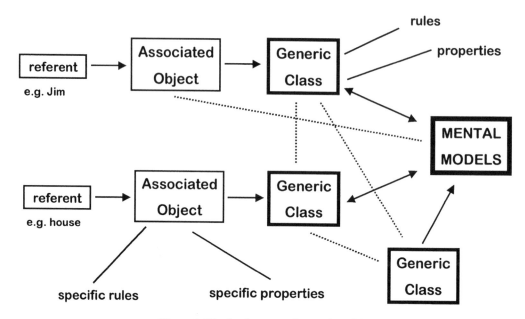

Figure 4. The development of mental models.

Of course, mental models do not only apply to computer systems. They apply to everything that we do. This point has been made very cogently by a number of authors including Norman (1990), Rogers et al (1992), Goei (1994), Seel (1995) and van Merriënboer (1997).

Obviously, Faulkner's comments on the relationship between human–computer interfaces and mental models are extremely important. As we have shown in Figure 1, this importance arises because end-user interfaces not only have to support the development of mental models relating to software operation, they may also have to project domain specific models relating to the tasks to be performed within some underlying application domain.

Of course, within the context of both interface and system design (and subsequent use) the importance of metaphors has to be emphasised (Barker, 1998; Hron, 1998). Metaphors are important because they can be used to initiate cognitive transfer between different subject domains and/or mental models. From a design perspective, when a metaphor is embedded in an end-user interface it usually takes the form of a graphical user interface (GUI). An important aspect of such interfaces is the set of icons and scenes that they contain. These are normally designed in such a way that they trigger various mental models relating to the tasks that can be performed within the application domain that the GUI provides access to. As we shall discuss later, the icons that are embedded in an interface often 'carry over' to a user's mental representation of a system.

Icons in the Mind

Text versus Pictures

According to Eysenck and Keane (1995), research in cognitive psychology has investigated several different types of mental representation (of knowledge). Figure 5 summarises the different types of representation identified by these authors.

In this diagram, the first distinction to be made is between external and internal representations. External representations exist in the 'outside' world, whereas internal representations exist 'in the mind'. External representations can be pictorial – in the form of pictures or diagrams; however, they can also be linguistic. Pictures and diagrams are 'closer' to the world since their structure resembles the structure of the world more closely. This structural resemblance is often called analogical. Linguistic representations are usually not analogical – as the relationship between a linguistic symbol and that which it represents is arbitrary. Linguistic representations consist of discrete symbols; they are explicit in the sense that objects and relations between objects are represented; they are abstract; and they are grammatical (their organisation follows a set of rules). Pictorial representations, however, are not made up of discrete symbols; they are implicit in the sense that they do not use symbols to represent relations between objects; they are concrete; and there are no clear rules for combining them.

Internal representations can be symbolic or distributed. In the traditional dominant symbolic view, a pattern is stored in long-term memory which denotes or refers to something outside itself (Vera and Simon, 1994). In the distributed view, distributed representations are stored as patterns of activation in connectionist networks. In the symbolic view (listed in Figure 5) analogical and propositional representations are distinguished. Analogical representations tend to be images in one of the sensory modalities. Propositional representations are language-like representations that capture the ideational content of the mind, irrespective of the original modality in which that information was encountered (Eysenck and Keane, 1995). Similar distinctions exist between internal analogical and propositional representations as between external pictorial and linguistic representations.

Within the context of human-information processing, psychologists often refer to 'iconic memory'. This terminology is used to refer to the temporary persistence of visual impressions after the stimulus that causes them have been removed. This paper, however, investigates more permanent pictorial (iconic) knowledge structures. Indeed, the teach-back experiments that we have conducted (and which are described in detail later) were intended to explore how people externally represent their internal (analogical and propositional) knowledge of word-processing systems.

Paivio's (1991) dual coding theory discusses the nature of analogical and propositional representations and the relationship between them. Eysenck and Keane (1995) illustrate this theory using a diagram similar to that which is depicted in Figure 6.

They then go on to summarise the main features of this theory as follows:

1. Human cognition depends upon two basic independent (but interconnected) coding/symbolic systems: non-verbal and verbal.
2. These two systems are attuned to the encoding, organising, storing and retrieval of distinct types of information.

149

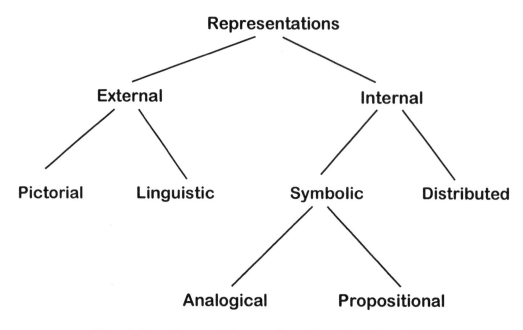

Figure 5. Types of representation according to Eysenck and Keane (1995)

3. The non-verbal (imagery) system is used for processing non-verbal objects and events (i.e. processing spatial and synchronous information) and thus enters into tasks like the analysis of scenes and the generation of mental images.
4. The verbal system deals with linguistic information and is largely employed for the processing of language; because of the serial nature of language this system is 'customised' for sequential processing.
5. Each system is further subdivided into several sensorimotor sub-systems (visual, auditory and haptic).
6. Each system has basic representational units: logogens for the verbal system and imagens for the non-verbal system; these come in modality-specific versions in each of the sensorimotor sub-systems.
7. The two symbolic systems are connected to two different input and output systems; the symbolic systems are interconnected by referential links between logogens and imagens.

From the perspective of this study, an important consequence of the theory is that it would be easier to externalise verbal representations through verbal responses (which are directly connected) than through non-verbal responses (which require referential links to the non-verbal system and then non-verbal responses). Similarly, it would be easier to externalise non-verbal representations in a non-verbal way than through verbal responses.

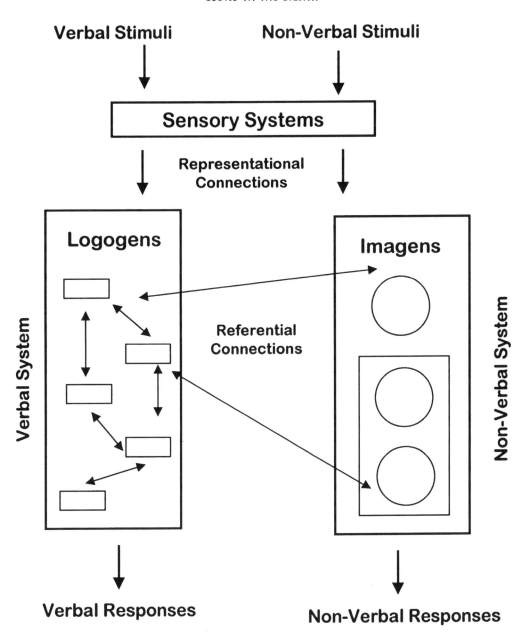

Figure 6. The major components of dual coding theory (Pavio, 1986)

Iconic Representation In Mental Models

In this section we discuss two important issues relating to iconic representation in mental models. First, we outline various methods for measuring mental models; these all involve the exteriorisation of knowledge – from reality to representational space (as depicted in Figure 2). We then go on to discuss the various forms of iconic representation that are often embedded within these externalisations.

Measurement of Mental Models

In order to study mental models, various methods are available – such as ratings, sorting, laddering, concept mapping, verbal protocols, teach-back and action sequences. We have described these techniques in detail elsewhere (Barker and van Schaik, 1999). Of the methods that are available, laddering and concept mapping are particularly important to the work described in this study because they make it possible to study abstract pictorial external representations of mental models. These consist of discrete elements; they embed explicitly represented relations; they are abstract and they may have rules for combining elements. Therefore they are more like linguistic than pictorial representations.

The teach-back method makes it possible to study iconic external representations of mental models. Therefore we will focus on teach-back to externalise mental models pictorially. Using this method, after exposure to some target system, participants are asked to describe (on paper) to another person how to perform a given task using that system. In doing this, subjects use their own preferred mode or representation. According to van der Veer (1990) these descriptions can then be scored to measure the following aspects of mental models: completeness, correctness, interaction levels and style of representation. The main assumption being made here is that users who can explain or teach back how to use the interface at higher or more detailed levels of interaction abstraction have a richer mental model of the interface. Knowledge captured by this method can be procedural (description of action sequences at the syntax level), goal-plan hierarchies (descriptions of how to achieve a goal – broken down into sub-goals at the task level) and concepts (physical and informational objects that are manipulated by actions at the semantic level).

Iconic Representations in Externalised Mental Models

In his investigation of students' mental models of operating systems, van der Veer (1990) used the teach-back method. He distinguished the following 'representation styles' to analyse teach-back protocols: verbal description, visual-spatial image, use of icons, sets of production rules and programs. Each of these is briefly discussed below.

Verbal descriptions. Van der Veer describes these as 'any representation which is completely or partially composed of language fragments that may be considered sentences in natural language. These sentences may be incomplete, words may have been skipped, abbreviated or misspelled. Nevertheless, the verbal statements will have to be longer than one word.'

Visual-spatial images. 'Any drawing or scheme that depicts at least two elements of a representation and at the same time indicates a spatial relation between the two is scored as a visual spatial image. The spatial relation may indicate a location/position of an element relative to another, or a flow of information, or a flow of control.'

Icons. 'Icons are graphical representations of any element in the description, that are drawn in such a way that no relevant structural details are visible. Icons may appear instead of words in a verbal representation, or as atomic elements in a visual-spatial image.'

Production rules. According to van der Veer, a set of production rules 'consists of at least two rules'. In this context a rule is defined as 'containing two elements, a header and a body. The header explicitly refers to a task and is clearly separated from the body. The body indicates how the tasks or actions are accomplished, or provides a decomposition.'

Programs. 'Programs are representations of tasks or actions, in which the flow of control is made clear for example by spatial layout, arrows, flow-chart like notations or by verbal constructions such as 'after that', 'if. . . then. . . else', 'for. . . do', 'repeat. . . as long as' or the equivalent of these in natural language.'

Case Study – Results Of A Teach-Back Study

As part of a wider study on mental models in relation to task performance, a teach-back task was carried out. In this task, a number of Final Year students studying a modular computing degree scheme acted as participants. The experiment was conducted as part of an optional module on Human–Computer Interaction. In this module the subjects had gained substantial experience in the use of word processing (using the MS-Word system) through a series of five practical exercises. Ten students participated in the teach-back task.

The MS-Word system embeds various interface agents such as menu bars, tool bars, dialogue boxes and, of course, icons. These icons may perform either of two basic representational functions: they may denote control commands that the user may issue (for example, print, bold, undo, redo and so on); or they may represent feedback about the state of the system (for example, saving, busy, printing, out-of-paper and so on). In keeping with what we have said earlier, the icons used by MS-Word may be either of a static nature (such as the print icon) or they may be dynamic (for example, the 'hour glass').

Materials. For the teach-back task a scenario involving a document was used. This scenario is presented in Barker and van Schaik (1999, Figure 5). The material which is referred to in this scenario is available as a hyperlink from this figure. In addition to the scenario material, answer sheets were used which participants filled in using a pen or pencil.

Procedure. Participants were asked to imagine a person (X) who is familiar with using MS-Windows but not MS-Word. In addition, this person is familiar with loading, printing and saving files. Participants were then asked to use diagrams and/or words to show how they would explain to X how to use MS-Word to accomplish the task described in the scenario.

Analysis. A 'theoretical' analysis of the teach-back task was undertaken by producing a scoring scheme with a complete set of actions required for teaching back how to produce, print and store the document used in the scenario. The scoring scheme was then tested and revised. It was then used to mark the teach-back protocols (produced by the students) for completeness, correctness, misconceptions and the use of representation styles.

The present study focuses on the analysis of the use of representation styles. We analysed the teach-back protocols at three levels; these are shown in Figure 7.

The three levels we used were: 1) the types of external representation employed; 2) the nature of the pictorial representation used; and 3) and types of icon. At each level we analysed both the frequency distribution of the types of representation and the purposes for which they were used. At level 1 we also analysed the redundancy of coding. The following possibilities were considered in the analysis of the teach-back protocols: single-style coding (pictorial or linguistic); pictorial and linguistic non-redundant coding; and redundant pictorial and linguistic coding.

Results

The results that we present below are organised according to the three levels of analysis that were introduced in the previous section.

Level-1 Analysis Table 1 shows the extent to which interface agents have been externally represented (pictorially and linguistically) and the teach-back elements coded most frequently.

The majority of elements (74 per cent) are linguistically coded, a minority are coded linguistically and pictorially at the same time (24 per cent). Among the most frequently coded elements there is little overlap between linguistic coding and combined linguistic and pictorial coding. For the five most frequently linguistically–pictorially coded elements, two abstract and three concrete icons were used. There is some overlap between linguistically and pictorially non-redundant and redundant coding of

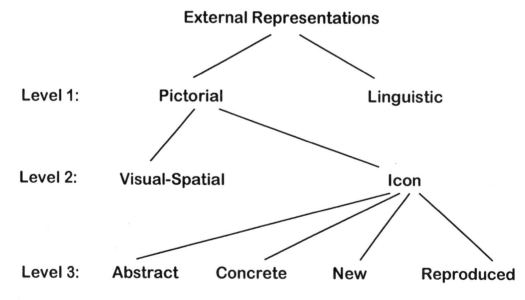

Figure 7. Analysis of teach-back protocols

(n=10)	Total	L*	LP	LP subdivided	
				LPN	LPR
Mean	23.0	17	6.0	1.0	5.0
(sd)	(6.25)	(5.25)	(3.88)	(3.29)	(2.68)
View header	5	5			
Type in text	34	34			
Save document	5	5			
Copy text	5	5			
Create matrix (table)	11	7	4	1	3
Create page	9	9			
Produce bullet points *(c)*	8	1	7	5	2
Set text bold *(a)*	10	2	8	8	0
Centre paragraph *(c)*	7		7	3	5
Underline text *(a)*	10	2	8	3	5
Print document *(c)*	6	1	5	1	4

* L: linguistic; LP: linguistic and pictorial; LPN: linguistic and pictorial non-redundant; LPR: linguistic and pictorial redundant; *(a)*: use of abstract icons; *(c)*: use of concrete icons

Table 1. Frequency of types of representation in teach-back protocols

elements. No production rules were found in the teach-back protocols. Seven out of ten teach-back protocols were coded (overall) as a sequential procedure. However, one protocol did use three repetitive structures to code individual teach-back elements (for copying text, creating a header and creating text).

Table 2 shows correlations between the quality of represented knowledge and representational style.

The significant correlations of completeness and correctness with the frequency of linguistically coded elements indicate that the quality of knowledge is strongly affected by the use of linguistic coding. The nearly significant correlations of completeness and correctness with the frequency of pictorially and linguistically coded elements indicate that the quality of knowledge is only weakly related to the use of pictorial and linguistic coding combined.

Level-2 Analysis Visual-spatial images and visual-spatial descriptions indicate the extent to which relations between interface agents are represented. Visual-spatial images were used sparingly in two ways. First, to represent relevant parts of the MS-Word menu structure in relation to one another (coded once). Second, to show groups of related interface agents which are represented iconically in MS-Word (coded four times). Visual-spatial descriptions are textual descriptions of icons in relation to each other. These were used only sparsely to represent: a) dragging an image to a location

Number of coded elements (n=10)	Completeness	Correctness
Linguistic	0.84*	0.80*
LP	0.52**	0.49**
LPN	0.33	0.33
LPR	0.26	0.22

* p < 0.05, one-tailed; **0.5 < p < 0.10, one-tailed

Table 2. Correlations between quality of knowledge and representation styles

on the screen (coded once) and b) to locate an item on the toolbar or the desktop (coded twice).

Level-3 Analysis None of the icons in the teach-back protocols were new; all were reproduced from the MS-Word system. Table 3 shows to what extent abstract and concrete icons were produced and the purposes for which they were used.

On a 'per icon' basis, concrete icons were coded almost twice as often as abstract icons. This indicates less variability in the coding of concrete icons compared to abstract icons; this difference is due to the frequent coding of the 'align paragraphs' function by concrete icons. Abstract icons were used most frequently to represent the formatting of text. For concrete icons, the function 'align paragraph' was by far the most often coded; next in order were the icons for producing bullets and producing borders. In Table 3, the right-hand column represents the concrete icons results with the effect of the 'align paragraph' icon removed.

Discussion

In this section we summarise our findings and then discuss them in relation to previous work. On average, at Level 1 (types of representation), the largest part of each teach-back protocol was coded linguistically; smaller fragments were coded both linguistically and pictorially. We found a complete lack of the use of production rules and only a sparse use of program structures; the over-whelming majority of linguistically coded elements were verbal descriptions. There was little overlap between the linguistic coding of elements and the combined linguistic and pictorial coding. A statistically significant correlation of quality of knowledge was found with the use of linguistic coding but only a weak correlation with combined coding. At Level 2 (nature of pictorial representation), visual-spatial images and visual-spatial descriptions were used sparsely but separate icons were used frequently. At Level 3 (types of icon), there was more consistency across participants in the use of concrete icons rather than abstract icons, which was due to the coding (with concrete icons) of 'align paragraph'.

Using Paivio's dual coding theory, we now consider the external representations found in the teach-back protocols as indicators of internal representations. Primarily, we treat verbal expressions as evidence for propositional internal representations and

(n=10)	Abstract icons*	Concrete icons**	Modified Concrete icons***
Mean - per icon	2.06	3.73	2.27
Mean - per participant	2.1	5.6	3.4
(sd)	(2.01)	(16.05)	(9.84)
Underline text	7		
Set text bold	7		
Align paragraph		22	
Produce bullet points		8	
Produce border		8	

*   In total 16 different abstract icons were coded
**   In total 15 different concrete icons were coded
*** In total 14 different icons, with icons for the function 'align paragraph' excluded

Table 3. Frequency of abstract and concrete icons in teach-back rotocols

non-verbal expresions as evidence for analogical internal representations. The majority of protocol elements were coded linguistically (verbal responses in Paivio's theory) indicating possible propositional (verbal) representations in order to generate non-verbal responses (see Figure 6). A minority of elements were coded using a combination of pictorial and linguistic coding – indicating possible analogical representations of interface agents. The sparse use of visual-spatial images and visual-spatial descriptions constitute a lack of evidence for analogical and propositional internal representations of relations between interface agents. However, other evidence was found for internal analogical representation of individual interface agents through the use of icons in the protocols; we also found evidence that concretely represented agents in the interface may be more consistently represented internally across participants than abstractly represented agents.

We next compare our findings of the use of representation styles with the results obtained by van der Veer (1990). In a study of a 'direct manipulation' interface (a graphical user interface), van der Veer found that 93 per cent of the teach-back protocols were verbal descriptions (compared with 100 per cent in our study). He also found: 20 per cent with programs (70 per cent in this study); none with production rules (just as in our study); 36 per cent with visual-spatial images (40 per cent in this study); and 37 per cent with icons (90 per cent in this study). The most striking difference is the much larger percentage of protocols using icons in our study. This may be related to the fact that our participants were experienced computer users who will have been exposed to and used iconically represented interface agents extensively, whereas those in van der Veer's study were relatively inexperienced computer users. Both studies found consistently that production rules were not used.

Interestingly, all of the students involved in our teach-back exercise had been exposed to the use of meta-notations (British Standard 6154:1981) and production rules for defining objects and processes encountered in human–computer systems. For example, they had previously used these techniques for defining memos, letters, files, screen-layouts, books and so on. We anticipated, therefore, that students might have used constructs of the following type within their teach-back protocols:

> *<document> ::= [<page>]^3*
> *<page> ::= <header> <body> <footer>*
> *<body> ::= <lead-page-body>| <next-page-body>*
> *<lead-page-body> ::= <address-part> <table-part> <promise-part>*
> *<next-page-body: ::= <table-part> <promise-part>*
>   *etc.*

However, despite their exposure to production rules, there seemed to be a complete lack of the use of this technique in the teach-back protocols that we observed in our study. This observation may be taken to reflect the fact that there may be some 'delay period' between a student's exposure to a particular technique and his/her ability to use it in a problem-solving context. Alternatively, it may well be that the students involved in this experiment could not see the relevance of the technique with respect to the teach-back task that they were asked to perform.

We believe that a close comparison of our results with those of Van der Veer is difficult since he only presented overall results for teach-back protocols. The results at the level of individual teach-back elements are more useful since they tell us how frequently particular types of representation are used throughout a protocol. For example, the use of a visual-spatial image already classifies a protocol as using this type of pictorial representation even if it only appears once in the whole protocol. As another example, the finding that 74 per cent of elements were coded linguistically and 26 per cent were coded pictorially would not be noticed if we were to compare the 100 per cent of protocols that used linguistic coding versus the 90 per cent that used icons.

Conclusion

Icons can provide a rapid and effective mechanism for communicating ideas, concepts and messages in coded form. Because of this, they now play an important role in many human–machine and human–human systems. Along with their auditory counterparts (earcons), icons are particularly important in the context of 'time critical' situations such as process control and traffic management. In this paper we have explored the use of icons for facilitating certain aspects of human-human communication within the context of a teach-back experiment that was intended to explore the nature of the mental models that people build as a consequence of their exposure to word-processing systems.

With respect to the use of human–computer interfaces, icons play an important role as short-cuts representing frequently used interface agents and status indicators that provide feedback. As was mentioned above, our study has explored the importance of icons in the knowledge representations developed by users of a word processing system. Although linguistic coding was dominant overall, for interface agents that were available in the MS-Word system (as either commands or icons), icons were the predominant external pictorial representational style. We found evidence for both analogical and propositional internal representations of interface agents through both linguistic and combined pictorial and linguistic expressions. Linguistic representations were strongly related to the overall quality of externally represented knowledge (both in terms of completeness and correctness) whereas combined pictorial and linguistic representations were only weakly related to this quality. However, particular interface agents were predominantly (or only) used with combined linguistic and pictorial coding – thereby underlining the importance of pictures. The specific example of the pictorial coding of 'align paragraph' shows how important iconic representations can be. This would suggest that appropriately designed icons can have a very important role in representing knowledge about a human–computer interface.

Regarding future research in this area, we believe that further work needs to be undertaken in order to investigate the effectiveness of the coding of interface agents (as icons) in terms of the knowledge representations that users develop. Some of the important issues to explore would be: a) which interface agents require representation as (permanently visible) icons; and b), for those that are to be represented by icons, what icons should be used? In addition to the design of effective icons, the saturation level with respect to 'visual clutter' would need to be investigated. That is, the number of icons, their purpose and their location on the screen would need to be studied in relation to the efficient use of the total available screen space and the need to find the required interface object represented by an icon quickly and accurately.

In order to investigate how well users might employ styles of representation as an indication of their internal representation, they could be prompted in a teach-back task with specific instructions as to the style to be produced. For example, one group of subjects could be prompted to use linguistic coding, a second group could be asked to use pictorial coding and a third group could be allowed to use their own preferred style of representation. The resulting teach-back protocols could then be analysed for: a) the actual use of the representation styles (compared to the styles they were asked to use); and b) their quality – in order to further establish the relation between coding styles and quality of knowledge.

References

Barker, P.G. (1998). 'The Role of Models and Metaphors in CAL Design', 346-8 in *A Worldwide Network of Learning: Opportunities, Challenges and Contrasts, Proceedings of the 15th International Conference on Technology and Education*, Santa Fe, New Mexico, ICTE Inc, Texas.

Barker, P.G. and van Schaik, P. (1999). 'Mental Models and Their Implications for the Design of Computer-Based Learning Resources', 1-12 in Section A1 of *Proceedings of CBLIS '99 (Computer-Based Learning in Science) International Conference*, Edited by G. Chapman, University of Ostrava, Czech Republic. The World Wide Web address given below refers to two files: paper.doc (containing an electronic version of the CBLIS '99 conference paper itself) and figures.doc (which contains all the figures and associated materials referred to in this paper). These files can be found within the CBLIS '99 directory at the following address: *http://www.isrg.co.uk.*

Barker, P.G., van Schaik, P. and Hudson, S.R.G., (1998a). 'Mental Models and Lifelong Learning', *Innovations in Education and Training International*, 35(4), 310-8.

Barker, P.G., van Schaik, P., Hudson, S.R.G. and Tan, C.M., (1998b). 'Mental Models and Their Role in Teaching and Learning', 105-10 in *Proceedings of ED-MEDIA/ED-TELECOM '98 - 10th World Conference on Educational Multimedia and Hypermedia and World Conference on Educational Telecommunications*, T. Ottmann and I. Tomek, (eds.)Association for the Advancement of Computing in Education, Virginia, USA.

Carroll, J.M. and Olsen, J. (1988). 'Mental Models and Human-Computer Interaction', 45-65 in *Handbook of Human-Computer Interaction*, M. Helander, Elsevier, (ed.) Amsterdam.

Eysenck, M.W., Keane, M.T. (1995). *Cognitive Psychology: a Student's Handbook*. 3rd Ed. Taylor and Francis, Hove.

Faulkner, C. (1998). *The Essence of Human-Computer Interaction*, Prentice Hall, London.

Goei, S.L. (1994). *Mental Models and Problem Solving in the Domain of Computer Numerically Controlled Programming*, Doctoral Thesis, Department of Instructional Technology, University of Twente, Enschede, The Netherlands.

Hron, A. (1998). Metaphors as Didactic Means for Multimedia Learning Environments, *Innovations in Education and Training International*, 35(1), 21-28.

Merriënboer, J.J.G. van. (1997). *Training Complex Cognitive Skills – a Four-Component Instructional Design Model for Technical Training*, Educational Technology Publications, Englewood Cliffs, New Jersey, USA.

Norman, D.A. (1990). *The Design of Everyday Things*, Doubleday, New York.

Paivio, A. (1986). *Mental Representations: a Dual Coding Approach*, Oxford University Press, Oxford.

Paivio, A.. (1991). Dual Coding Theory: Retrospect and Current Status, *Canadian Journal of Psychology*, 45, 255-87.

Rogers, Y., Rutherford, A. and Bibby, P.A. (1992). *Models in the Mind: Theory, Perspective and Application*, Academic Press, London.

Seel, N.M. (1995). 'Mental Models, Knowledge Transfer', and Teaching Strategies, *Journal of Structural Learning*, 12(3), 197-213.

Seely Brown, J. and Duguid, P. (1998). 'Organising Knowledge', 29-46 in '*Web-Weaving: Intranets, Extranets and Strategic Alliances*', P. Lloyd and P. Boyle (eds.), Butterworth-Heinemann, Oxford.

Vera, A. and Simon, H.A. (1994). 'Reply to Touretsky and Pomerleau: Reconstructing Physical Symbol Systems', *Cognitive Science*, 18, 355-60.

13. Designing and Evaluating Icons

Philip Barker and Paul van Schaik

Introduction

The discipline of human–computer interaction (HCI) is concerned with the scientific study of the effects that computer technology has on the end-users of that technology. Implicit in this definition of HCI is the idea that computers have end-user interfaces that facilitate a person's interaction with the underlying hardware and software subsystems. We have previously discussed the important relationships that exist between a computer, its end-user interface(s), its user population and the cognitive effects (such as the creation of mental models) that the technology has upon members of that population (Barker and van Schaik, 1999a; 1999b).

Increasingly, within end-user interfaces there is a movement away from the use of text-based 'command line interfaces' towards the more extensive use of 'graphical user interfaces' (GUIs). This transition has occurred because GUIs can be inherently easier to use – if they are designed correctly. An important characteristic of such interfaces is the way in which they combine multimedia and multimodal interaction techniques in order to achieve efficient and effective communication. Another important feature is the way in which GUIs can use various sorts of 'pictorial form' to facilitate interaction; this usually involves direct manipulation using a mouse. Nowadays, the majority of GUI-based end-user interfaces are object-orientated. This means that they embed various types of object that perform different kinds of interface function.

In our previous paper (Barker and van Schaik, 1999a), we referred to the notion of an 'interface agent'. Bearing in mind what has been said above, these are simply objects within an end-user interface that perform various functions on behalf of the computer or its users. Previously, we identified eight different types of interface agent that are often used to construct GUIs. The items within our list included text, icons, drawings, widgets, images, video, sound and tactile sensations. Unfortunately, as far as we are aware there is currently no adequate 'science of interface design' that prescribes how these interface agents should be designed and combined in ways that guarantee the production of an effective and efficient end-user interface. Sadly, much of interface design is, at present, still a 'hit and miss' process.

In view of what we have said above, we have been attempting to collect and collate knowledge that will help us to create a set of guidelines that will make end-user interface design a more scientific process. In order to realise this objective we have been conducting a programme of research into the design and development of icons. This research forms the basis of this paper. We believe this work is important because icons are now commonly used as a component within GUIs (Horton, 1994; Sassoon and Gaur, 1997). However, there is much contention about how these icons should be designed (De Carolis et al, 1995) and the functions they should perform – particularly in terms of their mappings onto application domains (for example, word-processing and information retrieval) and support tools (such as web browsers and word-processors).

It is our opinion that the roles that an icon (or more usually, an icon set) plays within an end-user interface is similar to those illustrated schematically in Figure 1.

Essentially, an icon acts as a vehicle of communication. It thus behaves as a message-passing agent – either between an end-user and a computer or between a computer and an end-user. However, from a cognitive perspective, we believe that an icon acts as a stimulus that triggers one or more mental processes that subsequently lead to some form of action being taken. In our previous work we have studied the nature of the mental models that users develop as a consequence of their exposure to icons and graphical user interfaces within word-processing systems (Barker and van Schaik, 1999b)

Because of the growing importance of icons in graphical user interfaces – particularly, the Internet and the World Wide Web (Honeywill, 1999) – it is obviously necessary to ask the basic question: *'What makes a good icon?'* Research into icons suggests that the quality of an icon can be defined in terms of both its physical characteristics and the effects that it has on its users (Rogers, 1989; Gittins, 1986; Lohse et al, 1991; 1994). Some of the more important of these properties that we have identified are illustrated schematically in Figure 2.

A good icon should be easy to learn, easy to remember and be distinctive (in relation to others with which it is used within an icon set for a particular application). By 'intuitiveness' we mean the ease with which a user can deduce its meaning without having had any previous experience of it (within a computer interface). There are two other important characteristics of an icon that also need to be considered. First, the strength of the stimulus that it generates – this usually depends upon the objects that it embeds and various physical characteristics such as its size, shape and colour. Second, its recall effectiveness – that is, how effectively its meaning is able to be recalled by a user from his/her long-term memory.

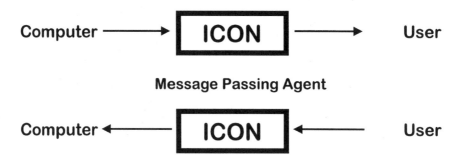

Figure 1. The role of icons in interfaces

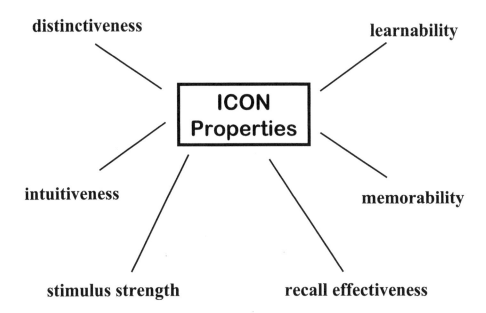

Figure 2. Important properties of icons

In an attempt to answer the important question that we posed above ('what makes a good icon?'), we have undertaken a series of experiments to study the design and evaluation of icons. The remainder of this paper therefore outlines the work that has been undertaken. The next section discusses the rationale for the work. We then describe our experimental method and the results obtained. These results are subsequently discussed and some conclusions presented.

Rationale

Bearing in mind the importance of designing good icons, we believe that it is necessary to consider the factors that are likely to have an influence on icon design. Furthermore, it is also necessary to 'scientifically measure' both the characteristics of good icons and the effects that they have on their users. In addition, from a design perspective, we need to consider techniques for evaluating icons (and icon sets) and to quantify those factors that are likely to influence their design – for example, the effect of previous icon design experience in a given domain and the role that expertise (in icon design) plays.

Because of our interest in the cognitive aspects of HCI, we believe that it is important to study what happens when an end-user of a computer is exposed to an icon. In particular, we need to consider the nature of the cognitive processes that are involved in processing an icon. In our view the basic processes (and some of the factors that influence these) can tentatively be summarised by a simple model that is similar to that which is illustrated schematically in Figure 3.

We use this diagram in order to suggest that when an icon (considered in isolation) is presented as a stimulus to an end-user, he/she could process it in either of two basic ways. These differ in the number and nature of the cognitive processing steps that are involved. The simplest way, involving least cognitive processing, occurs when the end-user makes a correct (or incorrect) direct association with the function that the icon represents. However, an alternative mechanism, involving extra cognitive processing, occurs when the end-user recognises one or more objects that are embedded in the icon and he/she is able to deduce the function that the icon represents.

Of course, in reality, icons are often not used in isolation. Therefore, additional factors are often present that can influence the cognitive processing of an icon. Some examples of factors that act in this way include: metaphors that may be embedded in the end-user interface; the context in which an icon appears (for example, printing or searching); the application within which the icon is embedded (such as a word processing system or a web browser); and experience. There are four types of experience that we feel are important. First, experience with using particular applications (for example, specific electronic mail systems or web browsers). Second, experience within particular domains (for example, information retrieval). Third, experience of designing icons for particular domains; and, finally icon design expertise. Of course, within any given application, an icon is normally a member of an icon set for that application (Rogers, 1989). This situation also provides contextual clues about the meaning of that icon.

Previous related work that is relevant to the study described in this paper has been reported by a number of researchers. This work has involved the role of design experience (Pitman and Payne, 1998), preference studies (Yamakawa et al, 1997), a

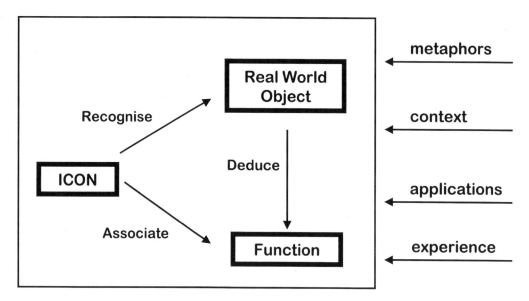

Figure 3. A simple model of icon proscessing

model of iconic reference (Familant and Detweiler, 1993), and the classification of icons (Rogers, 1989; Gittins, 1986; Lohse et al, 1991; 1994).

In their research Pitman and Payne described two experiments (relating to file naming for information retrieval) in which they explored the influence of design experience. They found that 'the names chosen by designers were better for other people than the names chosen by the self-choice group'. In this work, 'self-choice' subjects were ones who designed file names only for use by themselves while 'designers' had to produce names for use by other people. We argue that an analogous situation arises with respect to icon design. That is, design experience in a particular domain should lead to the creation of better icons.

Preference studies on icons for computer interfaces have been conducted by Yamakawa et al. In their research, they used a set of 96 icons in order to study whether or not subjects showed any preferences for particular icons and if any preferences that were observed could be used in predicting icon recognition. An important conclusion from their work was the suggestion that 'user preferences play an important role in the design if icons'. They also suggest that any icon that requires more than three guesses (to determine its function) should be replaced by a more effective one.

An important foundation for our work on icon design is the model of icon processing that we presented earlier in Figure 3. Work on models that is related to our own study has been described by Familant and Detweiler. Their models are presented in Figure 4.

Two variants are proposed: one for direct reference and one for indirect reference. As can be seen from a comparison of Figures 3 and 4, the major difference between our model and that of Familant and Detweiler is the absence, within the latter, of any form of direct association between the 'signal' and the 'denotative referent'. Of course, an important consideration when end-users process icons is the ways in which they themselves cognitively code and process knowledge. As we have discussed elsewhere (Barker and Schaik, 1999a), Pavio's dual coding theory would seem to be very relevant in this context. However, despite its appeal, we believe it has substantial limitations in that it does not provide any mechanism for distinguishing between the direct and indirect referencing of icons that was discussed above.

The Icon Classification Hypothesis

We believe that the quality of an icon (in terms of function identification) should be based upon the important measurable characteristics of that icon. Indeed, according to the icon classification hypothesis, the quality of an icon is a function of its characteristic properties as are derived from a suitable classification scheme. This relationship can be expressed as follows:

$$Q = F(\{p_i\} \text{ for } i = 1 \text{ to } N)$$

In this expression, p_i represents one of the characteristic properties – there being N such properties within the classification scheme that is used. Of course, the usefulness of a classification scheme can be assessed by analysing the correlation between

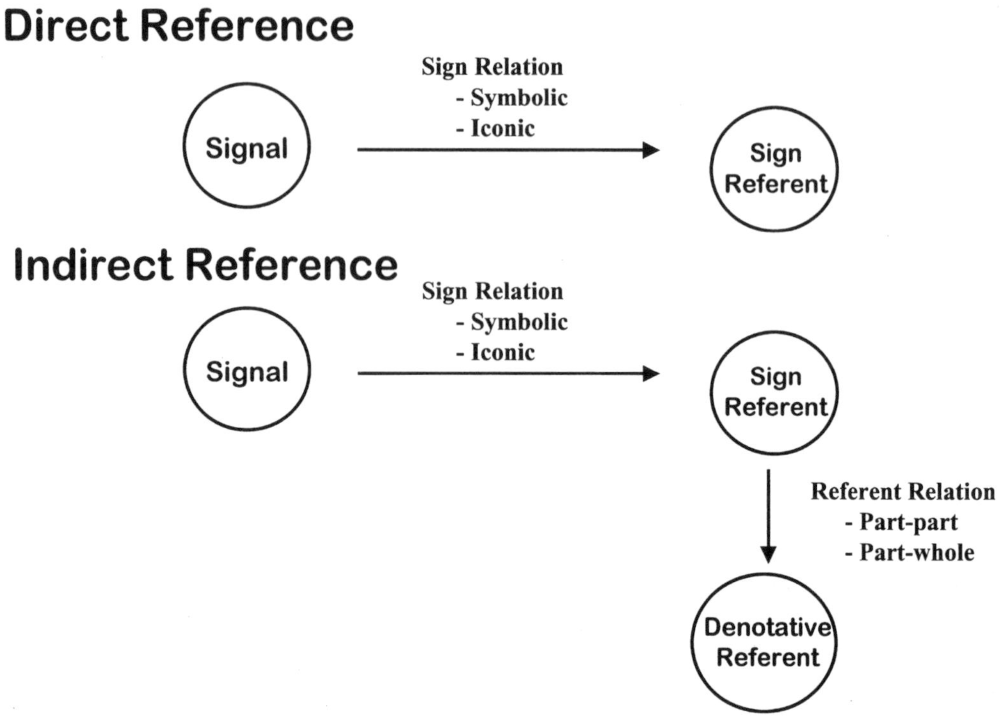

Direct Reference

Indirect Reference

Figure 4. Familant and Detweiler's model of icon referencing (1993)

function identification performance and the measured classification of icons according to the classification scheme.

Various examples of classification schemes have been cited above. We have found that there is some limited overlap between them. Rogers's classification is illustrated schematically in Figure 5.

Unfortunately, no quantitative scales have been developed to measure the characteristics of icons according to Rogers's scheme. However, Lohse et al (1994) have proposed an alternative classification that is based upon empirical research into the classification of visual representations. They produced and used 10 nine-point Likert scales based upon a frequency analysis of keywords that subjects used to describe the visual representations that were used in their previous research. The 10 scales and their anchor-point phrases are listed in Figure 6.

In our view, the work of Lohse et al (1994) is also important since it provides support for the icon classification hypothesis; they maintain that 'empirical work is required to discover and elaborate the basis on which people organise visual information'. This provides us with considerable motivation for carrying out the work that is described in the remainder of this paper.

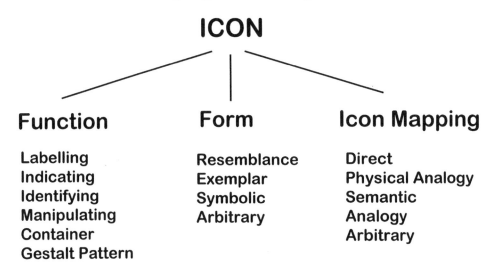

Figure 5. Icon classification according to Rogers (1989)

Experimental Methods

The study described in this paper is based on the results of two experiments that were conducted over a period of two weeks. The first experiment involved a design exercise while the second involved various evaluation tasks. Each of the experiments is briefly described below.

The Design Experiment

For this experiment the subjects (N=30) were randomly split into two equal groups (A and B). Group A was required to design a set of 10 icons relating to the domain of electronic mail (e-mail) while Group B had to perform a similar task for an information retrieval (IR) application. Each group was given a colour-coded (pink for e-mail or blue for IR) design booklet that contained: a) instructions on what to do; and b) a list of 10 functions for each of which, each individual in a particular group had to design an icon. The functions for which subjects had to design icons are listed in Table 1.

Within the design booklets, subjects were given, for each icon, a rectilinear area (measuring 32 mm x 28 mm) within which they had to produce their 'pencil and paper' designs. Some space was also provided (alongside the design space) so that subjects could briefly explain the rationale underlying their designs.

The design booklets were produced in such a way that subjects were not exposed to any particular design task until it was time for them to attempt it. Subjects were allowed 3.5 minutes to design each icon. At the end of the experiment the design booklets were collected in and used to prepare the materials for the second experiment.

The Evaluation Experiment

The evaluation experiment was conducted two weeks later. The two-week gap was required in order to prepare the resources that were needed. This experiment was more

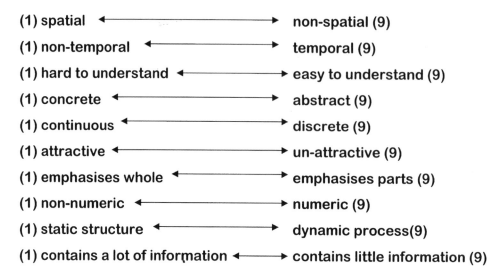

Figure 6. Icon classification according to Lohse et al (1994)

involved and required the preparation of three sets of overhead transparencies, a set of answer sheets and an evaluation workbook containing selections of icons. Icons for these studies were selected both from professional sources and from those designed by the subjects. The professional icons were taken from Windows 95 (for general icons), Microsoft's Outlook Express (for e-mail icons) and Internet Explorer (for IR icons).

The experimental design for the objective evaluation tasks employed three independent variables. The variables were design source (student or professional), design experience in a particular domain (e-mail or IR); and domain (e-mail, IR or general). The design is presented in Table 2.

The first three tasks in the evaluation experiment were used to evaluate icons objectively. The transparencies referred to above were used for this purpose. Each set of transparencies contained a total of 30 icons. The same icons were used in the three sets but the order in which they appeared within each set was different and random. Of the 30 icons, 10 were general function icons taken from Windows 95. Five were e-mail icons from Outlook Express and another five were icons (designed by students from Group A in the design experiment) for the same e-mail functions. A further five icons were IR functions taken from Internet Explorer and the final five were icons designed by students (from Group B in the design experiment) for the same IR functions.

The first icon set was used to evaluate function recall; the second set was used to investigate object recognition; and the third set was used to explore whether or not subjects were making any initial association between embedded object and icon function. While performing these evaluation tasks, subjects were exposed to each icon (using an overhead projector) for a period of 30 seconds. Subjects were given answer sheets upon which to record their responses – one answer sheet for each evaluation task.

Group A: Electronic Mail
Function 1: *Compose a Message*
Function 2: *Create 'Carbon Copy' of Message to Secondary Recipient*
Function 3: *Send Message*
Function 4: *Read Message*
Function 5: *Reply to Message*
Function 6: *Forward Message*
Function 7: *Archive Message*
Function 8: *Manage Mail Folders*
Function 9: *Manage Address Book*
Function 10: *Manage Distribution Lists*

Group B: Information Retrieval
Function 1: *Local Search of Current Document*
Function 2: *Global Search Using a Search Engine*
Function 3: *Display Next Set of Results*
Function 4: *Display Previous Set of Results*
Function 5: *Save Search Results in a Local File*
Function 6: *Cancel Search*
Function 7: *Search Abstracts*
Function 8: *Search Full-Text*
Function 9: *Go Back One Step*
Function 10: *Go Forward One Step*

Table 1. Icon design tasks

The evaluation booklet was used to evaluate icons subjectively by investigating subjects' preferences for icons. The booklet contained two sections – one for the electronic mail icons and one for the icons relating to information retrieval. Each section of the book contained 10 pages (one per function) and each page contained a matrix of 15 icons (labelled 1 through 15) that were taken from the results of the design experiment. The last page in the evaluation booklet contained a questionnaire that was employed in order to identify the e-mail packages, Web browsers and Internet search engines that the participants claimed to have used.

As directed by the experimenter, subjects worked through the evaluation booklet one page at a time and were allowed 30 seconds to select their preferred icon from the array presented on a given page. During the 30-second period, and prior to turning to the next page, subjects were required to enter 'the number' of their preferred icon (for that page) into a box that appeared at the bottom of the page. At the end of the experiment all the answer sheets and evaluation booklets were collected. The data that they contained was then transcribed into a Microsoft Excel spreadsheet (in order to extract basic statistics) and subsequently processed using the SPSS package.

	Email			IR			General		
	Prof.[1]	Student[2]		Prof.	Student		Prof.	Student	
		Self[3]	Other[4]		Self	Other		Self	Other
Group A Email designers (n = 12)	5[5]	5	-	5	-	5	10	-	-
Group B IR designers (n = 14)	5	-	5	5	5	-	10	-	-

1 professionally designed; 2 designed by students; 3 designed for this domain themselves in the design experiment; 4 other group designed for this domain in the design experiment; 5 number of icons presented

Table 2. Experimental design for objective evaluation tasks

Demographic Details

Demographic data was collected at the beginning of both the design and the evaluation experiment. This was obtained using forms that were embedded at the front of the booklets and answer sheets that were used in each of the experiments.

The subjects involved in the study were all students studying a final year module in human–computer interaction (HCI). For the evaluation experiment there were 31 subjects, 26 of whom had participated in the previous design experiment. Of these, 12 had been in the e-mail group and the other 14 were members of the IR group. The remaining five had not participated in the design experiment. The average age of the participants was 24.3 years (SD = 4.2). Considering both experiments together, there was a total of 7 females and 28 male participants. The distribution of academic subjects (by degree course) for the group was as follows: Information Sciences (11), Informatics (7), Software Engineering (2),Computer Science (8), Information Technology (2) and Business Computing (5).

On average, for the second experiment, participants claimed to have had used two Web browsers, two e-mail packages and three search engines. The most popular packages were: Pegasus Mail (27), Microsoft Outlook (13) and Pine (10) for e-mail; Netscape Navigator (29) and Internet Explorer (24) for Web browsing; and Yahoo (25), AltaVista (24), Infoseek (13) and Lycos (14) for Internet searching.

Results

In this section we discuss the results obtained from the experiments that have been undertaken. Particular attention is given to the effects of the independent variables on icon function identification, our model of icon processing, icon quality and participants' preferences for icons.

Effects of Independent Variables on Icon Function Identification

The effects of various independent variables on the correctness of function identification ('function recall') have been examined. The relevant descriptive statistics are presented in Tables 3 through 6.

The e-mail and IR groups did not differ when recalling:

(a) functions in a particular domain (e-mail or IR) for which they had designed icons themselves;

(b) icons in a particular domain for which they had not designed icons themselves (but for which the other group had designed icons); and

(c) general icons, that is, not specific for a particular domain (Table 3).

These findings are confirmed by statistically significant results from t-tests: (a) $t(24) = 0.476$, $p = 0.639$, (b) $t(24) = -0.821$, $p = 0.420$, (c) $t(24) = 0.853$, $p = 0.402$.

When investigating the effect of design expertise, it was found that the e-mail group was better at recalling:

(a) e-mail icons that were designed professionally compared with e-mail icons that the e-mail group had designed themselves; and

(b) IR icons that were designed professionally compared with IR icons that the IR group had designed (Table 4).

Finding (b) was confirmed with a significant test result ($t(11) = 4.170$, $p = 0.002$) while finding (a) was nearly significant ($t(11) = 2.092$, $p = 0.06$).

The IR group was better at recalling:

(a) IR icons that were designed professionally compared with those that the IR group had designed themselves; and

(b) e-mail icons that were designed professionally compared with those that the e-mail group had designed (Table 4).

Both of the above results were statistically significant: (a) $t(13) = 9.824$, $p < 0.0001$; and (b) $t(13) = 4.650$, $p < 0.0001$.

When studying the effect of design experience, it was found that the e-mail group was better at recalling e-mail icons designed by the group itself than it was at recalling IR icons designed by the IR group (Table 5) – a statistically significant result ($t(11) = 3.275$, $p = 0.007$). Similarly, the IR group was better at recalling IR icons designed by

	Email group		IR group	
Self-designed	41.6667*	(23.2900)**	37.5000	(21.3713)
Other-student designed	20.8333	(17.9435)	25.7143	(12.2250)
General icons	54.1667	(15.3864)	48.2143	(19.5239)

* mean; ** standard deviation;

Table 3. Function recall for the two groups

	Email group		IR group	
Self-designed	41.6667	(23.2900)	37.5000	(21.3713)
Professionally designed	55.5556	(16.1422)	88.5714	(15.1186)
Other-designed	20.8333	(17.9435)	25.7143	(12.2250)
Professionally designed	58.3333	(23.2900)	47.6190	(17.1184)

Table 4. Function recall and design expertise

the group itself than it was at recalling e-mail icons designed by the e-mail group (Table 5) – again a statistically significant result was observed ($t(11) = 2.552$, $p = 0.024$).

The investigation into the effect of domain revealed that the IR group was better at recalling specific (e-mail and IR icons) than it was at recalling general icons (Table 6) – a statistically significant result ($t(13) = -3.356$, $p = 0.005$). There was no difference in recall for specific compared to general icons for the e-mail group (Table 6).

Evidence for Model of Icon Processing

Correlations over 27 of the 30 icons used in the recall tasks (tasks 1, 2, and 3) were used to obtain empirical evidence relating to our model of icon processing. Three icons that had a function recall of 0% were excluded from the analysis. Significant correlations were found between the percentages of correctly recalled objects and correctly recalled functions ($r = 0.437$, $p = 0.023$) and between the percentages of correctly recalled functions and an initial link being made between icon and object before identifying the function ($r = -0.615$, $p = 0.001$). This means that there is a positive correspondence between the recall of an icon's function and the ease with which the object embedded within that icon is recalled. There is also a negative correspondence between the recall of an icon's function and the likelihood of an initial association being made. A trend towards a significant correlation was found between the percentage of correctly recalled objects and an initial link being made ($r = -0.333$, $p = 0.09$).

A multiple regression showed that function recall was significantly related to both object recall and an initial association being made – with $R^2 = 0.439$, $F(2,24) = 9.399$, $p = 0.001$. This means that 43.9% of the variability in function recall was accounted for by object recall and an initial link being made.

Quality of Icons in Relation to Model of Icon Processing

Icon quality can be related to our model of icon processing based on the following considerations:

(a) correct function recall without an initial association being made involves less cognitive effort than (and is therefore preferred over) correct function recall with such an association; and

(b) correct function recall combined with correct object recall will make incorrect function identification less likely when the icon is used repeatedly in an end-user interface and is therefore preferable over correct function recall combined with incorrect object recall.

These observations lead us to propose the gradation of icon quality that is presented in Table 7.

	Email group		IR group	
Self-designed	41.6667	(23.2900)	37.5000	(21.3713)
Other-student designed	20.8333	(17.9435)	25.7143	(12.2250)

Table 5. Function recall and design experience

	Email group		IR group	
General icons	54.1667	(15.3864)	48.2143	(19.5239)
Email and IR icons	56.9444	(14.9381)	68.0952	(12.9241)

Table 6. Functions and recall domain

The best icons are those that do not involve an initial association but where the object is correctly recalled (Q1). Second best are those icons for which the object is correctly recalled and an initial association is made (Q2). The third best are those that do not involve an initial association and where the object is not correctly recalled (Q3). Finally, the worst icons are those that do involve an initial association but where the object is not correctly recalled (Q4).

Two analyses were carried out to provide evidence for our gradation system.

First, excluding the three icons that had a function recall of 0 per cent, we compared the percentage of quality gradations of the four icons with best function recall with those of the 23 other icons (see Table 7). There was a significant difference between the four best icons and the other icons for Q1, Q2 and Q4 (Q1: $t(22) = -6.469$, $p = 0.000$, Q2: $t(22) = 2.429$, $p = 0.024$, Q4: $t(22) = 2.748$, $p = 0.012$) but not for Q3.

Second, over 27 icons (excluding three icons with 0 per cent function recall), correlations between the percentage of correctly recalled functions and the percentage of quality gradations showed that Q1 was significantly positively correlated with function recall and Q4 was significantly negatively correlated with function recall; neither Q2 nor Q3 were correlated with function recall (Table 8).

A multiple regression showed that function recall was significantly related to both Q1 and Q4 with $R^2 = 0.245$, $F(2,24) = 3.885$, $p = 0.035$. This means that 24.5 per cent of variability in function recall was accounted for by correct object recall without initial association (Q1) and incorrect object recall with an initial association (Q4).

Quality of Icons in Relation to Icon Characteristics

The 10 nine-point rating scales from Lohse et al. (1994) were used to rate each of the 30 icons used in the recall tasks. Two judges independently rated the icons. After debate some scores were modified to accommodate the results of the discussion. The two ratings for each icon were averaged and, if the average was a fraction, rounded towards the more extreme end-point of the scale. If raters showed different polarity, the middle scale value (5) was taken; these scores were discarded in the final analysis. Analysis of correlations showed that none of the scales was significantly correlated with function recall.

	Icon recalled	Object recalled	Initial association made	Percentage‡	Percentage†
Q1	Correctly	Correctly	No	59.20 (13.34)	25.27 (25.00)
Q2	Correctly	Correctly	Yes	28.79 (6.20)	43.68 (29.00)
Q3	Correctly	Incorrectly	No	6.45 (6.35)	5.411 (8.25)
Q4	Correctly	Incorrectly	Yes	5.56 (6.42)	25.63 (34.26)

‡ data from the 4 best icons (function recall ≥ 90%);
† data from 23 icons, excluding the four best icons in terms of function recall

Table 7. Gradations of icon quality for the four best icons

N = 27 icons	Icon recalled	Object recalled	Initial association made	Correlation with percentage of correct function recall
Q1	Correctly	Correctly	No	0.437 (p = 0.022)
Q2	Correctly	Correctly	Yes	0.090 (p = 0.654)
Q3	Correctly	Incorrectly	No	0.076 (p = 0.705)
Q4	Correctly	Incorrectly	Yes	-0.452 (p = 0.018)

Table 8. Function recall correlated with icon quality gradations

Preference

The frequency of preference for each icon that was included in the preference rating task was calculated for both the e-mail and the IR group. The difference between the groups was calculated for the icons representing each function. On average there were small differences in preference for icons: 6.67 per cent for e-mail icons and 4.89 per cent for IR icons.

Overall, preferences for icons were equally spread. However, 13 out of 300 icons were preferred by more than 25 per cent of participants. These are presented in Figure 7.

The same procedure as was described above was used for rating the 13 most preferred icons. Table 9 shows the rated characteristics of these icons. The most prominent characteristics of the icons were that they were concrete rather than abstract, discrete rather than continuous and non-numeric rather numeric.

Discussion

Our research has explored the effect of the following variables on icon function identification: design expertise; design experience in a particular domain; and icon domain. More specifically, our results indicate that: professionally designed icons were better recalled than those designed by students; design experience in a domain enhanced recall in that domain; and specific icons were better recalled than general ones by those who had designed icons for information retrieval.

Our model of icon processing (see Figure 3) proposes that there are three possible cognitive steps involved in identifying an icon's function. According to the model, the best icons are those for which: a) the function is correctly recalled; b) the object is correctly recalled; and c) no initial association is made. Our results show that object recall is positively correlated to function recall and that making an initial association is negatively correlated to function recall.

Furthermore, with correct function recall, the best icons were found to have:

- a higher percentage of correct object recall combined with no initial association being made;
- a lower percentage of correct object recall combined with an initial association being made; and
- a lower percentage of incorrect function recall combined with an initial association being made.

These findings and significant correlations between function recall and our gradation system for icon quality (in particular, the highest and the lowest gradation) support this system that is based on our model of icon processing. These results also provide evidence for the effects of 'external' influences within the model of icon processing.

Although existing icon classifications such as Rogers's (1989) and Lohse et al's (1994) do not seem to have been produced with the aim of predicting icon quality in mind, we have argued that the usefulness

Figure 7. Most preferred icons in the evaluation experiment

of any classification should be judged by its correlation with correct function identification. This will make it possible to predict the quality of icons based on their characteristics as defined by a classification. Our study found that the rating scales from Lohse et al's (1994) classification did not correlate with correct function identification.

Our study found that participants' preference for icons is not affected by design experience in a particular domain.

A limitation of the current study is that the student participants were only allowed a short time to design icons, although designing 'good' icons will usually take more time. Related to this, the study did not include a 'control' group of professional designers designing within the same time constraints as the student designers. The present study included three domains: e-mail, information retrieval and general. In order to generalise our findings, more domains would need to be studied. Of course, the bandwidth of the icons that were used in the evaluation experiment was limited

		Mean	s.d.
Spatial	Non-spatial	3.54	2.50
Non-temporal	Temporal	3.08	2.47
Hard to understand	Easy to understand	7.23	1.42
Concrete	Abstract	1.46	.78
Continuous	Discrete	8.46	1.66
Attractive	Unattractive	3.12	1.46
Emphasises whole	Emphasises parts	7.31	2.84
Non-numeric	Numeric	1.00	.00
Static structure	Dynamic process	2.69	2.39

Table 9. Rated characteristics of the 13 most preferred icons

since all the icons that were used in the recall tasks (tasks 1, 2, 3) had to be redrawn by hand.

Conclusions

Within most interactive computer systems, graphical user interfaces (GUIs) and the icons that they embed are important 'interface agents' that can be used to facilitate effective and efficient human–computer interaction. However, the design of icons and icon sets for particular applications is often quite problematic because of the many 'uncontrollable' variables and design parameters that are involved. Bearing this in mind, in this paper we have discussed some of the problems of designing and evaluating icons for use within particular application domains.

Two experiments have been described: a design experiment and an evaluation experiment. In the design study, two groups of students each designed an icon set for use within a particular application domain (either electronic mail or information retrieval). In the evaluation study the same students, acting as a single group, evaluated a 'mixed' selection of icons. The icons in this 'evaluation' set originated either from the design experiment or from a professional source. In order to investigate the influence of domain and prior experience on recall and preference, the data that we have obtained has been subjected to statistical analysis. This paper has described the findings from our research and we have discussed their implications with respect to developing a basic model for designing icons.

Regarding icon design, we argue that theoretical guidelines, backed up with empirical evidence, are needed. These need to be based on research, as exemplified by the present study, which investigates what happens when a user is exposed to an icon.

Related to icon evaluation, our model of icon processing (that can be viewed as an extension of previous models of icon referencing) has been backed up with empirical evidence. The model determines the evaluation methodology of icons in terms of tasks to be completed in evaluation experiments (function recall, object recall, initial association between icon and object). The icon classification hypothesis provides a way to determine the usefulness of icon classifications and should stimulate further classification development.

References

Barker, P.G. and van Schaik, P. (1999a).' Icons in the Mind', Paper presented at the 2nd International Workshop on Iconic Communication, University of the West of England, Bristol, UK (See Chapter 12 of this book).

Barker, P.G. and van Schaik, P. (1999b). 'Mental Models and their Implications for the Design of Computer-Based Learning Resources', 1-12 in '*CBLIS 99 – Proceedings of the Fourth International Conference on Computer-Based Learning in Science*', G. Chapman (ed.), University of Ostrava Press, Czech Republic.

De Carolis, B., De Rosis, F. and Errore, S. (1995) 'A User-Adapted Iconic Language for the Medical Domain', *International Journal of Human-Computer Studies*, 43(4), 561-71.

Familant, M.E. and Detweiler, M.C. (1993). Iconic Reference: 'Evolving Perspectives and an Organising Framework', *International Journal of Man-Machine Studies*, 39, 705-28.

Gittins, D. (1986). 'Icon-based Human-Computer Interaction', *International Journal of Man-Machine Studies*, 24(6), 519-43.

Honeywill, P. (1999). *Visual Language for the World Wide Web*, Intellect, Exeter, UK.

Horton, W. (1994). *The Icon Book: Visual Symbols for Computer Systems and Documentation*, John Wiley and Sons, NY.

Lohse, G., Walker, N., Biolsi, K. and Rueter, H. (1991). 'Classifying Graphical Information', *Behaviour and Information Technology*, 10(5), 419-36.

Lohse, G. Biolsi, K., Walker, N., and Rueter, H. (1994). 'A Classification of Visual Representations', *Communications of the Association of Computing Machinery*, 37(12), 36-49.

Pitman, J.A.and Payne, S.J. (1998). 'Choosing and Using Names for Information Retrieval, 102-103', in *HCI '98 Conference Companion*, HCI Specialist Group, British Computer Society, UK.

Rogers, Y. (1989). 'Icons at the Interface', *Interacting with Computers*, 1(1), 105-17.

Sassoon, R. and Gaur, A. (1997). *Signs, Symbols and Icons: Pre-History to the Computer Age*, Intellect, Exeter, UK.

Yamakawa, J.K., Miller, N. and Hutchinson, R.D. (1997). 'An Evaluation of Icon Performance Based on User Preferences', chap. 4 (pp. 35-50) in J.Carey (ed.), '*Human Factors in Information Systems: the Relationship between User Interface and Human Performance*', Ablex, London.

14. Evaluating Appropriate Interface Metaphors

Paul Honeywill

Overview

Observing people using computers might suggest that those who don't ask for assistance or an explanation are probably achieving their task. This is an assumption – an empirical approach would be to get behind the interface and track, monitor and generate a computer report on how users react to different interface metaphors which range from abstract to representative and among their own family compound icon groups, to discover without bias what precisely happens. This chapter is in three parts: 1) an explanation of an interface that has user tracking and monitoring built into the program so that the data will record the users' exact positions and routes through an interface, 2) system interface iconography, and 3) identifying interface visual language that has naturally evolved throughout the World Wide Web and how this will determine which interface icons might be a stating point to build a test interface that tracks, monitors and reports on user comprehension.

Introduction

Aaron Marcus (1999) declares that 'shockingly, in some of our projects, our clients never do call in users. . . however, we work as designers to prepare prototypes that are then evaluated by users'. Judith Sims-Knight (1992, pp.324-87) is a Professor of Psychology at the University of Massachusetts; she considers that users should be 'presented with scenarios, which allowed users to experience the interface behaviourally'. Judith Olson and Thomas Moran (1996, p.271-2) believe that for the evaluation of interfaces there are 'few complete methods'. They do, however, consider that approaches such as 'Cognitive Walkthrough' allow designers to improve interfaces when the user 'first walks up to it'. Cognitive Walkthrough asks questions of the user about how easy it was for them to 'discover how to do the next step'. Olson and Moran go on to say that users should also be observed and invited to join and influence the design process. One problem is that the users then become removed from 'stepping up' to the interface for the first time. They begin to form certain biases and assumptions that are no different from the designers themselves. A method for evaluating interfaces requires achieving results that are repeatable and possibly carried out on a test group or groups that have some incentive to engage with an interface. Before users 'step-up', as Olson and Moran have already said, they should first know what those benefits actually are and 'perhaps even enjoy using it'.

The ARC Interface

If learner investment is through incentive, to gain from that investment knowing what that investment is helps to decide how far a lexicon can go for a group that has an interest in using a particular interface. The ARC (Arts Research into Communication) was a series of innovative projects through 'virtual collaboration' with two institutions in the United Kingdom and one each from France and Spain and between campuses of the University of Plymouth. This series of projects is known as the Atlantis InterArc EC Research Programme. The first phase established parity for shared screen and simultaneous voice communication via ISDN (Integrated Services Digital Network) Planet II. The establishment of a 'Virtual Studio' at each location allowed each group to exchange files, see other computer screens at remote locations and operate other computer systems. The purpose of the project was to evaluate the convergence of technology between computers and communication and the natural development of computer compound icons within the group. Comprehension of specific navigational interface icons was designed in such a way that the interface could track, monitor and report back user comprehension, learning time and navigational preferences.

Stuart Card, Thomas Moran and Allen Newell (1983, p.404) state that 'the basic performance variables of a human–computer system are concerned with what tasks the system can do (functionality), how long it takes to acquire the functionality (learning), how long it takes to accomplish tasks (time), how frequently errors occur and how consequential they are, how well tasks are done (quality)'. For this reason the title screen of the ARC has four hidden 'rollover' navigation points; all are visible on mouse-up; each individual compound icon is visible on rollover. Once these points are learned they continue to be located in the same positions in the actual content of the ARC and therefore the user learns the rollover positions and knows their navigational significance. The advantage of this is that the content is not cluttered with compound icons, leaving the graphical user interface clear to perform the functions of the ARC's content. The home screen contains all the navigational icon points and on mouse-up the user is required to return to the home screen via the initial set of rollover icons. The four hidden rollover icons on both the title and home screen remain constant throughout. Once their position and action has been learned the user can always expect to find them at these navigational points. These four compound icons represent the 'Oops button', which takes the user back one screen; 'Volume button' which adjusts the sound levels; 'Home screen button' which returns the user to the home screen; and 'Help button' which explains how to navigate, this is for users who are lost but would still like to browse the ARC (Figure 1).

The home screen contains three of these icons, as the home screen button is not required. This screen contains a further two sets of compound icons. The first set is concerned with the classification of the contents of the ARC, i.e. Timebased, Sound, Still and Interactive. These icons closely resemble each other and because the differences are minimal their function is only apparent on mouse-up when they become motion dynamic. These icons require the user to make distinctions between icons which closely resemble each other. The only other distinguishing feature of the compound icon is its location. However, to track and monitor user learning, the icons

Figure 1. a) The title screen for the ARC. b) On mouse-up all screen navigational icons are visible

are clustered closely together near the centre and bottom of the screen (Figure 2b). Upon entrance to the content of the ARC a second set of compound icons appear as a new bottom row. These additional icons are also designed as part of the representational family group of compound icons (Figure 3b, bottom row, beginning left); firstly listing the artists in that category, secondly comments by the originator of that specific work and, thirdly other titles of work by that artist contained within the ARC.

The ARC Evaluation

To evaluate the ARC interface 10 test subjects were asked to complete the same task three times and then change the sequence and repeat that task twice. The combined purpose of the tasks was to understand how the user acquires the denotative values of interface metaphors. The test subjects were divided into two groups of five and choice of group was left to individual members. Those who felt less confident about using a computer gravitated towards the 'with lexicon group' (Group A), whereas more experienced subjects saw a non-lexicon test as a challenge (Group B). After the grouping was decided each test subject was individually instructed before launching the program. On entry to the program Group A was directed to the 'help' button while Group B was told not to select help if that target compound icon was rolled over. The task for both groups was to locate and select (click) four navigational compound icons; IA Interactive Artists (Figures 4a static, 4b dynamic) and TA Timebased Artists (Figures 4c static, 4d dynamic) – one static/representative; V Volume (Figure 14a) – one dynamic/representative; Q Quit (Figure 4f static, 4g dynamic). The task also had to be carried out in sequence, IA* TA* V* Q* (three attempts) and then change sequence to evaluate spatial memory to IA* TA* V* Q* (two attempts). This would generate five reports on each subject.

 The reports that were generated log the time spent at a target location. For example, 'starting now 1:51:26 pm Monday 22 February 1999, home screen at: 1:51:28 pm Monday 22 February 1999, rolled over volume at: 1:51:29 pm Monday 22 February 1999, changed volume at: 1:51:29 pm Monday 22 February 1999, home screen at: 1:51:31

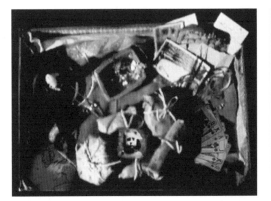
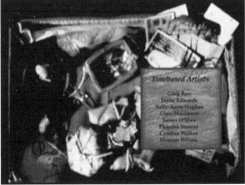

Figure 2. a) On entry no icons are visible. b) Positions of all navigational icons.
c) Timebased icon up on rollover. d) Animation of icon and selection window on mouse-up.

pm Monday 22 February 1999'. This five-second example shows that the user launched the program at 1:51:26, the cursor then moved across a non-target area (the home screen) until the volume control icon was reached three seconds later. The volume was changed immediately; the test subject then stayed within the volume control for a total of two seconds before moving on. The detail of the reports for 10 users record the average time spent on all five tasks as 4 minutes and 52 seconds generating 19,915 icon names, times, events and subsequent actions. A second report was written to extract the required data for each of the five attempts – duration, quit, time spent at the interface, return visits to icons, target icons that were rolled over, target icons that were selected (clicked), off target icons that were rolled over or selected, and if the final sequence was accurate. The actual sequence was also included with selection indicated by * and hit icon targets indicted with bold type. For example, 2D* TA 2D AN AN IA LG* Q* (Figure 5, legend). The second report also allows for additional observations such as recovery time by the subject when off target. There are many occurrences in the later reports where the earlier reports indicate that the target icons have been visited, for example, in subject eight, the third report includes the recovery time between Q Q* as 1 second and between TA TA IA* as 2 seconds. These reports

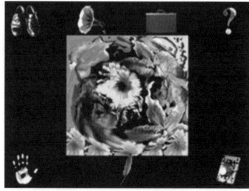

Figure 3. a) On entry no icons are visible. b) Positions of all navigational icons.

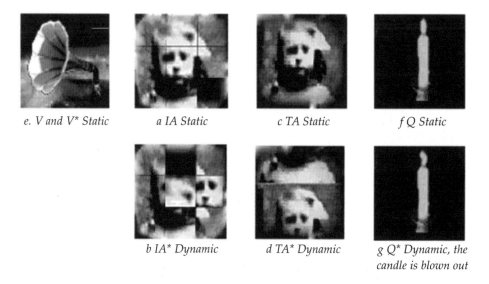

*Figure 4. The icons and their actions that had to be selected by each test subject. Within the data collection * indicates that a selection (click) has been made.*

establish that the test subject understands the lexicon but that the sequence was technically incorrect.

The second report was used to generate a table of key interface events for all five reports and included technically incorrect but where the subsequent reports show the sum total of correct target icon hits with no attempt to select the off target icon, and that the recovery time is within 3 seconds. On the second launch of the program four members of Group A had successfully selected all target icons; by the third launch all members had been successful (Figure 6.1). Group B fared less well and had not

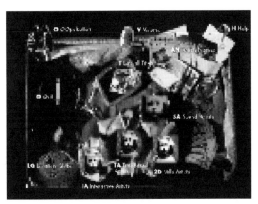

Figure 5. Legend of all possible target icons. For example, the actual sequence of test subject 10 (Group B, without lexicon), first report O O AN H AN T Q LG IA IA TA 2D 2D LG* IA IA* TA TA* TA 2D T Q O V H V V TA V* O H H 2D TA T LG LG O H AN T Q LG IA TA 2D T Q T Q T Q T * Q* and test subject ten final report V* IA* TA* Q*.

identified all target icons until the last attempt. During the first attempt all members of Group A, except one, had selected the target icons, whereas Group B members had not identified all target icons until the fifth attempt (Figure 6.7). Learning time was greater during the first attempt by Group A with an average of 1 minute 45 seconds learning the lexicon and an average of 1 minute 44 seconds hunting for compound icon locations within the interface. Upon the second attempt, this group spent an average of 26 seconds attempting to accomplish the task. Group B took five times longer during the second attempt and parity was reached during the third and subsequent attempts.

Group B hit nearly double the amount of target icons during their first attempt and 13 times more target icons during the second attempt (Figure 6.4). This is partly due to a missing lexicon which was still incomplete for one member until the final attempt (Figure 6.3). Also during the second attempt Group A returned to the target icons 12 more times than was necessary, whereas Group B returned 114 times to confirm the compound icons meaning (Figure 6.9). Not all of these returns were to target icons; off target icons had to be explored so that they could be dismissed. However, there are more compound icons that need to explain themselves by becoming motion dynamic than there are representative static compound icons. It is not shown in the table but in the actual reports the least hits were on icons that represented what they are; all reports showed that their position was known but was not considered a target and most compound icon hits were ones that required the subjects to learn their meaning.

Low hits and no selection of the representational buttons are probably due to an attribute of the cursor that was not disclosed to either groups which was the 'all icons displayed' feature. This shows all interface icons when the mouse is held down on the home screen. All subjects found and used this feature from the first report to the last and therefore all subjects were aware of representational compound icons on the interface. Off target representational icons were hit such as 'Oops back one screen' but only three times by Group A and 22 times by Group B. Compared to other off target compound icons which need further explanation (T AN SA 2D and LG), the hit rate was low and no test subject attempted to select the 'Oops' icon, indicating that it did not represent a target compound icon, and its meaning in this context appears to be understood.

Returned Data from the Report Logs

Time Spent at Interface and Use of Lexicon

Minutes:seconds	A With Lexicon 5 Subjects					B Without Lexicon 5 Subjects				
	Time	1	2	3	4	Time	1	2	3	4
First Report	3:29	0	0	4	92	2:38	0	0	3	159
Second Report	0:26	4	2	5	7	1:23	1	0	3	91
Third Report	0:18	5	3	5	3	0:21	4	1	5	8

Changed Sequence

	Time	1	2	3	4	Time	1	2	3	4
Fourth Report	0:20	5	1	5	8	0:21	4	1	5	13
Fifth Report	0:13	5	3	5	2	0:15	5	2	5	4

Total Time Spent   4:46   Average at help 1:45   4:58

Use of lexicon cont.	A With Lexicon 5 Subjects					B Without Lexicon 5 Subjects				
	5	6	7	8	9	5	6	7	8	9
First Report	74	68	19	6	142	90	133	15	12	150
Second Report	23	9	20	0	32	67	67	16	9	134
Third Report	23	1	20	0	24	28	4	19	0	32

Changed Sequence

	5	6	7	8	9	5	6	7	8	9
Fourth Report	29	2	20	0	31	33	4	19	0	37
Fifth Report	21	0	20	0	21	23	1	20	0	24

1. Technically Incorrect but with lexicon understood (previous reports form each test subject show the sum total of correct icon target hits).
2. Technically correct with no OFF target hits and where all icons have been selected (clicked).
3. Number of subjects that have identified dynamic, static/representational and dynamic/representational target icons.
4. Return visits to OFF and ON target icons.
5. ON Target icons hit.
6. OFF Target icons hit.
7. Selected motion dynamic, static/representational and dynamic/representational ON target (excluding duplicate hits). 20 individual hits required for full lexicon.
8. Selected motion dynamic, static/dynamic representational OFF target (excluding duplicate hits).
9. Total icon hits.

Figure 6. The Key data from these tables have been highlighted to show when full use of the lexicon is understood and what those implications are across a range of interface events .

By deploying user tracking behind the interface compound icons can be evaluated and those that are least successful can be exchanged allowing the interface to be re-evaluated through the data that is impartial and without bias. However, it must be recognised, as stated by Card, Moran and Newell (ibid. p.404), that 'users vary widely in general intellectual ability, experience with computers, specific knowledge of the task, specific knowledge of the computer, cognitive style, and perceptual-motor skills. . . finally there are variables concerning the user's subjective feeling about the system'. In order to apply the ARCs approach to program interface icons, user goals need to be known; therefore further tests are carried out to gauge user comprehension and assumption when using icons as function.

User Goals and Sub-Goals

David Canter (1978, p.261) writes that 'to evaluate systems for people who have particular goals to achieve it is necessary to identify what those characteristics are which lead to people needing to rely upon the system provided. It is then necessary to identify what are the family of goals and sub-goals which these users are likely to have.' Card, Moran and Newell (1983, p.10) write of applied psychology in the context of user goals and state that 'humans behave in a goal-orientated way. Within their limited perceptual and information-processing abilities, they attempt to adapt to the task environment to attain their goals.' Microsoft Word is one of many word processing programs which enable the user to carry out a number of tasks – the user has incentive to learn how to use this program but has to learn the lexicon to engage in a dialogue. However, much of this can be achieved through a user's 'one-way pidgin' version of human–computer discourse through what they already know (in the sense that it is derived from a language, creates its own method of use by adapting syntax and where the outcome is recognisable but the method is not necessarily desirable). In order to address this Olson and Moran (1996, p.272) suggest that the user must perceive a benefit from using the interface as it was intended. However, many actions are learned and habits are formed before this point is actually reached.

The Program Interface

Word is similar to other programs in how it functions by relying upon Apple's original approach of 'hey you – do this'. As pointed out earlier, to aid user comprehension requires standardisation across programs. The program uses many icon elements to build compound icons which are used within other programs, yet it also uses icon elements that are specific to Microsoft Word. In order to gauge user comprehension 20 test subjects were asked to use the program. This ensured that 'pointing and clicking' on an icon was in context. The results were divided into two groups, those that used Microsoft Word as their main word processing program (14) and those that used a different word processing program (5, with 2 invalidated). All test subjects where first year undergraduates who had received computer induction before the test, all had used word processing programs but not necessarily Microsoft Word (Figure 7).

Overall both groups paralleled each other in their comprehension of what individual and family groups of compound icons meant. Although Denis McQuail and

185

	1	2	3	4	5	6	6	8	9	10	11	12
1) User Correct	12	12	10	14	11	10	5	2	12	1	-	5
2) Correct Context	1	-	1	-	1	-	-	2	-	4	5	6
3) Attempted/Incorrect	1	2	3	-	2	2	6	8	-	5	6	2
4) No attempt	-	-	-	-	-	2	3	2	2	4	3	1
5) Non-User Correct	3	3	3	5	5	3	2	1	3	-	-	3
6) Correct Context	1	1	-	-	-	-	-	-	-	3	3	-
7) Attempted/Incorrect	1	-	2	-	-	2	2	4	1	-	-	-
8) No Attempt	-	1	-	-	-	-	1	-	1	2	2	2

	13	14	15	16	17	18	19	20	21	22
1) User Correct	11	6	5	8	8	1	4	4	-	7
2) Correct Context	-	1	4	2	2	7	1	2	1	-
3) Attempted/Incorrect	1	3	1	2	2	2	1	4	4	-
4) No attempt	2	4	4	2	2	4	8	4	9	7
5) Non-User Correct	4	1	2	2	2	2	2	2	-	2
6) Correct Context	-	1	-	1	1	1	1	-	-	-
7) Attempted/Incorrect	-	1	-	-	-	-	-	-	2	-
8) No Attempt	1	2	3	2	2	2	2	3	3	3

	23	24	25	26	27	28	29	30	31
1) User Correct	1	3	-	-	-	2	4	11	2
2) Correct Context	1	1	-	-	-	5	1	1	2
3) Attempted/Incorrect	9	6	10	7	5	1	1	-	10
4) No attempt	3	4	4	7	9	6	8	2	-
5) Non-User Correct	-	-	-	-	1	1	2	5	1
6) Correct Context	-	-	-	-	-	-	-	-	1
7) Attempted/Incorrect	3	2	2	2	1	1	-	-	-
8) No Attempt	2	3	3	3	3	3	3	-	2

186

	32	33	34	35	36	37	38	39	40	41	42	43	44
1) User Correct	11	11	12	10	13	13	13	1	1	8	11	6	1
2) Correct Context	1	-	-	-	-	-	-	1	1	3	1	2	2
3) Attempted/Incorrect	-	-	-	3	-	-	-	7	7	1	2	4	5
4) No attempt	2	3	2	1	1	1	1	5	5	2	-	2	6
5) Non-User Correct	4	4	4	3	4	5	5	1	1	4	4	1	-
6) Correct Context	-	-	-	-	1	-	-	-	-	-	-	1	-
7) Attempted/Incorrect	-	-	-	1	-	-	-	4	4	1	-	1	1
8) No Attempt	1	1	1	1	-	-	-	-	-	-	1	2	4

	45	46	47	48	49	50	51	52	53	54	55	56	57
1) User Correct	11	11	12	10	6	6	1	1	1	1	1	-	-
2) Correct Context	-	2	1	1	4	5	3	3	-	1	1	-	-
3) Attempted/Incorrect	2	-	-	-	-	-	2	2	1	1	2	1	1
4) No attempt	1	1	1	3	4	3	8	8	12	11	10	13	13
5) Non-User Correct	3	3	3	2	1	1	1	1	-	-	-	-	-
6) Correct Context	-	-	-	-	1	1	1	1	-	-	-	-	-
7) Attempted/Incorrect	-	-	-	1	1	1	-	-	-	-	-	-	-
8) No Attempt	2	2	2	2	2	2	3	3	5	5	5	5	5

	58	59	60
1) User Correct	-	-	-
2) Correct Context	3	1	-
3) Attempted/Incorrect	-	2	-
4) No attempt	11	11	14
5) Non-User Correct	-	-	-
6) Correct Context	1	-	-
7) Attempted/Incorrect	-	2	-
8) No Attempt	4	3	5

Figure 7. Results divided into two groups, those that used Word as their main word processing program (14) and those that used a different word processing program (5, with 2 invalidated) (reproduced from the Microsoft Word 5 interface).

187

Sven Windahl (1986, p.60) discussed the effects of mass communication on culture and society that relates mainly to 'influence which is long term, unplanned, indirect and collective. . . our attention is directed not as separate 'messages', but at whole sets or systems of messages which have similar features', they were referring to informal learning of social roles and from effects which relate to the 'receiving end' of communication. This can also be true of compound icons learnt through similar systems. Of this Philip Gough (1972, p.291-320) writes that 'it would seem that prior context would determine the course of lexical search', and this is evident where confusion has occurred when an icon or element of an icon represents other means in different programs (7.3). How this impacts upon user interfaces is through how the user perceives events and reacts. The results of the test indicate that compound icons fall into certain divisions and that there are certain expectations of what their denotation is. Icon use fell mainly into the categories:

a) Those that have been learned and are understood by both groups having encountered the icon before in that context – the printer can be found in many application programs (Figure 7.4).
b) Those that are least understood through little or no use, such as repaginate (Figure 7.21).
c) Those that are generally specific to one program but can be found in other specialist software other than word processing, such as nested paragraphs (Figure 7.11).
d) Those that are used in another program with a different connotation, such as 'save', 'software library' 'inserted disc' and so on (Figure 7.3).
e) Those that have a greater connotation as something else – most respondents read 'print preview' as 'add picture' (Figure 7.25). The test subjects have assigned a meaning with neither group giving a correct response or identifying the context in which it would be used. This compound icon has a higher number of respondents giving a similar incorrect answer.
f) Those that are abstract and have been learned requiring prior knowledge, such as tabulation. Only one test subject appears to use tabulate left, centre and right (Figure 7.53 – 7.55), but does not use the decimal tab or vertical line insertion (Figure 7.56 – 7.57). All respondents failed to identify the table margin compound icon (Figure 7.60).

Individual test subjects who used Microsoft Word as their primary word processing software were asked about their understanding of the compound icons used. The first category of icons have been learned through user preference – this can be considered as their usual routine of using the program. Comprehension of the compound icons reflect the test subject's use of the program to achieve a task. Primary events show user comprehension, such as 'creating new documents', 'saving', 'printing', 'spell checking', 'making style changes' to the type and so on. There was free admission that to perform tasks which are not part of the user's normal routine, other methods were used. For example, nested and unnested paragraph compound icons were rarely used and for those that did nest paragraphs, it was achieved using 'pidgin' discourse by using the tab key or the word space bar to create the desired outcome. Of those that understood and used nested paragraphs in the correct context, denotation was learnt through

WWW software where the compound icon is similar for nesting and unnesting and is regularly used (Figures 7.10 and 7.11).

Investment in learning appears to be through the incentive to gain something through use of a program or, as McQuail and Windahl (1986, p.19) state, the 'transactional' way of looking at perception. McQuail and Windahl then go on to state that 'human communication process may be regarded as subjective, selective, variable and unpredictable and that human communication systems are open systems'. This partly explains why only one person adjusted the tabulation points (Figures 7.53 to 7.55), instead of using the preset tab key default spaces. Individuals were staying within the parts of the program metaphor that allowed them to perform a task and no more. These 'events' appear to have been learnt and used in the correct context. Other sub-goals functions were achieved by other means, or simply not used and this was true of both groups. Therefore, ideally icons are better understood if they are frequently encountered regardless of the interface.

World Wide Web Interfaces
To find out which interface metaphors might be more appropriate than others a survey was undertaken of 192 countries spread across six continents between the period 7th January and 20th April 1999. The purpose of this was to evaluate icons that have naturally developed throughout the Internet. The search was limited to ISPs for each country to establish how icons appear on their interfaces and to explore the notion that they do indeed influence each others' development in some form. The reason for choosing ISPs was that many of these companies design websites for other organisations; therefore this influence possibly continues to other parts of the Internet. To logically follow through on these further connections was considered inappropriate. This was a small-scale investigation which attempted to make some sense of what de Bono (1971, p.243) considers as something that is recognised 'only after it has brought something about'. De Bono (ibid. p.240) uses an analogy to describe this as being unable to 'plan a new style in art, but once it has come about it creates its own validity'. This also helps to explain why computer compound icons used as interface navigation go unchallenged.

Computer Interface Compound Icons from around the World
The small-scale investigation was limited to Yahoo and to a set sequence; therefore if an ISP was not registered with this search engine then their domain name would not appear. For instance, the search result using this criteria for Japan reveals 29 results, yet if the search instruction was altered to 'Japan ISP' then the result would be radically different. The other criteria for the search was that the first entry listed in the Yahoo search result would be the link used to provide the data, also countries with many ISPs searching was limited to the first 50. Not all service providers have icon-driven interfaces; the average seems to be one in six. Another point to remember is that the amount of registration constantly changes; for example, during February 1999 the United Kingdom as a search result was changed from the United Kingdom to its constituent parts of England, Scotland, Northern Ireland and Wales. Some smaller

countries had no ISPs while Texas (1310) had twice the provision of the entire Austalasian continent (836). California (2894) was over double the provision of Texas. Therefore America was surveyed by state. The list below identifies three links, the first Internet Services (Figure 8a) shows fourteen records for Taiwan; further down the listing are Internet Services, Web Services (Figure 8b) with five records which include five ISPs from the first list (Figures 8a3, a4, a5, a6 and a8) and finally Internet Services, Web Services, Designers (Figure 8c) which contain one record (Figures 8a3, b1) which can be also found on the other two links (Figure 8).

a) Business and Economy > Companies > **Internet Services** > By Region > Countries > Taiwan

1) BST - FaxNet, Internet dial-up, Internet and Intranet solutions, home page designing, virtual hosts, I-Phone solutions.
2) Chiayu Information Ltd.
3) E Design - design, produce, and maintain websites for companies and individuals
4) Evolve New Media - solutions to your Internet and new media needs.
5) Greenworld Network Co.,Ltd
6) I-site Taiwan
7) Pinho Internet Service Co., Ltd. - offer computer mail order and Internet server technology services.
8) Starnet Internet Service Corp.
9) Tainan.com - with news, organizations, and hosting services.
10) Taoyuan Metro - shareware, current events, education, entertainment, and travel news and listings in Chinese.
11) TaoYuan Network - includes information about Taoyuan, electronic shopping and KiSS.
12) Trace
13) TTN Internet Service
14) Yangyi.com - Chinese-English homepage design & translation. Complete international internet services

b) Business and Economy > Companies > **Internet Services > Web Services** > By Region > Countries > Taiwan

1) E Design - design, produce, and maintain websites for companies and individuals
2) Evolve New Media - solutions to your Internet and new media needs.
3) Greenworld Network Co.,Ltd
4) I-site Taiwan
5) Starnet Internet Service Corp.

c) Business and Economy > Companies > **Internet Services > Web Services > Designers** > By Region > Countries > Taiwan

1) E Design - design, produce, and maintain websites for companies and individuals

Figure 8. a) The higher order of listing contains 14 search results, 5 of which can be found in b). c) has only one service provider that can be found on the other two. This indicates the growth pattern of ISPs in Taiwan with the Yahoo search engine.

Africa 114 ISPs

Algeria(0), Angola (2), Benin (0), Botswana (0), Burkina (0), Burundi (1), Cameroon (0), Cape Verde Islands (0), Central African Republic (0), Chad (0), Comoros (0), Congo (0), Djibouti (0), Egypt (27), Equatorial Guinea (0), Eritrea (0), Ethiopia (0), Gabon (0), Gambia (0), Ghana (5), Guinea (0), Guinea-Bissau (0), Ivory Coast (0), Kenya (5), Lesotho (0), Liberia (0), Libya (1), Madagascar (1), Malawi (0), Mali (0), Mauritius (2), Mauritania (0), Morocco (3), Mozambique (0), Namibia (6), Niger (0), Nigeria (0), Rwanda (0), Sao Tome and Principle (0), Senegal (0), Seychelles (0), Sierra Leone (0), Somalia (0), South Africa (86), Sudan (0), Swaziland (0), Tanzania (0), Togo (0), Tunisia (0), Uganda (0), Zaire (0), Zambia (1), Zimbabwe (6)

Guest book   Help desk   Write to webmaster
Angola *Static* http://www.ebonet.net/home.html

Download   Site map   launch your website   Spice up your business
Egypt *Static* http://brainy1.ie-eg.com

Business   Interact with   Go to net 2000   Leisure
             WWW
Kenya *Static* http://www.net2000ke.com

About us   Chat   Feedback   Search   Sitemap   Market
South Africa *Static* http://www.os2.iaccess.za

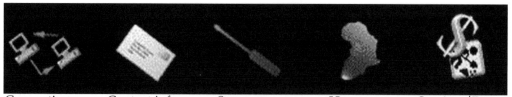

| Connections | Contact info | Support | Home | Services/Rates |

South Africa *Dynamic* http://www.pe.co.za/index2.htm

Feedback   About us   Search   Sitemap   Chat

Namibia *Static* http://www.iafrica.com.na

Web design   Email   Search   Network Internet Solutions

Zimbabwe *Static* http://www.icon.co.zw

Asia 1004 ISPs

Afghanistan (0), Bahrain (2), Bangladesh (10), Bhutan (0), Brunei (1), Cambodia (2), China (229), India (197), Indonesia (34), Iran (0), Iraq (0), Israel (42), Hong Kong (77), Japan (29), Jordan (6), Kazakhstan (1), Kirgyzstan (0), Kuwait (0), Laos (0), Lebanon (12), Malaysia (31), Maldives (0), Mongolia (0), Myanmar (if no try Burma) (0), Nepal (2), North Korea (0), Oman (0), Pakistan (21), Philippines (51), Qatar (0), Russia (29), Saudi Arabia (5), Singapore (131), South Korea (13), Sri Lanka (4), Syria (0), Taiwan (14), Tajikistan (0), Thailand (40), Turkmenia (0), United Arab Emirates (16), Uzbekistan (1), Vietnam (4), Yemen (1).

FIND   **Service and Support**

China *Static* http://www.vtech.net

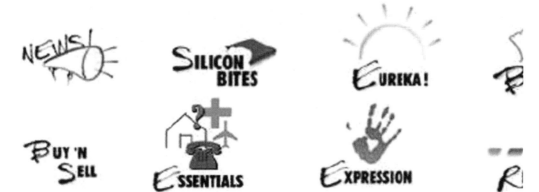

India *Static* http://www.karnataka.com/megha/

Israel *Static* http://www.zahav.net.il

Lebanon *Dynamic* http://www.netways.com.lb

Computers   e-mail   Information   Notepad   Download   Money
Indonesia *Static* http://www.medan-link.com

Malaysia *Static* http://www.myartists.com/gv/

Pakistan *Static* http://www.mags.net.pk/

About us   Clients   Contact us   E-mail   Faq

Hosting   Members   Sign up   Web page

Philippines *Static* http://www.filbiznet.com

Search	Dial in	People	Russian network

Russia *Static* http://www.komitex.ru

about us	search	contact us	download	sitemap	sitetour
Product & Services	Pricelist	Member's Privilege	Node & Phone Numbers	Member Support	Account Management

Thailand *Static* http://www.loxinfo.co.th

Australasia 886 ISPs

Australia (683), Fiji (6), Kiribati (0), Nauru (0), New Zealand (187), Papua New Guinea (6), Solomon Islands (0), Tonga (2), Tuvalu (1), Vanuatu (0), Western Samoa (1).

Info	Links	News	Search	Internet help

Australia *Static* http://aardvark.apana.org.au

Contact	Home	Links	News

Australia *Dynamic* http://www.at.com.au

Consulting   Design   Hosting   Portfolio   Resources   Marketing

Fiji *Dynamic* http://www.InternetFiji.com

Information   Contact us   Online   News   Services

New Zealand *Static* http://www.dtl.co.nz

Europe 1325 ISPs

Albania (0), Andorra (1), Armenia (5), Austria (34), Azerbaijan (5), Belgium (29), Belarus (4), Bosnia-Herzegovina (0), Bulgaria (8), Croatia (1), Cyprus (14), Czech Republic (5), Denmark (21), Estonia (6), Finland (7), France (51), Georgia (3), Germany (147), Greece (23), Hungary (7), Iceland (9), Irish Republic (0), Italy (300), Latvia (7), Liechtenstein (2), Lithuania (9), Luxembourg (13), Macedonia (7), Malta (17), Moldova (0), Monaco (4), Netherlands (169), Norway (14), Poland (17), Portugal (27), Romania (24), San Marino (1), Slovakia (4), Slovenia (2), Spain (206), Sweden (29), Switzerland (41), Turkey (26), Ukraine (26),

Chat   Forum   Links   Search

Andorra *Static* http://www.andornet.ad

Ftp Homepages Information Search

Austria *Static* http://www.vip.at

Home   About us   Links   Pages   Prices   Systems Info

Bulgaria *Dynamic* http://www.netbg.com

Home   Advice   Contact Form   Contact   Design Service   Email

Hosting   Information Introductions   Links   Search   Snail mail

Cyprus *Dynamic* http://infowebNET.com/index1.htm

General Information   Products

Denmark *Static* http://www.fenestra.dk

actualité   contact   particuliers   recherche   revendeurs   agences

France *Static* http://www.pandemonium.fr/pandemonium.html

Germany *Static* http://www.global.de/global/ga/who1a.html

Information   Contact us   Search
Switzerland *Static* http://www.quaras.ch

Europe – United Kingdom 702 ISPs

England (633), Northern Ireland (16), Scotland (40), Wales (13).

England *Static* http://www.advantage-rt.co.uk

Mail form   Home
Northern Ireland *Static* http://www.pmworkshop.co.uk

North America excluding USA 1590 ISPs

Antigua & Barbuda (2), Bahamas (5), Barbados (6), Belize (4), Canada (1338), Costa Rica (21), Cuba (0), Dominica (0), Dominican Republic (16), El Salvador (9), Greenland (0), Grenada(0), Guatemala (8), Haiti (3), Honduras (9), Jamaica (3), Mexico (144), Nicaragua (6), Panama (10), Puerto Rico (0), St. Kitts-Nevis (0), St. Lucia (0), St.Vincent &The Grenadines (0), Trinidad and Tobago (6).

About us   Contact us   What's new   Alliances
Canada *Static* http://www.racsa.co.cr

Internet   Manuals   News   Opinion   Services
Costa Rica *Static* http://www.racsa.co.cr

Children

Company Information

Contact us

Home

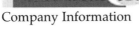
Members only

National Guide

News

Search

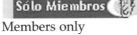
Select sites

Services

Software

Tourism

Guatemala *Static* http://www.infovia.com.gt/indexfr.htm

About us   Clients   Net services   Hardware sales

Software   Tech support   IT support   Technology online

Jamaica *Static* http://www.digtechinc.com

Culture   Events   Ideas   Sites of interest

Mexico *Static* http://eureka.tamnet.com.mx

Culture   Education   Finances   Information   Internal organisation

Items for sale   Medicine   Professional   Services   Software &
                                                                    qualifications

Nicaragua *Static* http://www.ibw.com.ni

North America - United States of America 15,419 ISPs

Alabama (119), Alaska (58), Arizona (265), Arkansas (50), California (2894), Colorado (340), Connecticut (182), Delaware (31), Florida (987), Georgia (516), Hawaii (85), Idaho (69), Illinois (624), Indiana (204), Iowa (94), Kansas (83), Kentucky (74), Louisiana (128), Maine (76), Maryland (362), Massachusetts (571), Michigan (346), Minnesota (384), Mississippi (51), Missouri (223), Montana (58), Nebraska (69), Nevada (118), New Hampshire (88), New Jersey (411), New Mexico (89), New York (897), North Carolina (339), North Dakota (19), Ohio (400), Oklahoma (108), Oregon (310), Pennsylvania (426), Rhode Island (45), South Carolina (114), South Dakota (27), Tennessee (175), Texas (1310), Utah (122), Vermont (34), Virginia (481), Washington (645), Washington DC (0) (comes under Washington), West Virginia (33), Wisconsin (235), Wyoming (23)

ABOUT US   WHAT'S NEW   SUPPORT   CONTACT US

Florida *Static* http://www.javahausweb.com/nhome.htm

Nebraska *Static* http://adnet.net

Company Info   Products   Projects
New Hampshire *Dynamic* http://www.atypica.com

About us   Contact us   E-mail us   Services   Support
New York *Static* http://www.ythis.com

201

Search
Oregon *Static* http-//www.teleport.com/~avfx/

Home   Our Agency   Portfolio   Results   Teamwork   What's New   Contact Us

Rhode Island *Static* http://americahouse.com

Clients   Contact us   Home   About us   Web work

South Carolina *Static* http-//www.9voltnet.com

Client sites   E-mail   Flash quote   Marketing   Our mission   Prices and services

Wisconsin *Dynamic* http://www.bytesites.com

South America 537 ISPs

Argentina (96), Bolivia (8), Brazil (340), Chile (19), Colombia (19), Ecuador (15), French Guiana (0), Guyana (3), Paraguay (7), Peru (16), Suriname (0), Uruguay (3), Venezuela (11).

Ftp   Ideas   Links   News

Brazil *Static* http-//www.bluenet.com.br

Chile *Static* http://www.cybercenter.cl

Figure 9. Icons from different ISPs from around the world.

As mentioned, this is only a small-scale investigation and does not begin to fully tackle the magnitude of the task of measuring the development of natural language used throughout the Internet. What is immediately apparent at the time of this survey is that the largest number of ISPs are spread throughout the United States of America with an overall lower concentration of services providers in the southern and mid-western states, although Texas appears to be the exception to this rule being the second largest state service provider. Overall the United States of America has at this point 15,419 ISPs, which is just over two and a half times greater than the provision for the rest of the world. Of the English speaking countries, USA has 15,419, UK has 702, Australia has 683, New Zealand has 187 and South Africa has 86, including Canada (although it's French speaking citizens must be taken into account), of the 21,577 servers in recorded use at this point only 3,162 were potentially for non-English use, although English appears to be a dominant factor of these ISPs. Africa has the least provision with 114 ISPs of which 86 are from South Africa and have been included in the English speaking account (Figure 9). Size does not necessarily reflect quality both aesthetically or semantically. The United States of America might have the largest global provision, yet small countries such as Costa Rica, Zimbabwe or even Nicaragua appear to rival or better American provision; but empirical proof will take extensive research beyond the scope of this study.

Conclusion

This small-scale investigation into which icons are used within one sector of the Internet conclusively indicates there are extensive possibilities for further research. The methods developed for the ARC to track, monitor and report on user comprehension of compound icons used on interfaces is a valid method of researching the lexical and semantic values of compound icons. Nothing is straightforward, and although the Microsoft Word questionnaire was used in conjunction with the interface and therefore in context, human response can be diverse. Even the program itself proved disruptive through semantic interference when the overall connotation of compound icons had been assigned a different meaning in another program and context. This implies that prior knowledge merely alters the degree of disorientation according to the individual's experiences. Therefore further research should be with icons that have been chosen through collective diachronic natural user selection. That these compound icons acquired throughout the Internet should have a singular purpose, be iconic in what they represent and with all the necessary design criteria applied to measure visual readability. Each compound icon can then be placed into categories that are identified through associated basic word commands such as 'search', 'about us', 'contact us' and so on. Finally, because language is in a constant process of change, further research would serve as a synchronic point in time for which future measurements could be made from and referred to.

References

de Bono, E. (1971). *The Mechanism of Mind*, Penguin Books.

Canter, D. (1978). 'Way-finding and signposting: penance or prosthesis'. in Easterby, R., Zwaga H. (eds): *Information Design*, John Wiley and Sons, New York.

Card, S., Moran, T., Newell, A. (1983). *The Psychology of Human-Computer Interaction*, Lawrence Erlbaum Associates, New Jersey.

Gough, P. (1972). 'One Second of Reading', *Visible Language* VI (4) Autumn, p.291-320, The Cleveland Museum of Art, Cleveland.

Marcus, A. *The Design Process for Information Products* (Internet). Downloaded from the WWW 6th April 1999. http://www.amanda.com/publications.

McQuail, D., Windahal, S. (1986). *Communication Models: For the study of Mass Communications*, Longman, New York.

Olson, J., Moran, T. (1996). 'Mapping the Method Muddle: Guidance in Using Methods for User Interface Design'. in Rudisill, M., Lewis, C., Polson, P., McKay, T. (eds): *Human-Computer Interface Design: Success Stories, Emerging Methods, and Real-World Context*, Morgan Kaufmann Publishers, Inc., California.

Sims-Knight, J. (1992). 'To Picture or Not to picture: How to Decide', Visible Language 26 (3/4), p.324-87, Rhode Island School of Design, Providence.